The World of Jia Zhangke

The World of Jia Zhangke

by Jean-Michel Frodon
Translated from the French and with additional research by Sally Shafto

THE FiLm DeSK

ISBN: 978-0-9994683-7-1
Library of Congress Control Number: 2021934924

All writing reprinted with permission of rights holders

1st edition of 1,500, 2021, Film Desk Books
Jake Perlin and Jim Colvill, publishers

© Jean-Michel Frodon, 2016
Foreword © Dudley Andrew, 2021
Translation © Sally Shafto, 2021

The publishers extend their grateful appreciation to
Jean-Michel Frodon, Sally Shafto, Dudley Andrew, Aliza Ma,
Laura Coxson, and Carla Brookoff

All photos © Jia Zhangke, except those on pages 34–35, 62–63,
177, 194, 200–201 (© Walter Salles), and 169 (© Cohen Media Group)
Cover image © Walter Salles

Designed by Brian McMullen
Map designed by Donato Ricci
Printed at Sheridan Books, Inc. in Michigan

Also published by The Film Desk:

François Truffaut by Lillian Ross,
from *The New Yorker*, 1960–1976

John Huston by Lillian Ross,
from *The New Yorker*, 1949–1996

Philippe Garrel — *L'Enfant secret*

Pasolini in New York

Duras/Godard Dialogues

Table of Contents

Translator's Note 8

Preface 11

Foreword
    The Poet of Post-Mao China by Dudley Andrew 15

Across Generations 23

Jia's Films
    Jia Before Jia (But Already Jia): *One Day, in Beijing*
        (1994) and *Xiaoshan Going Home* (1995) 37
    The Zigzag of the Little Thief: *Xiaowu* (1997) 38
    What Time is the Train for Youth?: *Platform* (2000) 40
    Singing in the Pain: *In Public* (2001) and
        Unknown Pleasures (2002) 43
    A Network Film: *The World* (2004) 46
    Beauty Equation: *Still Life* (2006) 50
    The Art of Portraiture: *Dong* (2006) 53
    A Film in Volume: *Useless* (2007) 56
    Like Milk on a Stone: *24 City* (2008) 59
    They Used to Write Poetry: *Cry Me a River* (2008) 61
    Shanghai and its Memories: *I Wish I Knew* (2010) 63
    A Touch of China: *A Touch of Sin* (2013) 67
    How Jia Moved Mountains: *Mountains May*
        Depart (2015) 69

A Heroine of the Century: *Ash Is Purest White* (2018) 71
So Close to Their Land: *Swimming Out Till the
    Sea Turns Blue* (2020) 74

Interviews with Jia Zhangke
Jia Speaks 83
On *Mountains May Depart* 162

Interviews with Jia's Collaborators
Zhao Tao, Actor 169
Yu Lik-wai, Cinematographer 177
Zhang Yang, Sound Engineer 187
Lin Xudong, Editor 194

By Jia
The Films of My Life 203
My Helpless City, My Homeland 211
How Many Trees Are Needed to Cover
    Tiananmen Square? 217

Afterword
Ulaanbaatar by Walter Salles 223

Appendix
Songs from Jia's Soundtracks 235
Map 236
Suggested Further Reading and Viewing 238
Filmography 241
Index 251

TRANSLATOR'S NOTE

In China surnames are cited first, followed by the given name. Jia is thus the filmmaker's patronym, indicating he's the son of the Jia family, and Zhangke, his personal name. With regard to the romanization of Chinese personal names, there is a great deal of inconsistency in how they're treated in English in the literature on Jia, as well as in the credits of his films in their English-language releases. I have followed the Hanyu Pinyin romanization, which in Mainland China has replaced the earlier Wade-Giles system and the place name spellings of the *Postal Atlas of China*. In Hanyu Pinyin, romanized personal names are spelled without hyphens, apostrophes or an extra space. Pinyin is spaced according to words, not characters. Thus, the name of the title character of Jia's 1997 film is Xiaowu (and not Xiao Wu as it's usually cited).

Taiwan and Hong Kong, however, don't always use Hanyu Pinyin romanization. I have thus retained the hyphen in the following names as is common usage: Yu Lik-wai, Lau Kar-leung, Hou Hsaio-hsien, Tsai Ming-liang, Chow Yun-fat, Wong Kar-wai, Li Kit-ming, Wu Nien-jen, Chow Chi-sang, Li Han-hsiang. For more on this topic, please see the *Chicago Manual of Style*, 17th edition: 11.82, 11.83, 11.84, and 11.85.

In Western literature Jia Zhangke is often repeatedly cited by his entire name. We have here followed Western and Chinese practice of initially referring to him by his full name and then by just his last name.

preface

IT WAS A JOYFUL dinner in the autumn of 2009. Leon Cakoff wasn't sick yet, or if he was, it wasn't apparent. In a small courtyard restaurant he welcomed some guests from *his* festival, the São Paulo International Film Festival. Leon created the festival in the darkest hour of the Brazilian dictatorship and it had become a space for freedom, invention, and exchange. A space that he continually expanded with the help of the radiant Renata de Almedia by his side.

The need for Leon's festival remained great, even with the restoration of democracy in the mid-1980s. One of his many countless initiatives to develop this artistic and democratic torch at the heart of the megalopolis was the launching of a collection of books devoted to the great filmmakers of our day. Manoel de Oliveira, Abbas Kiarostami, and Amos Gitai were the subject of top-notch publications, accompanying retrospectives that established or re-established their eminent place. Even seemingly canonized filmmakers need their reputations reinforced by new generations.

That year my friends Leon and Renata had invited me to take part in the Festival jury. Joining us that evening was another old friend, Walter Salles, filmmaker, generational figurehead, and also—something little known outside of Brazil—champion of an elevated concept of cinema: a producer of young filmmakers and a tireless defender, in the media, of the art of cinema in its most diverse forms, contemporary and historical, from fiction to documentary. More than ten years earlier we organized together a screening of Mário Peixoto's pioneering masterpiece *Limite* (1929) at the Cinémathèque française—Walter was responsible for resurrecting and restoring this long forgotten film.

In discussing this series of books, Leon suddenly asked me who I thought was "the greatest filmmaker working today." The answer—*my* answer—I knew already, having often been asked the question before. Usually I would have to justify my choice, and even introduce the filmmaker to my unknowing questioners. But that evening it was not necessary to defend my choice: Jia Zhangke. As a filmmaker at the vanguard of contemporary inventions in the art of cinema, Jia employs the very best resources of documentary as well as fiction film; he invents inspired forms that reflect the great art of his country, a daring cinema that utilizes the newest technological and aesthetic developments. All this makes him the preeminent witness to the greatest transformation in our world today: the upheaval experienced by a billion-and-a-half Chinese. To my mind, he unequivocally merits this epithet, despite its pretentiousness.

And that's how we agreed to not only do a book that I would write, but also a film by Walter, who knows his Chinese colleague's work intimately. During the course of that serendipitous dinner, I also learned that Walter had gone to China to make a documentary at the end of the 1970s.

But there were a few obstacles to be overcome. We couldn't do the book and the film without Jia himself being available. Although he was very enthusiastic about the project, he was preoccupied by a demanding workload, of which the making of his own films was only the most obvious part. There were also problems with funding. And then Leon fell gravely and increasingly ill. Of course we stayed in touch by cell phone and exchanged emails. Jia wanted to do the book but couldn't immediately as he had lost funding on a film. And then, on October 14, 2011, Leon died. Everything came to a halt. It seemed to be one sadness after another.

But Renata refused to give up. She said we should still do it, do it in Leon's memory and because it's right that the book exists. She re-imagined the conditions that would make the project possible, thanks to the support of an exceptional publisher, Florencia Ferrari, who worked for the highly esteemed Brazilian publishing house, Cosac Naify. Walter Salles raised money and found interested partners. Everyone made room in their schedules. Jia became available in the midst of a storm—the preparation of the Chinese release of *A Touch of Sin* (its release was canceled at the last minute by the authorities, a worst case scenario). Jia also gave us access to documents, photos, and archives. With a small crew hired by Walter Salles—Maria Carlota Bruno, Inti Briones, and others—and completed by Jia's own collaborators, we set off together for his native city, Fenyang. We traveled and met his family, his childhood friends, his collaborators. We ate and drank, roamed the streets, listened to the voices and sounds, discovered landscapes, and recorded traces of memories. The collaborative work that Walter Salles and I undertook was nourished as much by these situations as by the traditional process of interviews and research. And of course we spent time with Jia, a lot of time—some of it joyful, some serious, and some anxious. Jia gave generously and unstintingly. We also spent time with his wife and principal actor Zhao Tao, who endows the couple with a halo of thoughtful grace and gentle beauty, frequently rendering words unnecessary. Many of Jia's other collaborators and fellow adventurers were also spoken to, whom we will encounter again in the following pages.

From all of this was born Walter Salles' documentary *Jia Zhangke: A Guy from Fenyang*, a remarkable film of one filmmaker's appreciation—accompanied by admiration, intelligence, humor, and deep affection—for another. Another result was this book, the original version of which was published by Cosac Naify in Brazil. Jia Zhangke, Walter Salles, and I together presented the fruits of our labor in an intense moment of joy at the São Paulo Festival in October 2014. Then Jia made another absolutely fascinating film, *Mountains May Depart*, which was the occasion for a new interview added as a bonus to the subsequent French and English editions of this book. And then he directed two more feature-length films, the fiction *Ash Is Purest White* and the documentary *Swimming Out Till the Sea Turns Blue*, both of which are now introduced in this English edition.

This book is dedicated to Leon Cakoff, to Renata de Almeida, and to all those who supported this often difficult but heartfelt endeavor on a great body of work of contemporary cinema.

Jean-Michel Frodon

Besides those whose names appear above, I would also like to acknowledge and thank for their assistance a few other friends and supporters: Jay Yo Chen, Agnès Devictor, Joanna Collier, Gregory Gajos, Isabelle Glachant, Arthur Hallereau, Alexandra Henochsberg, Laurence Herszberg, Hsieh Chinlin, Shôzô Ichiyama, Guy Jungblut, Mathieu Laclau, Ricardo Lelis, Li Danfeng, Lin Xudong, Justine O, Charles Tatum Jr, Wang Hongwei, Pascale Wei Guinot, Xiao Xi-nan, Yu Lik-wai. In addition, Casper Leung provided some very precious information. Many thanks too to the translator of the Chinese version of this book, professor Kong Qian.

I am grateful to Dudley Andrew for his constant support, his immense knowledge and the friendly conversations we so often had about Jia (and so many other topics), to the commitment of Jake Perlin without whom this book would never had existed and for his loyalty to me and to the project during the very difficult period all of us went through while the book was being made, to the constant and imaginative implication of Sally Shafto and her immense work on the translation, and to Jim Colvill for the quality of the proposals and improvements he provided as the publisher.

Finally I wish to express my deep gratitude to Donato Ricci whose friendship and skills made possible the making of the map at the end of the book.

foreword

The Poet of Post-Mao China
by Dudley Andrew

THIS CENTURY BELONGS, we are told, to China, whose national cinema is said to be reaching a scale equivalent to Hollywood's in its heyday. While China's industry aims to copy Hollywood in infrastructure, genres, and marketing (thus becoming, in my view, progressively less urgent and more banal), outside the Chinese studios one can still find the legacy of the "urban generation," those filmmakers of the late 1990s, who registered with raw images the consequences of China's market socialism and the unprecedented urbanization it produced. Those films definitely felt urgent, reaching audiences through clandestine routes and from scarcely identifiable sources. They were often illegally made and screened, and in any case cut off completely from the state-supported studio system that, since the 1980s, had been reliably turning out 150 rather predictable films a year.

Nothing was predictable in the Sixth Generation, at least not immediately. Festival programmers had to rely on word of mouth to locate the most promising films and trends without the aid of box-office buzz or local Chinese festivals or official critical reactions. Yet You Le, Wang Xiaoshuai, Zhang Yuan, and others captivated the interest of cinephiles, for they gave evidence of a vibrant marginal movement, from which emerged a great many strong films, and one of the most significant cineastes in the world over the past two decades, Jia Zhangke. This poet of post-Mao China has been chronicling the experience of over a billion people across an unprecedented economic revolution: in only a few years China went from being a static, fully socialist, and largely rural culture to a hyper-dynamic urban one, fueled by the sudden unleashing of entrepreneurial energy and of State capital, resulting in the licensed displacement of people, incalculable numbers of people. Jia Zhangke's art has brought into view the millions who live in the limbo between hometown and city center: construction workers, entertainers, gamblers, tradesmen, migrants of every stripe. His masterpieces of 2004–2006, *The World* and *Still Life*, displayed, on the one hand, the implacable structure of the new cut-throat economic system, and, on the other, the "structure of experience,"—the class feeling—that this produced within those caught up in it.

In *The World* drifters from Shanxi and other provinces, often speaking dialect, are tossed together in the bowels of a Beijing theme park that advertises a tour of the world without leaving home. But having left their homes, these workers are stranded on the edge of the metropolis, exploited to entertain the new urban class. Russian women arrive, driven into the sex trade that's just a step down from where the heroine, Zhao Tao, finds herself. She forms a sympathetic link to the construction laborers drawn from Shanxi, one of whom works himself to death in the capital. His family, arriving to claim his body, seems indifferent to the indemnity paid them in cash but they then honor the boy's spirit when funeral money is burnt on the very site where he lost his life. He sacrificed himself for minor debts he could only pay off by joining the risky economy's building rush. The high-rises for whose swift construction he died, would soon house others like him, already making their way to the capital where they too will labor in social alienation. A Shanxi relative who brought this dead worker's parents to claim his body, becomes the migrant hero of Jia's next film, *Still Life*. Traveling south in search of the wife and daughter whom the economy has drawn away from home, he lands in the midst of the monumental Three Gorges hydropower dam project, that displaced some half-a-million people, while it temporarily attracted bands of itinerant work crews. The film ends with the hero gesturing to some fellow migrant-workers to follow him north to the mines he knows so well. Given Jia's view of contemporary China, this almost amounts to an ironic happy end, for we can imagine their life in the mines.

Jia's genius stems from his having intuited the appropriate scale at which to view, record and then sketch Chinese life in transition. His fictions and his actors (some of whom return film after film) can be quite involving as we follow their private concerns and dreams; but they're also always involved in a world beyond their personal drama, a world populated with others facing them down, a world of institutions, regulations, technology. Background and foreground interact so intricately that we give up trying to distinguish pertinent gestures, actions, words and scenes. In *The World* and *Still Life*, we cannot tell what relates directly to the characters named in the credits as opposed to what belongs to the setting or environment. Everything is germane; everything is in some sense "documentary." In following the fates of the featured players to the end, we follow a mass movement and the conditions that have brought this movement about and that it in turn affects.

Jia has succeeded in something rare, something for which Neorealism provided a template: he's brought into sudden focus, and then articulated, a previously unremarked on, even unseen, reality, that of an entire class of unclassified human beings. They now have been given a face and something of a voice in the social geography; and that geography is now visibly more complicated, hence more tragic, than had been thought. This effort to "figure" the invisible and the ignored is what art, at its most consequential, has always aimed for. Political art, when it recognizes its historical moment and races ahead of it—like Goya in painting or Malraux in fiction—exposes the system that devastates its subjects. Jia Zhangke intuited a form that cinema needed to adopt to reach this political edge; he photographed the bodies of migrant laborers, and the particular dramas of a couple of these, in an economy that consumes them while they do what they can to disturb or transcend that economy.

In succession his major films have progressively zoomed back to take in wider aspects and dimensions of the socio-economic changes that bewilder not just his characters but an entire nation. *The World* stuck close to the conditions and dreams of those who work literally under the World theme park or in the construction zones of the capital city. In *Still Life* he focused on two different characters coming from the same place who wind up in the same changing landscape, thanks to distinct personal plots. With *A Touch of Sin* he pulled back further still to grasp something common across the national map via four brutal vignettes in each of which the flayed bodies of characters are somehow strong enough to disrupt the machinery of what the state considers progress. Traditional values—values that seem quaint in our cynical era—steel a small spectrum of people against the indignities of their situations, as all are chewed up by the coldly economic values of contemporary China. This synchronic montage of a brutal nation gives way in a later feature, *Ash is the Purest White*, to a diachronic representation of this clash of values in three historical slices (2001, 2006, 2018). Touching several of the locations of his earlier films, but set primarily in Datong, the capital of Jia's native Shanxi Province, progress and decadence are graphically visible on the faces and living conditions of its characters.

Like no one else, Jia has pictured the roil of China in movement. In his "Hometown Trilogy" he tracked a society's gradual emergence from a quarter-century of Mao's ironclad control (Jia was six when this leader died). The music, images, and fashions that appear in those films, particularly *Platform*, feel like wind filling the sail of a boat picking up momentum. Sometimes breezes could be felt coming intermittently from the West, as if carried by the strains of Western pop music that pass through his films. China sailed into the 1980s toward what seemed like limitless horizons. Like quite a few other Western scholars at the time, I was privileged to feel the gathering momentum of China's drive toward modernism when I was invited to Beijing in 1988, on the eve of the Tiananmen massacre. The diligence, concentration, and hopes palpable at the Beijing Film Academy where I gave a series of lectures, had not completely dimmed when, five years later and despite Tiananmen, Jia arrived there to study film history and theory. Effectively he grew with the country that he soon set about documenting and expressing.

A teenager in the 1980s, he was, like the new market economy, wildly rambunctious and naive, pushing forward and not knowing quite what was "out there." The music, breakdancing, football, motorcycling, and minor hooliganism that he and his Shanxi friends engaged in are local manifestations of an entire country preparing for a future where the rules had yet to be set. This included businessmen and bureaucrats in Beijing and Shanghai who felt licensed to try out high-stakes initiatives, where the risks too often fell on the shoulders of unsuspecting others. *Platform* embodies this moment of personal and cultural adolescence as it was about to confront the paternal figure of State power (at Tiananmen square). But nothing could stop these Shanxi characters from wanting to look beyond home toward the "unknown pleasures" of China's megalopolises. And nothing could keep Jia Zhangke from looking beyond China toward the world of world cinema. He claims he was the only one of his buddies to leave their hometown; still, they spent their youth dreaming together about ways to move beyond their circumstances, if only to drive off on their motorbikes, shirt flapping behind them. In just this way, the exuberant and expectant 1980s, even with all its privations and frustrations, were fondly remembered a decade later by many Chinese who became entrepreneurs and cosmopolitans.

Jia wants never to leave his hometown and his formative period completely behind; this was the source of his growth spurt; and so he regularly returns to shoot his films in Shanxi to tap that energy and the sentiments he feels there, as well as to grasp through his camera and microphone the special texture of the architecture and populace, especially their gestures and dialect, their silly jokes or absurd rituals. The least successful of his films among the critics and the public has been *I Wish I Knew*. Although I wrote an affectionate article about it, I believe this film started from an emotional deficit, as it were. Commissioned for the Shanghai World exposition, it was cut off from Jia's past, and from the repertoire of language and habits that make up his expressive universe. Knowing the danger of losing touch, of taking on subjects of the upper crust world that his fame inevitably lifted him into, Jia has taken care to keep close to Fenyang, where he grew up. That's where he helped establish a literary festival in 2019, after setting up his highly publicized Pingyao October film festival.

But there's no use pretending he's an ordinary guy. Today Jia must go undercover in Shanxi, for he's become, with or against his will, a national spokesman and a citizen of the World. Yes, "The World." This is the title of the film that brought him exceptional international recognition, and ironically also the first of his works to be licensed for national distribution. So it occupies a crucial place in Chinese film history and a particularly crucial one in his oeuvre. It came after his first two films (*Xiaowu* and *Platform*) displayed, often with nostalgia, the failure of the pipedreams of provincial youth, and then after *Unknown Pleasures* left its deracinated and disillusioned characters suspended on an unfinished highway somewhere between a hometown that no longer felt like home and the burgeoning, inhospitable city they sensed before them. *The World* represents life in the center of China which is playfully figured to be the center of *The World* itself. The problem is that the film's location isn't exactly Beijing, but a rather tasteless theme park in the suburbs, and the characters aren't locals; they don't even speak Mandarin with each other but dialect. When not performing (a dancer from India, a flight attendant, an African in a New Year's cavalcade) they're held captive underground in depressing dormitories. Some of them, the Russians in the sex trade, are quite literally prisoners; their handler has confiscated their passports. In contrast Zhao Tao and her boyfriend seem free, but they have no passports and haven't the means to go it alone nor the will to return to Shanxi.

Much of this is eloquently represented in the remarkable opening credit sequence, the conclusion of which shows a ragman pulling his rucksack full of old clothes across the screen, then pausing to glance at the spectator, as if he were the director winking at us. Behind him, the park's version of the Eiffel Tower stands tall as the beacon of modernity. Two time zones are here superimposed, the slow time of the provincial rag-picker who gets up with the sun and finds a place to sleep when it sets, and the frantic all-hours life of the businessmen in Beijing for whom time is money, with Paris and Wall Street just a fax or a text message away .

An excellent recent book by Li Yang, *The Formation of Chinese Art Cinema, 1990–2003*, culminates in a chapter on Jia Zhangke, but it leaves him stranded in 2003 on the cusp of his best known films. Indeed Jia seems to have almost single-handedly brought about a caesura in Chinese film history at this time. For just as he was initiating production of *The World*, the Chinese Film Bureau finally officially recognized him and the other members of his generation, allowing them to operate on the margins, where of course they could be monitored. Effectively China's "underground filmmakers" had been recruited to work, like it or not, within the system, perhaps like the entertainers living underground who were conscripted to keep the theme park of *The World* functioning.

Jia's films, the early ones especially, maintain an allegorical aspect relating to the expanding sphere of his life and possibilities. Although it was distant from the place, culture, and even language of his birthplace, Beijing was the center of the Maoist world into which Jia was born in 1970 and toward which he inevitably gravitated during his adolescence; this period was also the adolescence of Modern China as we have come to know it. He and his country grew increasingly muscular and outward-looking during the 1980s and early 1990s. However, the world that he found when he arrived at the Beijing Film Academy in 1993 and that he would represent a decade later, felt increasingly disproportioned, out of scale, and unreal. Through a series of ingeniously interlinked film techniques, Jia represented Beijing's "World" as a "totality" (*pace* Fredric Jameson) by first extending the borders of the theme park that gives the film its name and holds its workers captive, and second by drilling down to the core of this (non)place and the culture it pretends to represent. The giant strides this director has taken since 2004 push off from the broad, rock-solid plateau of this magnificent film, which ironically grasps the depth of a culture void of substance.

Jean-Michel Frodon has measured the full breadth and depth of Jia Zhangke's "world" from first film to last. This book will reward any serious spectator and is particularly gratifying for me. My friendship with Jean-Michel began about the time Jia renewed my faith that cinema was alive and urgent. Thanks to Bazin, I met Jean-Michel a couple times a year at the office of *Cahiers du Cinéma*, where our wide-ranging conversations would inevitably turn to this Chinese master we both revered. Jean-Michel figures among that director's most articulate champions, and the enthusiastic review he wrote of *Still Life* from Cannes opened the film to me and to many others. In 2008 we were in Shanghai with Jia for a tribute to Bazin fifty years after his death. Jia's remarks about Bazin, highly informed, intelligent and moving, were poignant for us both. You can imagine that this sealed my nearly unconditional belief in the director. That meeting also made clear to me something that the subsequent dozen years have repeatedly shown, that Jia could not find a more lucid and perceptive writer outside China than Jean-Michel Frodon. Both men keep the largest human and social issues forefront, not as pundits do, or commentators, but through the most subtle interplay of the images and sounds that comprise events in cinema. Jia makes discoveries through these and builds his film worlds out of them, while Jean-Michel ferrets these discoveries from the films and articulates them in a style that's deceptively easy-going and always sharply focused. *The World of Jia Zhangke* is a rarity, for it comes from a sustained encounter of one of our greatest critics with one of our greatest directors. Thankfully both are still working at full tilt.

—New Haven, July 2020

Across Generations

Meeting Jia Zhangke is an unsettling experience that unites, to a rare degree, the ordinary and the extraordinary. The ordinary is simply a *way of being*, both natural and modest, where the mundane questions two people share when getting to know each other prevail. Right away, the *extraordinary* is felt in the different ways Jia occupies space and time: physically, emotionally, and intellectually. If you don't speak Chinese—and Jia himself isn't really fluent in any Western language—the language barrier changes nothing. Arguably the linguistic gap makes the density and lightness of his very *presence* even more palpable. An aristocratic aura emanates from some great artists, something many try to imitate. In contrast, Jia embodies a curious proximity with *beings* and *things*, and completely lacks arrogance, despite his extremely high standards. We will see in the following pages how his thinking and speech deepen this "feeling" that I felt immediately, and that's still so apparent after all the time we have spent together. What one feels in the company of this key figure of contemporary cinema illuminates how he has, under conditions of never-ending complexity, built a body of work whose importance and recognition continue to grow.

Jia occupies an essential, albeit difficult, place to define in the history of Chinese cinema, and in the history of cinema in general. The first reason for this difficulty is that his work is far from finished. Between 1995 (when he made *Xiaoshan Going Home*) and 2020 (when he released *Swimming Out Till the Sea Turns Blue*), he's made eleven feature films and as many shorts. Together, they testify to his great diversity of inspiration, technical approach and style. In the decades to come, we can presumably expect from him an equally abundant continuation and renewal. But, even if we stick to just what he's already accomplished, his importance should be considered and appreciated within the framework of several factors: the relevance of China and its cinema in the opening years of the 21st century, the evolution of contemporary cinema on a global scale, and the long history of Chinese cinema (or rather Chinese *cinemas*, including the Hong Kong and Taiwanese branches).

In attempting to understand Jia's place in contemporary cinema, we are confronted with a classifying system which, although useful, has since become burdensome and even out-of-date: the way in which Chinese filmmakers have been categorized by "generations." During the 1980s, Mainland Chinese cinema experienced an international recognition that was remarkable considering the country was only just emerging from the "black hole" of the Cultural Revolution (1966-1976). It was at this time that people began to divide Chinese cinema history into these "generations." The system had the advantage of delineating clear chapters in Chinese film history: the First Generation was that of silent cinema (1905–1930); the Second the period of the civil war and anti-Japanese resistance up to the Second World War and the Communist takeover (1930–1949); and the Third Generation covers when the studios were controlled by the State of the Popular Republic of China (1950–1965). After the Cultural Revolution, which essentially destroyed the film industry, came the Fourth Generation—also known as the "sacrificed generation"—which encompassed filmmakers whose careers should have begun in the 1960s. For artistic, ethical and political—not to mention financial—reasons this generation favored a modest, realist cinema that aimed to depict the daily life of both urban and country dwellers. Aesthetically, their principal reference was Italian Neorealism, and theoretically, André Bazin's writings. These directors made possible the appearance of the Fifth generation, the most well-known of them all.

Following their resurrection of the Beijing Film Academy, the Fourth Generation filmmakers became professors, mentors, and guardian angels for directors-in-the-making. This was the role performed by filmmaker Wu Tianming who, after becoming a studio head in the Shaanxi province, made it a welcoming place for the experiments of newcomers, the best known of which are Chen Kaige (*Yellow Earth* (1984), *The Big Parade* (1986), *King of the Children* (1987), *Life on a String* (1991)); Zhang Yimou (*Red Sorghum* (1987), *Ju Dou* (1990), *Raise the Red Lantern* (1991), *The Story of Qiu Ju* (1992)), and Tian Zhuangzhuang (*On the Hunting Ground* (1985), *The Horse Thief* (1986), *The Blue Kite* (1993)). Despite the major differences between them and their individual films, the style of these Fifth Generation directors can generally be said to be characterized by a visual experimentation that engages with the heritage of traditional Chinese painting and classical art forms. Thematically their works function as sensual fables, a break with the Maoist period right at the moment that China was entering into its "Reform Era," introduced by Deng Xiaoping.[1] The films are frequently set in the countryside—particularly in vast sparsely populated landscapes that evoke the empty spaces of classical painting—and inspired by the long years spent among peasants during the filmmakers' adolescence at the time of the "campaigns of re-education." Earthbound realism is combined with an interrogation of humankind's place in the universe. No room is left for socialist China's value system, and instead the films promote a youthful, rebellious energy, that's expressed, above all, in a longing for intimate relationships.

The first films by these directors were all banned. But their *auteurs* succeeded in finding recognition abroad, thanks largely to the major international festivals: Hong Kong played a leading role for *Yellow Earth*, and Berlin, Venice, and Cannes soon took over in promoting these new talents. In the 1990s, the Fifth Generation's two leading figures, Zhang Yimou and Chen Kaige, moved toward an increasingly decorative and spectacular cinema. They flattered the exotic tastes of foreign audiences with films increasingly less critical of the Chinese world until ultimately they themselves became the regime's official filmmakers. In the meantime, with the new decade, appeared the Sixth generation, the last one to date. Over the years these generational categories have somewhat lost their legitimacy.

The impetus for the Sixth generation resulted from a direct attempt to convey the economic reform of the 1980s, an endeavor blocked by the repression in Tiananmen Square in June 1989. Wu Wenguang, with his documentary *Bumming in Beijing: The Last Dreamers* (1990), and Zhang Yuan, with the fiction films *Mama* (1990), *Beijing Bastards* (1993) and the documentary *The Square* (1995), are this movement's two principal representatives. The filmmakers of this new generation, freely examining contemporary life's hardest aspects, were not interested in the countryside, preferring instead to devote themselves to urban areas and underprivileged neighborhoods, to the young dropouts with no future in sight. They wholeheartedly embraced lightweight, handheld cameras, and a "dirty" image, in great contrast to the previous generation's meticulously composed shots and sophisticated color experiments. Likewise, their often agitated and sometimes frenetic pacing,

---

1. The politician known as the "Architect of Modern China," Deng Xiaoping, came to power following Mao's death in 1976 and oversaw wide-ranging economic reforms. [Tr.]

accompanied by modern music, is lightyears away from the long takes and traditional music of which their elders were so fond.

Jia Zhangke emerged in the second half of the 1990s, gaining international recognition in cinephile circles with his first feature-length, *Xiaowu* (1997). The film takes place in a world marked by financial greed, the disappearance of law and order, and sexual repression, blending the daily life of ordinary people—and an interest in humdrum urban transformation—with a sensitivity for individual psychology. Shooting in his hometown, Fenyang, located in the central province of Shanxi, Jia avoids a binary representation of China that pits the countryside against booming megalopolises like Greater Beijing and Greater Shanghai. The China that he privileges may be invisible, but it's nevertheless becoming an integral part of the social fabric: hundreds of intermediary cities experimenting with, as best they can, the exit from a centrally planned economy, a rampant uncontrolled urbanization, and new and extreme forms of corruption that are accompanied by the arrival of modern entertainment, new media, and numerous amenities.

The film takes in the immense complexity of these issues while remaining focused on a down-on-his-luck youth roaming about in his own city. He's returned home only to discover he no longer belongs there. This introductory journey—an initiation in disgrace—is made using stylistic choices marked by the influence of Western modernism—mainly Italian Neorealism and Robert Bresson's work—and, at the same time, the aesthetic biases characteristic of China's Sixth Generation, particularly the rough documentary style of the images.

Xiaowu signaled the appearance of a new perspective in cinema, attentive to the most contemporary of realities, and capable of inventing modes of film production in sync with the singularly unprecedented size of, and violence at play in, China. This signal has been well received by world cinephilia, festivals, and critics. It's undoubtedly the clearest, but Jia's isn't the only one. He's been classified as part of a current that began at the beginning of the 1990s. Time has revealed him to be the most outstanding and most noteworthy member of this group of directors that includes Wang Xiaoshuai, Lou Ye, Zhang Ming, He Yi, Liu Jiang, Wang Chao, Jiang Wen, Li Yang.

Jia is the first to insist on this collective movement's importance, and has always understood that strength comes in numbers. As a student at the Beijing Film Academy in 1994, he created, with a dozen of his classmates, the Youth Experimental Film Group. Their meetings gave rise to heated and fruitful discussions that remain stamped in his memory. Above all, from the first signs of international recognition, Jia did something unique: as a guest at foreign film festivals he would bring DVDs of films by his compatriots. Thus he became a veritable ambassador for this new generation of filmmakers—if not of a new China—which is truly remarkable when taking into account the fiercely competitive climate that, everywhere in the world, young *auteurs* are subjected to, and the strategic importance of foreign validation for a director who is banned in his own country. This generosity and strategic intelligence is both exceptional and entirely characteristic of Jia.

At the start of the 21st century, Jia's renown was greatly expanded thanks to his next two films: *Platform* (2000), which won awards at both Venice and the Festival des Trois Continents in Nantes, and *Unknown Pleasures* (2002), which was included in the main selection at Cannes and hailed by North American critics. In 2003 he founded his company Xstream Pictures, with the producer Chow Keung and Yu Lik-wai, the cinematographer for most of his films. With the company, whose private funding comes from China, Hong Kong—where both Chow Keung and Yu Lik-wai are from—and abroad, Jia not only gave himself the possibility of producing his own films, but was also able to support other filmmakers in various ways: filmmakers including Emily Tang, Diao Yinan, and Song Fang. He also backed Yu Lik-wai's impressive features, *Love Will Tear Us Apart* (1999) and *All Tomorrow's Parties* (2003). Later, Jia created a major film Festival—in Pingyao, next to Fenyang—organized pedagogical programs for novice film critics, and launched the construction of movie theaters. These varied projects are evidence of his expansive vision. As a director, Jia is like an excellent Go player,[2] something that also requires knowing when to let go.

The unfailing support of Shôzô Ichiyama, producer at Takeshi Kitano's Office Kitano, as well as of several European partners, most notably in

---

2. Go is an abstract strategy board game invented in China more than 2,500 years ago. It's believed to be the oldest board game still in existence. [Tr.]

France, also contributes to the ongoing dialectic between the local and the faraway in Jia's films; a preoccupation with the relationship between a "here" and an "elsewhere." The strength of Jia's foreign partnerships was confirmed and bolstered by the Golden Lion for *Still Life* in 2006.

All the while Jia was engaged in an ongoing, uphill battle to escape the marginal world of underground cinema. Many other Chinese filmmakers, including some of the best, build a viewership willy-nilly through foreign visibility and domestic pirated DVDs, as opposed to the official state channels that guarantee theatrical distribution. In contrast, Jia has always wanted his films to be seen in regular movie theaters, so that his compatriots can easily see them. While putting into place a vast alternative network for his films relying on the internet and local cinephile groups throughout the country—thanks to which his unauthorized films were shown in cafés, galleries and private apartments—he never stopped wanting access to official distribution channels.

While his earlier films remained banned in China, this objective was finally achieved with *The World*, his fourth feature, in 2004. Instead of resting on his laurels with this personal victory—a victory nonetheless fragile as, at the end of 2013, it would be called into question with *A Touch of Sin*—Jia has dedicated time and energy to negotiating for a less restrictive and less arbitrary juridical structure, while also lending his support to censured colleagues like Tian Zhuangzhuang, Jiang Wen, and Lou Ye. The international recognition of Jia's films—a source of pride for many Chinese—offers him significant visibility in the media and on social media, particularly with his twenty million followers on Weibo, the Chinese Twitter.

Jia is rightly the filmmaker most closely associated with China's accession to the rank of superpower at the start of the 21st century. This new superpower status was accompanied by geopolitical, economic, social, technological, and environmental changes of an unprecedented nature and scale, changes that affected the stylistic and technological shift to digital filmmaking. As is often the case with great artists, Jia not only benefited from the emergence of new technologies, but also largely anticipated them. His first film shot with a digital camera was *In Public* (2002), but his three previous features had already foreshadowed the digital aesthetic, even though they employed traditional methods and were shot on celluloid. But it's not just a matter of filmmaking technology. The constant presence of the virtual and digital in the contemporary world is incorporated in *The World* through animated on-screen SMS messages, while in *Still Life* an apartment building transforms into a spaceship in a comic gag.

This "fantasy" moment intensifies the constant tension between documentary and fiction that exists in all of Jia's work. While this is a factor with all great filmmakers, no one has engaged with it in such a methodical and rejuvenated way as Jia has. Throughout much of his career, he's shot a documentary and a fiction in quick succession in the same location: the mining town of Datong for *In Public* and *Unknown Pleasures*; the Three Gorges Dam site for *Dong* and *Still Life*—in fact, in both these cases, the documentary actually gave birth to the fiction. Then came the creative merging of fiction and documentary in *24 City* (2008), an investigation on the transformation of a military factory into a luxury residence, and *I Wish I Knew* (2010), a portrait of the city of Shanghai through the stories of "witnesses" with positions as different as they're complimentary, accompanied by a ghostly heroine played with absolute grace by Zhao Tao.

Taken together, these artistic choices characterize an oeuvre that combines the most up-to-date sensibility with an openness to new technologies, and characteristics representative of the Second, Fourth, Fifth, and Sixth Generations of filmmakers, to invent a completely new and contemporary cinema.

Chronologically and stylistically, the similarities with the urban energy and grunge style of the Sixth Generation is obvious, even if it was never a question, for Jia, of letting himself be confined to just one style. With the Fifth Generation, his rapport is more complex. Jia has always asserted the decisive role played by Chen Kaige's *Yellow Earth*, which initially spurred his desire to make films and, from this generation, he's inherited a sense of reality and visual experimentation. From his second film *Platform* onwards, it was clear that Jia was assimilating filmmaking lessons from this generation of the post-Cultural Revolution Renaissance, albeit in order to do something new. For Jia has never hid that he feels betrayed by the leading players of this generation for their drift towards the official regime, something that served as a counterexample for him.[3] He hasn't, however, adopted an openly anta-

---

3. For example, Jia told the American scholar Michael Berry: "In 1997 I was getting ready to

gonistic posture toward the Chinese authorities, not wanting to force a break with the public-at-large.

Jia's artistic choices do have continuity with the films of the Fourth Generation, with their modest realism that's attentive to people's daily lives. On a formal level—his gaze directed at the realities of the world—Jia also asserts the Second Generation's legacy, characterized by both a formal exploration that comes from Brecht's theater, and a compassionate look at a people suffering from the earthquakes that shook the country between the 1910s and 1950s, from the Republican to the Communist revolutions. From this generation, Jia reserves pride of place for Fei Mu (1906-1951). Today Fei is regarded by many Chinese directors and critics as a tutelary figure, notably for his film *Spring in a Small Town* (1948),[4] shot just before the filmmaker went into exile in Hong Kong, where he would stay until he died. The interview with the director's daughter in *I Wish I Knew* plays a very significant role in the film, accompanied by numerous excerpts from classics of Chinese cinema that underline the prominent place, both on the level of historical testimony and artistic inspiration, that Jia attributes to Fei. Furthermore, Jia's cinema draws from other sources of Chinese cinema too, with clear references to the two great masters of Taiwanese New Cinema: Hou Hsiao-hsien and Edward Yang—both are regularly praised by Jia—and also to the legacy of martial arts cinema, above all that of King Hu, to whom *A Touch of Sin* pays homage.

Jia's films have continued to develop thematically and aesthetically without turning their back on the past. He escapes easy categorization, whether as a member of a Sixth, or Seventh, generation—any attempt to confine him in this way oversimplifies his accomplishments. For the framework of Jia's references, and his sources of inspiration, aren't limited to just China's

---

graduate from the Beijing Film Academy and, after four years of watching Chinese films, I still hadn't seen a single Chinese film that had anything to do with the Chinese reality that I knew. After the Fifth Generation's initial success, their artistic works started to undergo a lot of changes. But there was a very clear disconnect between these films and the current Chinese reality we were living in." In Michael Berry, *Xiaowu, Platform: Jia Zhangke's Hometown Trilogy*, BFI Film Classics (London: BFI, 2009), 128–129.

4. In 2002 Tian Zhuangzhuang paid homage to this film with his similarly titled *Springtime in a Small Town*.

cinema(s): we should not forget his substantial rapport with European cinema's long history of modernity. Clear echoes of Rossellini, Bresson, Pasolini, Antonioni, Godard, and Wenders resonate in his films.

Particular emphasis has been given to Jia's relationship with the history of his art—the cinema. But the universe of his references is far broader than just that. Among others, mention should be made of his very personal way his cinema is nourished with pictorial inspirations. His films successfully achieve a paradoxical association of influences usually considered contradictory, as they mobilize both classical Chinese art and European painting. Inspired by the former, a few scenes come to mind: in *Platform* when, against the walls of Pingyao, a young couple breaks up; the empty carcass of the weapons factory in *24 City*; the scene in *Still Life* in front of the Kuimen Mountains, immortalized in a thousand "mountain and water" paintings from the Tang, Song, Yuan, and Ming dynasties. In these paintings the landscape's grandeur is magnified by the compositional void, reinforcing humankind's small place within the vast cosmos, and reflecting an eastern philosophy of the world.

But other scenes come to mind as well: the peasants who settle down and wait for the theatrical performance at the beginning of *Platform*; an overcrowded public transit system in *In Public* where individuals are looked at one by one; the distressing faces of the elderly who attend the funeral ceremony in *Dong*. Together these individuals carry, to an extraordinary degree, what has been at the crux of Western painting since its origins in icons: the portrait, the face. To "hold together" and combine, in a dynamic and lively way sensitive to the fluctuations of reality, these two diametrically opposed aesthetics—and using an approach that sacrifices neither the individual, nor the vastness of the world—requires a filmmaker with exceptional sensitivity. The final sequence of *Xiaowu* exemplifies in a tense, dramatic, but light manner Jia's modus operandi: the fate of a fictional character set against the gaze of the city's local population.

Haunted by his country's long political and cultural history, Jia is a Chinese filmmaker to the core, a filmmaker of his time, a time defined by the internet and connections without borders. In order to occupy this era *cinematographically*, a special art of bifurcation is needed, an art of displacement whose centers and perspectives constantly realign—within each film and from film to film—the issues, the questions, the focal points of the time. Crystallization of this dexterity is never meaningless: it's the fortuitous meeting, on the side of a country road, between the fashion designer and the coal miner in *Useless*; it's the road that the poor cousin takes, moving away from the troupe in the truck in *Platform*; it's the very universe of *Unknown Pleasures* saturated with possibilities that never transpire; it's the anxieties visible on the prostitutes' bodies in *Dong*; and, of course, it's the movement between the different stories that make up *A Touch of Sin*.

This multiplicity finds a particularly visible and moving incarnation in the three faces present in nearly all of Jia's work. His longtime friend Wang Hongwei signals a loyalty to a modern cinema, open to the winds of current events; his nimble form reacts in the moment to instances of the real, whether standing still or in movement. Han Sanming—Jia's cousin and a close friend since childhood—always plays a version of himself. Palpably and silently, he embodies a social reality on which Jia hasn't turned his back, without giving it the dominant position it would have been given in a more message-oriented cinema. Finally, there is the actor Zhao Tao to whom Jia has been married since 2012. With an unpretentious grace she embodies the very idea of fiction, of translation, conveying different realities and feelings. The essential heterogeneity of these three presences translates—through gestures, voices, looks—the complexities that Jia's cinema never stops developing with the world.

Jia's Films

Jia Before Jia (But Already Jia)
One Day, in Beijing (1994) and *Xiaoshan Going Home* (1995)

JIA ZHANGKE SHOT his first film, *One Day, in Beijing*, in 1994 on an analog video camera that he borrowed from the Beijing Film Academy, even though he was enrolled in film theory and not directing. It is a ten-minute documentary that consists of a series of short portraits of people—mainly Chinese visiting the capitol—that Jia encountered in Tiananmen Square. Despite the setting, there is no overt reference to the dramatic events that took place there in 1989. This is in contrast to Zhang Yuan's *The Square*, also shot in Tiananmen Square in 1994, which offers an implicit memory of the "Tiananmen Spring" and its suppression.

The following year, Jia made his first fiction film, *Xiaoshan Going Home*, an hour-long fiction, with his friend and classmate Wang Hongwei in the main role of Xiaoshan. Shot during his studies at the Film Academy and under the banner of the Youth Experimental Film Group—which Jia founded—the film follows a young man in the streets of Beijing, given to disorderly meandering and torn between different loyalties.

Xiaoshan, with his disheveled appearance, long hair and omnipresent cigarette between his lips, works as a cook at an inexpensive restaurant. He quits his job, planning to return to his native province for the New Year's celebrations. Over the course of the film, he wanders aimlessly throughout Beijing and has a series of encounters: with an ex-girlfriend with whom he breaks up, with some pals with whom he engages in a bout of heavy drinking, with his former lover again for a short lived and joyless sexual tryst, and finally with an old friend who traffics in train tickets and gets severely beaten up. At the end of this pathetic odyssey Xiaoshan, who has failed to leave the capitol, shaves his head.

Throughout, Xiaoshan's decisions are motivated by a desire for adventure, a central theme of the film. It's shot with an unstable hand-held camera, attentive to the miniscule events of daily life that arise in the darkest streets of the world: in markets, in the subway, and near train stations. "New Wave" filming if you like, but pushed in a more slovenly direction, something echoed by the protagonist's appearance and his irrational and unpleasant behavior. Jia relies on a sort of raw energy, born from the capture of reality and a certain lack of polish, in order to continually engage our attention. This "dirty realism," deliberately focused on the least rosy of appearances, is a continuation of the Sixth Generation's style from the early 1990s, with its raw images, unstable framings, and muted colors. Jia's first feature, *Xiaowu*, from 1997 shares a similar aesthetic, and yet also affirms a more unique, personal style.

Stylistically, *Xiaoshan Going Home* rejects any idea of a simplistic naturalism. One example is Jia's shift from black and white to color during the first sequence and the shift back to black and white shortly before the film's end. Others are the awkward use of title cards, which provide useless or redundant information to what one sees—a process he would use again in *Xiaowu*—dialogue on a black screen, or the use of ironically kitsch elements like Xiaoshan's poem to his mother, or the maudlin pop song, used here as quirky commentary, rather than as a element of reality.

Xiaoshan Going Home is a kind of notebook on the malaise of Beijing's young migrant workers from the provinces. In a register that's deliberately non-narrative and non-aesthetic, it generally resists any overt technical mastery, preferring instead a vigorous affirmation of the freedom of film language. The film would prove to be a useful business card for Jia: selected in 1996 by the Hong Kong Independent Short Film and Video Awards, it won the top prize in the narrative short category, which allowed its young director to meet two of his most important partners for the coming years: the cameraman Yu Lik-wai[1] and the producer Chow Keung.

* * *

The Zigzag of the Little Thief
Xiaowu (1997)

RIGHT AWAY THE slightly dirty image in *Xiaowu* is bizarre, as if stolen on the fly, and yet it's elegantly exact. But ever since Robert Bresson's *Pickpocket*—an obvious but not overwhelming reference for this, Jia's first feature—it's been known what a precise art the filching of pennies or yuans

---

1. Yu Lik-wai's documentary, *Neon Goddesses*, won the Grand Prix at the Independent Film and Video Awards that same year.

from other people's pockets is. Every shot of this fictional reportage seems to vibrate with a mix of urgency, risks, and a somewhat forlorn humor.

The film's protagonist, Xiaowu,[2] is a pickpocket who returns to his hometown Fenyang, a small city in Northern China's Shanxi province with bleak and dusty streets. He crosses paths with a tourist in search of the exotic, but there's no silk or concubines here, not even the bright red of Maoist imagery. Xiaowu is coming back after a stay in prison. His newly rich childhood friend, Jin Xiaoyong—who has abandoned picking pockets for more lucrative trafficking—turns his back on him because he's getting married. This arriviste makes an appearance on local television, adopting the pose of the new middle class bred from China's economic reforms. Xiaowu's story is made up of a series of adventures, disappointing for him but instructive—for the viewer—on the state of contemporary China, with every scene filled with a potential for laughter that veers between complicity and irony.

Jia is a great filmmaker who, in his early years, occupied the unlikely aesthetic position of being the offspring of Maurice Pialat and Hou Hsiao-hsien. He films every glance as if he's recording an electric current; capturing the air that vibrates between bodies, and knowing this expresses more than sociology or psychology ever can. His subtle and efficient images, which might appear to be hastily shot, blow up the characters' interactions by capturing them in diametrically opposed movements, and he succeeds in making even banal relationships dramatic. *Xiaowu* is an extraordinarily dense and affecting film, composed of numerous memorable elements, including deliberate silences: the paid-for stroll with the sex worker Meimei in the streets and in the hair salon; Xiaowu's gentle thoughtfulness when he pays her a visit when she's sick; the carnal truth of his naked body in the public bath; the suggestive richness of the soundtrack woven from street sounds and television; the kitsch cigarette lighter that plays the song "Für Elise" (an ode to Chinese modernity).

The film culminates in the sequence where, arrested by a policeman—an ambiguous figure—the petty thief is displayed before a crowd. The sub-

---

2. Xiaowu is the protagonist's first name and refers in Chinese to a small bird (the little bunting). While the surname of his former partner-in-crime, Xiaoyong is several times mentioned (Jin), Xiaowu is consistently addressed, at least in the English-language subtitles, by only his given name. His father, however, reminds him that he's the son of Liang Changyau. [Tr.]

sequent 360° panoramic shot from Xiaowu's perspective goes further than simply showing the character's perspective, and the film's total immersion in his reality. It ultimately produces the effect that the people staring at the thief are looking directly at us, the viewers, and by extension the director. With the simplest of means, Jia explodes the voyeurism at play in any representation, by very simply revealing what's at play in the murky mysteries of the *mise-en-scène*. No one is safe here, not even the authorities or the public.

* * *

What Time is the Train for Youth?
Platform (2000)

"You can't even be bothered to imitate a train!" shouts the troupe leader at Cui Mingliang (Wang Hongwei) after he delays the group's post performance departure by bus. "How would I know how to imitate a train? I've never seen one!" replies the young man. This unseen train, leaving for an encounter with the world, symbolizes the aspirations of a generation. It's the manifestation of a technical, social, and economic shift that spreads across the mainland and connects it to the rest of the planet. It's also, like the first Chinese rock song, "Platform"—twice heard in this eponymously titled film—the manifestation of a vibrant energy.

Platform is the first film that Jia Zhangke wanted to make but, because he didn't have the funds to produce it, he instead began with *Xiaowu*, a simpler project. *Platform* is unusually complicated, even if it doesn't initially appear so. Beginning about twenty years earlier and spanning a full decade, the film features an ensemble cast, rather than a single protagonist. It's a highly ambitious work that addresses two fundamentally different transformations.

The first transformation is the passage from adolescence to adulthood of the four protagonists and their friends, akin to the conventional Bildungsroman of novels and cinema. The second transformation is infinitely more complex, and documents China's changes during the Reform Era of the 1980s, when Deng Xiaoping led the country from a planned economy based on agriculture and heavy industrialization to a consumer economy; from a country completely defined by the austere ideology and proletarian rhetoric of Maoism to one open to numerous western influences. These two transformations are, however, in no way equivalent and in many ways contradict each other. Jia is too subtle a filmmaker to reduce the upheaval of the Reform Era to a kind of national adolescence, or to equate the pangs of youth with an economic and social upheaval.

The film focuses on the members of an itinerant theater troupe that initially perform agit-prop scenes with slogans and red flags, and that later turn into a musical group called the Shenzhen All Star Rock and Breakdance Electronic Band. Naming their group after Shenzhen—far away from the young performers' home in the Shanxi province—isn't gratuitous as it was China's first openly capitalist city. Strictly speaking, *Platform* isn't an autobiographical film as Jia was considerably younger than his characters at the time. But it's dedicated to his father—with whom the independently-minded filmmaker had a very stormy relationship—and is deeply rooted in his own history and geography.

The first shots—of Fenyang in wintertime—give the impression that *Platform* continues *Xiaowu*'s aesthetic of documentary images captured on the fly. But this is contradicted by both the carefully composed shots with fixed frames and elegant panning shots, as well as by the use of sets.

The sets quickly create another atmosphere, another weight. Jia succeeds in imbuing his protagonists' youthful momentum with the cumbersome imperatives of the "revolutionary morality," a repetition of old traditionalist straightjackets dressed up in red verbiage. This double weight is characteristic of the period and a vestige of provincial and archaic society; it's embodied by the authorities and especially the father of the young woman Yin Ruijuan, played by Zhao Tao, working here with Jia for the first time. The streets and buildings of Fenyang also express a weight from which the characters wish to escape, as conveyed by the film's emblematic image of Wang Hongwei on the back of a bike, his arms open like wings.

The sad and dilapidated buildings that make up the film's urban landscape are surrounded by the majestic walls that encircle the city.[3] These walls testify to a bygone power and ambition, an earlier time of confinement. Their impressive mass contrasts with the delicate discussion Mingliang and Ruijuan have in a scene of overwhelming beauty. Here for the first time Jia exercises the singular power of his *mise-en-scène*, drawing on classical, even silent, cinema. And cinema itself is present within the narrative, due to the screening of *Awāra* (1951)—a film by Raj Kapoor, the "Indian Chaplin"—that's cut short when Ruijuan's policeman father forces her to leave the screening.

Chinese society's gradual liberation of individual desires is chronicled by new habits—new ways of dressing, new music, new dances—and matches a concomitant evolution in economics and technology. The theatrical troupe, adopting a fresh repertoire inspired by cassette tapes from Shenzhen and Hong Kong, performs in remote villages where the recently installed electricity serves to reinforce the power of the local bigwigs. There's a lot going on here and it's worth emphasizing Jia's mastery—he was then barely thirty—in juggling so many narrative strands. There is the mysterious train that never stops where the troupe is, reminding us of the forced inertia imposed on a people who need a passport to change cities within their own country. Or, more generally, the intense desire of these young people for changes that were systematically blocked in the immediate post-Mao era.

---

3. The surrounding walls recall those that still encircled Fenyang in the 1980s, but which were destroyed before filming began. These scenes were filmed in the neighboring city of Pingyao where very similar constructions remain standing.

An astonishingly dynamic film, *Platform* is also at times very funny. For example, the memorable hymn to Genghis Khan, transformed into a pop makeover of an unorthodox historical heritage: it's a Cantonese cover version by the Hong Kong singer George Lam of the 1979 hit by the German band Dschinghis Khan.

A film of infinite sadness, *Platform* is preoccupied with the many disappointments of the time. One scene in particular conveys the somber mood: Mingliang's impoverished cousin, Sanming—much poorer than the others who themselves are far from rich—before trudging off to work in a clandestine mine where he'll likely die, signs a contract absolving the mining company of any responsibility in the case of his death. He gives Mingliang five dollars to give to his sister, so she can leave Fenyang for university and never return. We are reminded that the country's economic changes and embrace of modernity, is accompanied by the suffering—and often death—of countless unfortunates.

At the end of the film we are left with a feeling of defeat: the once rebellious rockers and rebels have settled down to everyday life, with the television on in the background. *Platform* is the story of the Tiananmen generation, a generation who once dreamed that China's economic reforms would also lead to new *personal* freedoms.

* * *

Singing in the Pain
In Public (2001)
Unknown Pleasures (2002)

UNKNOWN PLEASURES IS a film of collisions. It's an intentionally disturbing film, with its jarring images of a vulgar self-obsessed capitalism that hasn't yet been restrained by middle-class decorum. The intrusive jingles and scrappy tunes commercializing anything and everything on the film's soundtrack are equally discordant. But, perhaps most of all, the film is jarring in its collision of a film genre with real life. The genre is that of the New Wave and its spin-offs—cinema that focuses on young people—as represented by a number of films from throughout the world: *Adieu Philippine*,

Black Peter, I Vitelloni, Saturday Night and Sunday Morning, The Unscrupulous Ones, Good-for-Nothing, etc.,[4] right up until Hou Hsiao-hsien's *The Boys from Fengkuei*. Usually these are films about nonchalant roguish youths who want to have fun and work as little as possible, who get by with sleazy tricks, and devote themselves as much as possible to the serious questions of quick sex and everlasting love. All these films—made during a period in which their country of origin was undergoing rapid modernization—depict their own social and economic environment. But until *Unknown Pleasures*, none of them made this the very core of the story. It's an extremely dark core, a darkness that constantly threatens the film's two young protagonists: best friends Binbin and Xiaoji.

For *Unknown Pleasures*, Jia returned to his home province of Shanxi, shooting in Datong, a mining city, instead of Fenyang, where his first two films were shot. Datong is a secondary metropolis, as different from the large town of Fenyang, as it is from the megalopolises of the east coast. It's one of China's second-tier cities and the kind of city that's rarely shown in cinema. The film turns its implacable gaze on Chinese society, specifically the commodification of human relationships that took place at the beginning of the 21st century. It was the time of a major boom, and of the brutal secret repression of the Falun Gong sect,[5] which Binbin's mother belongs to. It was also at this time that China was chosen to host the 2008 Olympic Games. The immense collective jubilation that followed this announcement echoes the circumstances that gave rise to the film: a paradoxical mix of the

---

4. *Adieu Philippine*, Jacques Rozier's 1962 film; *Black Peter*, Miloš Forman's 1964 debut film in Czechoslovakia; *I Vitelloni*, Federico Fellini's 1953 film; *Saturday Night and Sunday Morning*, Karel Reisz's 1960 English drama; *The Unscrupulous Ones*, Ruy Guerra's 1962 Brazilian crime film; *Good-for-Nothing*, Yoshishige Yoshida's first Japanese feature from 1960. [Tr.]

5. Falun Gong is a new religious movement established by Li Hongzhi in China in 1992. Falun Gong associates meditation, *qigong* exercises with a moral philosophy. It identifies as an offshoot of Buddhism but also incorporates elements from Taoism. Although the movement was initially condoned by Chinese authorities, it very quickly fell into disfavor because of its size (by 1999, there were some 70 million adherents of the movement), independence from state, and spiritual teachings. The authorities began circulating negative press about the movement and labeled it a cult. In April 1999, over 10,000 Falun Gong followers—the largest assembly in China since Tiananmen ten years earlier—demonstrated in Beijing, demanding legal status and freedom from state interference. A crackdown and ban on the movement swiftly followed. [Tr.]

urge to embrace globalization with a nationalist chauvinism that transcends both class and generation.

The omnipresence of American brands—or even the *Pulp Fiction* wig that the singer-call girl Qiaoqiao (Zhao Tao) wears when hawking an obviously undrinkable Mongolian wine—highlight China's market explosion. Her energy as a walking advertisement is in stark contrast to her peers' general inability to take decisive action in their lives. Xiaoji's romance with Zhao Tao's starlet is doomed to failure, even sexually. And the young man's pitiful imitation of a gangster leads nowhere. The film depicts the helpless state created by the surfeit of enticing signs that are intrinsic to a dynamic and greedy consumerism. This tension between bait and desire paralyzes the young characters' existences: adrift with no future in a world where they can only lay claim to chimerical signposts, they wear themselves out pretending to be someone they are not.

Unknown Pleasures valiantly attempts to break from this boisterously bleak environment with a long take of Cui on his motorbike in the arid steppe surrounding the city, an abstract space, completely untouched by the adjacent jungle of signs. It's an attempt to break away not just from Datong, but the entire universe of the film. The characters themselves ultimately realize there is no escape, and the film ends in the grip of police repression, Chinese society's old curse. This repression is no less present than before, made manifest by the extreme violence of an economic boom that destroys social ties and creates enormous inequality. The scene where Binbin begins to sing in the middle of the police station epitomizes the film's feeling of being on a collision course. In this moment there is a mingling—both grotesque and terribly sad—of rebellion with a kind of forced euphoria, as an impossible complicity is sought with the cop who, in the hope of forging a communal belonging, orders him to sing.

Jia made *Unknown Pleasures* right after the documentary short *In Public* (30 minutes), which is also set in Datong. *In Public* is Jia's first film shot on a digital camera (and *Unknown Pleasures* his second), and finds him observing passersby in various public spaces—a train station, a bus, the dance hall—without voiceover or dialogue. The film was commissioned by the Jeonju International Film Festival in South Korea, and its thirty minutes are a contemporary version of silent cinema's City Symphonies (Charles Sheeler and Paul Strand's *Manhatta*, Dziga Vertov's *Man with a Movie Camera*, Walter Ruttmann's *Berlin: Symphony of a Great City*, and Manoel de Oliveira's *Douro, Faina fluvial*[6]). For Jia the film gave rise to an identification less with places or passersby, than with the kinds of ambiances and moods that occur in public spaces.

While shooting in Datong, Jia said that he noticed an inexplicable and strange euphoria in its inhabitants. This feeling is echoed by the film's international title, *Unknown Pleasures*, suggested by Yu Lik-wai in reference to the English post-punk band Joy Division's debut album (the film's Chinese title—*Ren xiao yao*—is that of the Taiwanese pop melody sung by Binbin at the end). This troubling euphoria is caused by the joy of consumption, of getting rich—or at least living only for this goal—and, the film suggests, has become a universal mass experience. It's this realization that makes the film's violence all the more disturbing.

* * *

A Network Film
The World (2004)

"See the world without leaving Beijing." These words greet visitors to the theme park The World, endlessly repeated by a synthetic voice over loudspeaker (the park in the film is itself synthetic, a composite of two theme parks: one in Beijing, the other in Shenzhen). Jia Zhangke's fourth feature develops from a contradiction: China has entered into the globalized economy, all the while maintaining a strict political control that limits people's ability to travel abroad. Hence the symbolic role passports have in the film. They're only permitted for those of a privileged social class, so are the subject of multiple fantasies, even if "going abroad" only means a trip to neighboring Mongolia, whose capital Ulaanbaatar is prized for a certain exoticism, the local equivalent of say Samarkand or Timbuktu.

---

6. *Douro, Faina Fluvial* (*Labor on the Douro River*) from 1931 is Oliveira's first film and depicts his hometown of Porto. [Tr.]

The theme of an impossible journey, central to all of Jia's work, isn't just a question of geography, but also of blocked destinies. In *The World* airplanes replace the older modes of transportation in Jia's earlier films—trains, buses, trucks, and motorbikes—with the world no longer divided into a *here* and an *elsewhere*. The film is also concerned with two other issues: the introduction of the *virtual* in everyday life, and the social conditions in China at the start of the 21st century. It's extraordinary that a work of art, no matter its genre, is able to combine such complex and heterogeneous elements in a manner that's both legible and enticing.

Jia succeeds here because he is, to a rare degree, an artist aware of the realities of his country, and of his time. One characterization of his era is the profound upheaval caused by the deleterious intrusion of digital technology into human relationships. In *The World* Jia uses animation to visualize the characters' actions on their cell phones, something that's not merely decorative: although this new technology may be virtual, it has an unquestionable impact on the "real world." Hence, Jia isn't content with this animation just illustrating the private dreams and anxieties of his characters, instead according it the same primacy as "real" actions and words. He does this not for playful or formal reasons, but because the distinction between the physical and the virtual has been abolished in the contemporary world. It's not that reality has disappeared, but that these synthetic images are now *part of* reality. This is why *The World* is every bit as realistic as *Xiaowu* and *Unknown Pleasures*.

Jia is conscious of the fact that, when he shot *The World*, two-thirds of China's population—a billion people—had neither a passport nor a computer. A billion poorly educated, often illiterate, peasants and low-wage workers were completely bypassed by all the attention on the country's enormous developments in the third millennium. It's hardly surprising that these extraordinary changes should be the center of so much attention and although Jia is unquestionably their best cinematic chronicler—via both fiction and documentary—he's not the only one. But he *is* the only one to make the connection between China's lightning modernization and the profound effects it's had on its immense population,[7] while simultaneously refusing to limit his focus to just the abject poverty and terrible injustices that afflict so many.

The presence of the "Shanxi cousins" in the film illustrate this harsh injustice. They have come to Beijing to work on construction sites and the extreme precariousness of their situation as workers and exiles leads directly to the death of the cousin nicknamed "Little Sister." Jia's feelings for, and attentiveness to, these forgotten souls who symbolize the fate of so many of China's citizens, is palpable in his *mise-en-scène*. In a moving scene towards the end of the film funerary paper burns for them at the top of an unfinished concrete tower.

Where does Jia find the intuitive intelligence to bring to life such complex issues—both essential and abstract—in a way that's so profoundly credible and moving? The film's narrative construction is based on overlapping multiple bodies: that of the theme park, that of the capital in the throes of a major socio-economic upheaval, and that of an interconnected planet.

---

7. Very different, for instance, is Wang Bing's nine-hour opus *West of the Tracks* (2002), a documentary that focuses exclusively on the collapse of the industrial world from the previous era without addressing the effects of new technologies on ways of life.

Having characters say things like "I'm going to India," or "I'm going to Japan," before walking only sixty or so meters—to the faux Taj Mahal or the faux Kyoto pagoda—is the film's basic premise, and its running gag. But, accompanying this, is the film's engagement with a real, and harsh, material world: there is nothing virtual about exploitation, sexual deprivation, and the drive for domination.

In the opening scene, Zhao Tao, dressed as an Indian temple dancer, wanders the subway-like subterranean backstage corridors. From there the film continually takes the "tubes": the monorail, the elevator of the fake Eiffel Tower, various corridors, the train station, the airport, the bus. The highpoint is a visual and caricatural metaphor that we doubt really exists: a night-club brothel imagined as a golden intestine for the nouveaux riches. The animated SMS on cell phones is the visual, logical, and seamless extension of this transportation network. Together, these corridors and electronic communications connect all the protagonists with each other, allowing for the circulation of desire, fantasies, and power.

Our protagonists here are the couple, Xiaotao and Taisheng. Xiaotao is a dancer in the theme park. She constantly changes her outfits, each representing a different national culture—India, Egypt, Japan—and takes part in a never-ending show of glitzy clichés played to the sound of all-purpose muzak. Her boyfriend Taisheng is the head of security. The purity of their relationship does not preclude false pretense, even betrayal. Still, *The World* isn't so much a dramatic narrative in the classic sense, and instead showcases multiple protagonists, situations, and human relationships. Jia reveals to us the trafficking, score-settling, loyalties, and influence peddling that go on behind the scenes of this world.

It's a world we can no longer ignore, a world in which Jia manages to create moments of pure grace: from the Russian song Anna offers to Xiaotao to the animated image of Taisheng on horseback near a fake monument. Or, simply and marvelously, Zhao Tao's face framed in a window, her face open—open to the world—despite everything.

Beauty Equation
Still Life (2006)

FOUR MEN, BARE-CHESTED, sit side by side on a bed. They're eating, and don't invite the visiting stranger to join them. In the penumbra they look strong, perhaps even threatening. There is a complicated story between these four—whom we won't see again and don't know—and the visitor who humbly faces them. Selected almost randomly, this is just one scene from the film, and definitely not the most important one. But, by itself, it harbors a physical intensity; a multiplicity of possible meanings; an unresolved violence; a presence of bodies, objects, stories; and a humanity that even a hundred other films altogether can't match. That's *Still Life*, a film so powerful in its individual components that it's better to begin by discussing them, rather than the film's overarching themes. For, any hasty discussion of its broader themes would be to risk not fully comprehending Jia's achievement, an achievement that takes place incrementally, shot by shot, and sequence by sequence.

Some of these shots are famous for their exceptional nature: the film shifting to the fantastic when a building converts into a space rocket and flies away; the addition, via digital effects, of a flying saucer over the vast landscapes of the Kuimen Gate; the collapse of a gigantic building seen by a couple from the cut-out of a half-destroyed wall; a tightrope walker improbably crossing the sky above a seemingly infinite field of ruins. Despite these moments, the film isn't about magic tricks, but instead quite the opposite. For *Still Life* proposes that there is no division between realism and fantasy in a world that inflicts—on people and nature—a seismic event such as the construction of the Three Gorges dam. In this world, the supernatural is a daily occurrence to be found on every street corner.

For example, there is the nocturnal shot of an immense bridge over the Yangtze illuminated by an apparatchik's pure hubris; or the abstract choreography of miniscule workers destroying with sledgehammers the titanic pipes that pass over the frail silhouette of the unhappy young woman—she's a delicate figure, outlined in yellow, in the vast inhumanity of this Chinese *Metropolis*. Or the image of a quiet moment for the overworked diggers as they listen to a song and share a drink; or that of the body of a young man packed in a plastic gag; or the image of prostitutes on a half-destroyed balcony, as in a theater at the end of the world.

These are just a few examples of how each shot of the film carries an inexhaustible visual and political richness, filled with emotion. And from this array, Jia composes a first, a second, and then finally one hundred different stories that are ultimately one and the same.

Still Life's main story is that of the superhuman upheaval caused by the construction of the world's largest dam, the extreme brutality it imposes on people and nature. Every aspect has a truly mythological dimension: the expulsion of hundreds of thousands of inhabitants, corruption, chaos, hardship, exploitation of workers on the construction sites, coming ecological catastrophe, managerial hubris (with no distinction between corporate executives and party leaders), endless bitter disputes between the residents and the employees.

Two main narratives structure the film. First the story of Han Sanming, a poor miner from the Northern province of Shanxi. Han Sanming is the actor's real name, and in *Platform* he played the role of the poor cousin. Here he's searching for his daughter whom he hasn't seen since his wife—whom he bought from her parents—fled Shanxi sixteen years earlier to return to Sichuan. His long search—which leads him from encounter to encounter and forces him to work on the demolition of buildings—breaks to make room for the story of Shenhong (Zhao Tao), the abandoned wife of Guo

Bin, one of the supervisors of the dam construction. She too has come from Shanxi looking for her spouse.

A poster for this film that shows Han Sanming and Shenhong back-to-back in front of the Three Gorges Dam is misleading as they never actually meet (although they will be joined briefly when they both see the flying saucer from different places at the same time).

Han Sanming and Shenhong may be from the same province, but they're not from the same world, and their journeys aren't exactly equivalent. Shenhong is helped in her search by her husband's friend (Wang Hongwei). He would like to be her friend, but there's no room for love, or even friendship, in this place. Jia's camera itself seems to vibrate when filming Zhao Tao and this reverberates on everything around her, communicating the region's rising heat, matched by the stifling world being built. The building's take-off will be but a brief burst of freedom from this unbearable pressure.

As if it were the most natural thing in the world, the film resumes Han Sanming's story after Shenhong leaves. We watch him perform slave labor before finally he and his wife unexpectedly reunite.

The force and singularity of specific moments in the *mise-en-scène* has often been noted: a demolition site, a ferry descending the majestic course of the river, the air-conditioned offices of the companies building the dam, a cheap restaurant where co-workers share their misfortunes over noodles. The *collective* force of these moments should be noted—a magisterial gaze that magnifies seemingly trivial situations, giving equal place to each. However, this stylistic unity isn't uniform—the unity stems not from what is shown but from the coherence of Jia's *perspective*. The slow tracking shots, the carefully composed frames acutely attentive to every detail, the constant sensitivity to the tonality of light and sounds, to the scents and the heat, grants *Still Life* a similarity with the Yangtze River itself, an immense force heading into the future.

The film is able to communicate, if only in outline, the stories of one hundred other individuals: that of the young thug overcome with loneliness who ridiculously imitates Chow Yun-fat in John Woo's *A Better Tomorrow*; the old man who thinks he can house the demolition workers without being himself destroyed; "Little Ma," whose romantic dreams are dashed as she winds up as slave labor on a boat; and the demolition company's unseen manageress. Plus Wang Dongming, the courageous fellow played by Wang Hongwei, who, amidst the general destruction done in the name of progress, continues his archaeological excavations. Swimming against the tide, he still participates in his way in China's august history, from the Han emperors to Mao Zedong. Jia's equation here—the dam's construction plus the two main stories multiplied by one hundred—makes *Still Life* an astonishing achievement. With neither complacency nor oversimplification, the filmmaker depicts his country's colossal upheaval at the start of the 21st century.

* * *

The Art of Portraiture
Dong (2006)

FROM BEHIND WE think it's Han Sanming, the actor-character of *Still Life*, who is once again contemplating the Kuimen canyon—the most spectacular of the Three Gorges that gives the dam its name. But instead it's a strong young man, whom we subsequently see wandering in a landscape—where much of *Still Life* took place—that has been devastated by the demolitions making way for the dam. Later, he performs Kung Fu, alone in a desert ruin in the rain, and makes fun of himself: "a complete failure!" This man is the artist Liu Xiaodong, a friend of Jia's,[8] who visited the site of the Three Gorges' dam to paint one of his characteristically large frescoes. On the same terrace from which *Still Life*'s Shenhong and Sanming saw the flying saucer, he paints an enormous composition showing ten workers in briefs gathered for a card game, squatting slightly apart. Han Sanming, who is in the painting, looks at them.

Liu Xiaodong, wearing shorts, "directs"—or at least arranges—his models, simultaneously explaining his way of working in voiceover; his search for a distanciation, and a way of outsmarting his own technical skill. Later he praises the energy of the men, whose force and tension—including sexual—

---

8. An observant viewer will recognize Liu as one of the clients in the karaoke scene in *The World*; the filmmaker, Wang Xiaoshuai also makes a cameo appearance in this scene.

he's attempting to harness. These men are older than the often naked young men and women who are usually Liu's subjects.

Dong was shot before *Still Life* and observes Liu Xiaodong as he works at the site of the Three Gorges dam. Although the two films were released simultaneously, with the documentary becoming a de facto "complement" to *Still Life*'s fictional world, the filming of *Dong* actually served as a preparatory exercise for the later film. That said, for the viewer, what's most important is less the reverberations between these two films, and more how the painter's personality, preconceptions, and style are in sync with those of the filmmaker.

The school of painting to which Liu belongs has been called "neo-realist," echoing the movement of Italian Neorealism, to which Jia is a contemporary heir. The painter's "neo"-realism has, however, little to do with Rossellini's legacy. Liu's neo-realism represents an ironic and stylistic break with the Communist party's social realism that dominated Chinese painting between 1949–1980.

As Jia is younger than Liu, he didn't need to free himself from the equally overbearing social realist impulse in film, thanks to the work of his predecessors, the filmmakers of the Fourth and Fifth Generations. But the painter and the filmmaker do share a quest for dreams and fantasy in the everyday matter of life. When, in a single shot, the camera carefully watches Liu's large brush give form to Han Sanming, then slowly follows Sanming as he looks out on the vast landscape that fills the top half of Liu's canvas, reality and artifice, humankind and the natural world, come together miraculously under Jia's extraordinarily attentive gaze.

The film's focus isn't exclusively on Liu at work. Instead, accompanying Liu functions as a pretext for a continuation of Jia's own preoccupations: to observe, listen, and soak up the ambiance of the quotidian. In one scene Liu walks along the Yangtze with a young man and the shot—depicting two miniscule characters within a vast landscape surrounded by clouds and water—echoes the settings and composition of traditional Chinese painting.

In *Still Life* there is a scene in which the construction workers escort the body of a coworker, who has perished on the site, to the river. This scene is repeated in *Dong*, when one of the workers whom Liu is painting similarly dies. Bringing photos and gifts, Liu accompanies the worker's body to his family home in the hinterland. The distraught widow and children are joined by the whole village to take part in a ceremony that's immensely sad, and yet still celebratory. Jia films all of this with his camera, and does what he's been doing at least since *In Public*: filming faces with affection and exceptional attention. This is very far from classical Chinese painting, and instead close to Rembrandt. The portraitist tradition has existed for hundreds of years in the history of art—Rembrandt being a preeminent example—but hasn't really been recognized in film. If it were, Jia would surely be acknowledged as a foremost practitioner. It even seems likely that Jia shot *Dong* just to be able to capture three key shots in the film, each one devoted to an old peasant's face.

Later in *Dong* we find Liu on the ferry in the Three Gorges and, without transition, on another boat floating on a river in Bangkok, now wearing a short-sleeved shirt with flowers. From central China to the capital of Thailand, Jia does here, on a large scale, what he's always done on the smallest scale: bifurcations—never gratuitous—that enrich and deepen the film's meaning.

Far from his home country, Liu Xiaodong is in Thailand to paint a second fresco, one which functions as a companion to the one at the Three Gorges dam. This time, instead of eleven workers in their underwear, we have eleven Thai sex workers, also scantily dressed. This important bifurcation between China and Thailand, men and women, is relevant for its capacity—very meaningful in Jia's cinema—to render perceptible the world in all its complexity, as in the shift from the man's story to the woman's in *Still Life*, or later a reverse gender shift in *Useless*, when Jia switches point of view from the fashion designer to the miner.

This shift continues in Bangkok with the appearance of new characters: the wealthy, pious, patriotic Chinese-Thai businessman, proud of himself and his beautiful squadron leader uniform; or the female bartenders who, laughing out loud, launch into a parodic and lascivious dance, as one leaves to look for loved ones in the megalopolis; or the two blindmen begging in a tourist market. Facing these young prostitutes—so beautiful, fragile and tough all at once, some sick underneath their make-up—Liu Xiaodong paints. He paints them individually and together. He paints like one who practices martial arts, with precise gestures and a focus on breathing that releases energy. It becomes clear that this is also the way that Jia makes films.

Liu Xiaodong mentions that although he studied Western painting and sculpture he now prefers Chinese art of the 6th century. His admission reminds us of the work of appropriation that Jia similarly had to accomplish in order to forge his own distinctive style. By accompanying his painter friend, Jia is obviously also making a commentary on himself and his own art. Confronted with his huge painting of young women—young bodies vibrating with possible stories—Liu Xiaodong only mentions what to him, and Jia, is most important, saying: "I hope my work is able to reproduce something of the dignity that all human beings possess."

* * *

A Film in Volume
Useless (2007)

FOR ITS FIRST two thirds, *Useless* seems to be a regular documentary, and it would be magnificent enough if this were all it was. Its starting point is China's current position as "the world's factory," due to its immense manufacturing sites where clothes, cars, and telephones are mass-produced, twenty-four hours a day, for the entire planet.

Straightaway the camera's slow lateral movements linger, if only for a second, on faces, bodies, and manual labor, resisting mass-produced images of the workers as a contrast to the standardized nature of the factory's products. By speaking to these people about their lives, Jia recognizes them as human beings who must be treated as individuals, despite their poor living conditions that allow for little variation in their diet and certainly no up-to-date medical care. Out of this pairing of the manufacturing industry with those who work there, emerges the discovery of what initially seems to be the film's subject: the fashion designer Ma Ke, whose luxury boutiques are prominently situated alongside those of Louis Vuitton, Dior, and Yves Saint Laurent in the chic neighborhoods of Guangzhou and elsewhere. As if floating on a flying carpet, the film softly enters the young woman's workshop, and accompanies her as she searches for forms and textures. She explains her dual ambition: to create an internationally-known Chinese fashion brand, and to highlight the use of natural materials and an artisanal fabrication that's meant to last, in contrast to the industrial standardization and perishable imitations that surround her.

In this moment we understand that Jia has found in Ma Ke an alter ego. Her goals in fashion mimic his in cinema: to establish a Chinese name on the international stage, and to defend the values of a personalized approach, as opposed to the usually standardized practices of their respective industries. This parallel is further reinforced by the fashion designer's words and creations; although sophisticated, her designs are made from seemingly rough materials, as if taken live from nature or reality.[9]

In a provocative gesture that highlights the virtues of the superfluous, Ma Ke named her haute couture line Wuyong, meaning "useless." It's easy to imagine Jia adopting the same name for his cinema, a cinema that might seem at times meandering in its focus on individuals, but that's in fact concerned with vital, urgent matters.

Without forewarning, the film then transitions to Paris, where the parallel between fashion and film—between Ma Ke and Jia—continues apace as Ma Ke stages a fashion show. The similarity between Fashion Week and all the major international film festivals is clear, as is the importance of Western cultural endorsements for securing greater opportunities at home.

Ma Ke grew up near Jia's hometown in Fenyang. Back in China, we accompany her as she looks for a quiet corner in the Shanxi province to work, so that a contact with the nourishing earth, imbued with China's millennial history, may permeate her fabrics. Jia listens sympathetically to Ma Ke's New Age lingo, while the designer searches for a suitable place to rejuvenate herself. At the wheel of her Honda, she passes a worker dressed in tatters. It's here that the film suddenly takes on a new dimension, as vast as it is moving and unexpected. The moment recalls a similar scene in *Platform*, when the young troupe abandons the poor cousin Sanming on the side of the road as he goes to work in the coal mine. This time, however, the camera follows

---

9. Some of Ma Ke's rough-hewn, experimental designs also seem to borrow from the aesthetic of Joseph Beuys' art. Ma Ke is the designer for the contemporary folk singer Peng Liyuan, the wife of President Xi Jinping [Tr.]

the man, also a miner. We stay with him as he goes to Fenyang to settle a dispute with a tailor over a pair of his pants that will ultimately cost him two yuans (20 cents). This paltry sum sharply contrasts with the salaries and price of goods in the high-end fashion world where *Useless* began. Although still in the same *country*, we are now in a completely different *world*.

Useless then relocates to the workshop of the two women who work at the tailor shop. We eavesdrop on their conversations, then cut to the blackened miners showering at the end of their shift. One of them is a former tailor whose livelihood has been ruined by industrial manufacturing. There is a beautifully tender exchange between this shy man and his wife, for whom he's chosen a suit. He's proud of his choice, and of his wife, whom he finds beautiful—she too is proud, proud of his laconic pride. It's a moment of extraordinary respect. The implication is clear: taste and beauty aren't the exclusive domain of the high-end customers seen at the beginning of the film, gorging on luxury bags and petits fours.

To the sounds of a popular song that then changes into a daily hymn, we find the couple dressed up, riding a motorbike through the Shanxi landscape, like the heroes of a chivalric romance, or even the characters in *A Touch of Sin*. Continuing to weave threads between what is usually separate—even invisible—the camera crosses paths again with the miners, their faces lined with fatigue and grime, and watches them with the same affection it gave the young faces of the seamstresses. In fact, from the Guangzhou sweatshops to the Shanxi coal mines, rarely have faces been so well filmed. They remain anonymous, without identification or story, but nonetheless radiant with the light that is humanity itself.

Useless begins as an encomium to individual creativity and the need for this creativity to both continue on from, and break with, tradition. But the film does not stop there, as it opens up to the vastness of China and its people, rejoining the everyday world with all its contradictions and violence. More complex than *Still Life*'s two intersecting individual narratives, *Useless* instead addresses itself to Chinese society as a whole, with its profound depths of misery and breathtaking summits of dynamism and ingenuity.

Like Milk on a Stone
24 City (2008)

HOW TO CONVEY one of the greatest human sagas? The best Chinese filmmakers, with Jia at the forefront, are working relentlessly on this: to narrate—via cinema—the fate of the Chinese people since 1950. It's a truly staggering history, a weaving of a myriad of individual experiences of millions and millions of people forced to submit to daunting economic, political, and geographical constraints. But the best Chinese filmmakers aren't ideologues and their films aren't guided by an overarching thesis. Instead, their gaze is exceedingly attentive to the difficulty, complexity, and depth of all these men and women's experiences. This isn't just cinema's project, and many Chinese authors, photographers and visual artists have also assumed the challenge of telling this epic narrative from the perspective of daily life. In order to do this subject justice, new methods of film language have emerged; China's socio-political changes essentially spawning a substantial body of cinema.

Working with urgency—seven films of varying lengths from 2006 to 2008—*24 City* focuses on a very specific time and place. The place: Factory 420 in Chengdu, the capital of the Sichuan province, that has for decades been a flagship for the military aeronautical industry. The time: its conversion into a luxury residence called *24 City*. Jia uses several methods of narrative and *mise-en-scène* for a film that, although seemingly simple, is, in reality, very complex. His goal is to make perceptible exactly what this factory has represented over its nearly sixty years of existence, from its establishment in the middle of the Korean War up until its conversion. During these years the factory operated as a self-contained universe, with apartments, places of education and entertainment. *24 City* is built around eight to camera testimonies: those of six workers from different generations and those of two young people, the son and daughter of workers of Factory No. 420: he's a newscaster on local television and she's a professional shopper supplying the new local middle-class with luxury goods from Hong Kong.

Of these eight narrators, four are played by actors. The vast majority of Chinese spectators will certainly identify Lü Liping, a star in China, and perhaps also Chen Jianbin, who is fairly well-known. Aficionados of Jia's films will recognize Zhao Tao, and many viewers, in China and the West, will also recognize Joan Chen. She plays a worker nicknamed "Little Flower" due to her resemblance to the protagonist in Zhang Zheng's 1980 film of the same name, an enormous public success. Joan Chen herself actually played that character, back before she moved to the US, when her name was Chen Chong. Although the narratives these four "characters" recount are fictional—unlike the "real" witnesses—the film treats them no differently. There is no pretense in these performances, which are uninterested in the distinction between fiction and documentary, the implications of which Jia has long been exploring.

The film's core are these individual stories. They're the narratives—true, false, exaggerated, simplified—that fuel the lives of the population, organized so as to create the most meaning and emotion. These portrayals are true-to-life and include heart-breaking stories of uprooted individuals, and justify ways of life that are sometimes tragic, both individually and collectively. The stories are recorded in faces, in bodies, and in voices, like signs loaded with presence and meaning; like the logograms that punctuate the film. Jia intersperses throughout the eight testimonials numerous seconds long portraits: people of whom we know nothing, views of workshops, buildings and streets, and documentary sounds. This hints at the countless potential narratives that could develop beyond the narratives of these eight witnesses.

On the one hand, *24 City*'s *mise-en-scène* is less spectacular than the strange and poignant beauty of *The World* and a *fortiori* of *Still Life* with its striking, fantastic imagery and carefully constructed dramatic structure. On the other hand, *24 City* is both more austere, *and* more complex: its editing is admirable and its shots often supremely beautiful. The film's narrative drive is equally thrilling. All these narrative ideas—including the "in-joke" of casting Joan Chen as a character called "Little Flower"—prompt an intimate and emotional reaction. *24 City* provides many details on China's vast collective history, both what has happened in the past and what is currently happening.

This heterogeneous and very subtly arranged material is reinforced by a commentary that's both musical and poetic. On the soundtrack we hear not only Chinese pop music, but also orchestral music composed specifically for the film. By subtly mixing lyricism with triviality, the musical soundtrack cues an empathetic response completely in sync with the film's images. The addition of poems read in voiceover—these are primarily from the classic Chinese novel, *Dream of the Red Chamber*,[10] but the film also includes two poems by W. B. Yeats—construct contrasting, meditative echo chambers. The poems endow *24 City*—which documents the closing of a factory emblematic of Maoist China and its subsequent transformation into a condominium complex emblematic of the new, capitalist China of the 21st century—with much of its meaning and a great deal of its force.

Halfway through *24 City* there is a remarkable shot that condenses all the ideas-at-play in the film. While we hear a crowd sing "The Internationale" in Chinese, one of the Factory 420 buildings collapses in an immense cloud of dust, and Yeats' words appear on screen: "We that have done and thought/That have thought and done/Must ramble, and thin out/Like milk spilt on a stone."[11] Jia's mission is to preserve these traces of the thoughts and actions of an entire people, to remember them when they're fading, to summon them when they have disappeared, and to know to what extent they're ephemeral, and important. Therein lies the grandeur of Jia's cinema.

* * *

They Used to Write Poetry
Cry Me a River (2008)

JUST TWENTY MINUTES long, *Cry Me a River* is an important film in Jia's filmography. In the old neighborhoods of Suzhou—a large city one hundred kilometers from Shanghai and nicknamed the "Chinese Venice"—we see two men and two women amongst the picturesque canals and houses in a fantastic park. They will soon be forty years old, much like Jia in 2008, the year he made the film. We recognize Zhao Tao and Wang Hongwei but not

---

10. Written by Cao Xuequin during the Qing dynasty in the middle of the 18th century, it's one of China's four great classical novels. [Tr.]

11. From Yeats's poem "Spilt Milk." The other Yeats poem in the film is "The Coming of Wisdom with Time." [Tr.]

necessarily the other two actors: Hao Lei and Guo Xiaodong, who both debuted shortly before in Lou Ye's *Summer Palace* (2006). We don't know right away what unites these characters; out of habit we may assume (mistakenly) that they form two couples. It seems that each of them now lives in a different city and that their lives have followed different trajectories: one got rich, and two others had children. The four catch up with each other like friends who haven't spoken in ages.

It turns out that ten years earlier the four friends did form two couples. They were university students then: enthusiastic, in love, creative, and united. The time was the eve of the Tiananmen uprising, which was the subject of *Summer Palace*. Together they published a magazine called *This Generation* that only lasted one issue. They're meeting up in Suzhou to celebrate the birthday of their old professor, who introduces them to a businessman and university sponsor with these words: "They used to write poetry, but not anymore." The love that once tied Zhou Qi (Zhao Tao), who now lives in Shenzhen, to Ma Qiang (Guo Xiaodong), who remained in Suzhou, is also in the past, but she still shows great affection when she holds down the hood of his jacket as he washes his hair over the sink.

The model for *Cry Me a River* is Fei Mu's masterpiece from 1948, *Spring in a Small Town*. That film is a melancholic elegy on the impossibility of recapturing a lost love. Both the film and its director are important for Jia and many other directors from his generation. Fei was a crucial reference that allowed Jia and his peers to deny the radical break the regime wanted to establish between pre- and post-revolutionary cinema, between China before the Revolution and the country that was supposedly born in 1949. However, Jia's elliptical and delicate short is very much focused on his own generation, reeling from a decade of accelerated modernization.

It's easy to find in many countries across different time periods, films or novels that acknowledge how youth's promises aren't always kept in adulthood, that the world isn't what many once dreamed it would be. What is striking and profoundly moving about this film is its lack of *nostalgia*—the antithesis of *melancholy*, which permeates the film. The harshness of certain observations is offset by Jia's infinite delicacy in representing them. He does not judge his characters—nor does he absolve them—but instead just *ob-*

serves them: their relationship to money (omnipresent), their families, aging, and desire.

As for Jia, he's certainly not abdicated his youthful dreams, nor lost his enthusiasm and capacity to take risks. He still "writes poetry" with his camera. But this is his *generation*. *Cry Me a River* is perhaps his most personal film. We can feel his anxiety that this could have happened to him, and it did happen to many who are dear to him. It's a short film, composed of just a few shots and a few lines of dialogue, close even to a tourism film showing off the beauty of Suzhou.[12] Like the lyrics of the sad love song that gives the film its (international) title, the shots in *Cry Me a River* vibrate over time, arousing deep reverberations. Great artists also live in time, and time passes.

* * *

Shanghai and its Memories
I Wish I Knew (2010)

JIA IS CINEMA's leading filmmaker on the upheavals that contemporary China has experienced. His careful investigations into China's murky past help us understand its present. Of course he's not alone. Wang Bing, in particular—with his documentaries *Fengming, a Chinese Memoir* and *Dead Souls*, and the fiction film *The Ditch*[13]—has similarly embarked upon unearthing a taboo episode of Chinese history: the terror of the period of the "Great Leap Forward" at the end of the 1950s and the "gulags" of the Gobi desert. In *I Wish I Knew*, Jia also travels in time and memories in order to uncover what was once hidden, banned, or repressed. The film advances smoothly like the course of a river, and visual metaphors for liquid elements—river, harbor, rain—abound. Its fluid *mise-en-scène* accompanies, as in a dream, the urban

---

12. *Cry Me a River* was commissioned for dual exhibitions on the art and architecture of Chinese cities, including Suzhou. These exhibitions were organized by the Centre de Cultura Contemorània in Barcelona (CCCB) and in Paris by the Cité de l'architecture, the co-producers of the film.
13. *Fengming, a Chinese Memoir* (2007) and *Dead Souls* (2018) both premiered at the Cannes Film Festival; *The Ditch* (2010) premiered at the Venice Film Festival. [Tr.]

drifting of the young woman Zhao Tao plays. An ancillary character in the film, she's there to help trigger the meetings between the protagonists. The latter are all tied to a specific area—the city of Shanghai—that, although not the most archetypical of Chinese cities, nevertheless meaningfully distills many of the nation's trials and tribulations.

The choice of Shanghai as the film's setting is essential. The film was actually the result of a commission from the city of Shanghai to accompany the 2010 World Expo. Jia was asked to make a portrait of the city where this event—the pride of the whole country—was to take place. It was supposed to welcome visitors at the entrance to the Chinese pavilion, the jewel of the Expo. Since Jia had long been considered as a dissident filmmaker by the Chinese authorities, this official commission signals an important shift.

Ultimately, Jia made something very different from what he was originally commissioned to do. Rather than making something that simply extols Shanghai's greatness, he instead made a feature that evokes more than a century of its history. As a result, the Expo organizers initially rejected the film, and it was blocked at the event's inauguration, before ultimately being presented, in a somewhat watered-down version, outside of the Chinese pavilion.

The majority of the film consists of two kinds of testimonies. Accompanied by Lin Xudong—director, editor, and mentor to Chinese cinema's young generation—Jia collects the memories of eighteen people whose stories evoke an image of China's history that's defined not only by wars, revolutions, repressions, and exiles, but also by persisting dreams of freedom and progress, as well as loyalty to a culture long banished from collective memory.

Many of these witnesses are elderly. Some describe their parents' life, going back to the start of the previous century. Even for Western viewers faraway from this history, these testimonies are frequently moving, other times comic and intriguing. Exemplary in this sense is the story of a notorious gangster from the 1930s, a ringleader of one of the main triads, as told with filial devotion by his daughter.

From a Western perspective, the result—especially in relation to Chinese silence about its own history—recalls Marcel Ophuls' *The Sorrow and the Pity*: a testimonial film that's capable—far beyond what is explicitly said, which is already significant—of reconstructing a complete mental picture. But instead of the four-year period during the German Occupation of the city of Clermont-Ferrand that Ophuls addresses, *I Wish I Knew* surveys an entire century of history, illuminating it in a portrait of infinite nuance and richness.

This richness stems in particular from the attentive gentleness with which the characters are filmed by the talented cinematographer Yu Likwai. From the melancholic dance to the song by the crooner Dick Haymes—which lends the film its title and recalls the concerts at the Peace Hotel in the time of the Bund during the concession era[14]—to the pulsating streets of the contemporary city, or the pavilions in the traditional Yu Garden, it overflows with quasi-spiritism.

The film's gentleness should not, however, mislead. *I Wish I Knew* ultimately serves as a veritable assault on the wall that separates the world's largest country from its own history. It's a herculean task performed with a

---

14. The Bund, where the Peace Hotel is located, runs alongside the Huangpu River. It was Shanghai's most fashionable avenue during the period when the largest part of the city was divided into concessions allocated to the foreign forces who carved up China between the middle of the 19th century and the 1930s.

formidable tenderness, a tenderness countering both forgetfulness and manipulation.

Jia's intelligence and courage also brings him to Hong Kong and Taiwan in search of testimonies from those who were, until recently, banished from the historical narratives of the mainland—these people also have a stake in China's collective saga. Throughout he also includes other forms of testimony, including excerpts from other films, showing how Chinese cinema recorded traces of the country's reality that are important to understand and elucidate. These include clips of Chinese propaganda from the Communist party or the Kuomintang, independent films by filmmakers such as Hou Hsiao-hsien, Wong Kar-wai and Lou Ye, and even an excerpt from Antonioni's *Chung Kuo, Cina*.¹⁵ Once again evoking Marcel Ophuls, they're part of a relationship to the past both realistic and dreamlike, a past defined by historical fact *and* the imaginary.

Cinema itself is further evoked outside of the film excerpts that are used. For example, in the visit to the Shanghai film studios, where streets from the time of the concessions have been reconstructed as sets, or in the interview with Barbara Fei about her father, Fei Mu, whose film, *Spring in a Small Town*, was such an important touchstone for many contemporary filmmakers. Fei's ordeal—from Shanghai to Hong Kong to Beijing—speaks volumes about the century's atrocities and absurdities.¹⁶

---

15. Antonioni's documentary (1972) is a travelogue that observes the lives of contemporary working-class persons in China. It was attacked by both the Chinese authorities and the Italian Communist party. [Tr.]

16. Fei Mu's short life was indeed buffeted by the chaotic winds of history and successive wars. Born in Shanghai in 1906, he was an early film aficionado. He shot one of his first films *Blood on a Wolf Mountain* (1936) on the eve of the Second Sino-Chinese War (1937–1945). Allegorizing the conflict between China and imperial Japan, the film co-stars the actress Lan Ping, who was later known as Jiang Qing after she became Mao Zedong's fourth wife in 1938. Following the outbreak of the war, Fei, along with other artists and intellectuals, fled to Hong Kong where he met the producer Xin Jinmin. With the producer's support Fei returned to Shanghai to shoot his 1940 film *Confucius*. The film was made during the so-called Orphan Island period of the war when the Japanese occupied the Chinese sections of the city, but the international concessions remained free. The following year, however, Japan invaded Shanghai's foreign concessions and seized control of the film industry. Fei remained in Shanghai for the rest of the war. Not wanting to work under the Japanese, he turned to the theater. He shot his masterpiece, *Spring in a Small Town* in Songjiang, a small town not far from Shanghai. The location reveals the heavy bombing

A Touch of China
A Touch of Sin (2013)

THE FIRST SHOT is all that's needed to set the stage for the entire film. It's a powerful and unusual image, an unforgettable moment: next to an overturned truck, beside a sea of tomatoes scattered on the road, a massive man sits astride his motorbike meditatively tossing a tomato in the air. It's as if the precise and sensitive attention to his country's reality of Jia's cinema has suddenly received a contribution from an energetic stylist like Sergio Leone or Quentin Tarantino. Such is *A Touch of Sin*, a work that's not only gripping but also disturbing, comic, and terrifying.

Since his debut with *Xiaowu*, a key element of Jia's *mise-en-scène* has been his ability to organize scenes that frequently echo and resonate with others. In *Still Life*, the double narrative ultimately converges as the two independent characters nearly meet; and, in *I Wish I Knew*, Zhao Tao wanders across Shanghai, each step evoking memories and preparing new encounters. *A Touch of Sin* goes even further than these two in its weaving together of four distinct and separate narratives. Although perfectly intelligible separately, these four episodes are organized so that, collectively, they tell the much larger story of a country where the scale, brutality, and speed of social change has led to outbursts of unprecedented violence.

Each episode has a main character: a peasant who becomes a relentless executioner after being fleeced by the authorities and the *nouveau riche*; the hit man who makes a living as a conscientious small-scale artisan, and is respectful of tradition; the hostess of a bathhouse and brothel, Xiaoyu (Zhao Tao), who is confronted by the brutal arrogance of traffickers, and

---

the town had suffered in the still ongoing Chinese Civil War (1946–1949). In 1949 after the Communist Revolution and the founding of the People's Republic of China, Fei again fled to Hong Kong. A year later desiring to move back to his home city of Shanghai, Fei went to Beijing where he met with Jiang Qing, his former actress and now head of the Communist Party's Film Office. She advised him to write a confession, known as a *jiantao*, reflecting on his errors and explaining why he had moved to Hong Kong. Humiliated, he refused to comply and returned to Hong Kong. A year later he died while still in exile in Hong Kong, at the age of forty-four. His oeuvre fell into oblivion, particularly during the Cultural Revolution (1966–1976). With the reopening of the China Film Archive in the 1980s and the re-release of his best-known film, his work found a new audience in the 1980s. [Tr.]

the contempt of a middle class to which she aspires; and the young garment factory worker who, leaving his job to look in vain for a better fate, parodies Maoist imagery by wiggling his butt at a nightclub. Violence, indifference, and baseness reign in each of these stories. The miracle lies in Jia's approach, an approach that continually brings out humanity, tenderness, and the promise of human connection.

Situated in four different regions of the country and in four types of landscape—from the semi-desert plains of Shanxi interspersed with illegal mine shafts to the Sichuan mountains; from the global city of Chengdu to the southern region of Guangdong—the film composes a kind of virtual map of the extreme pressures China is currently undergoing, taking in all kinds of details and detours that give it a breathtaking sensuality and texture.

At the outset of his career, Jia established himself as a master of contemporary cinema, a filmmaker who knows how to narrate stories, and understands what's at stake in them—he films not just actions but also the reasons behind them, and their consequences. His first five fiction features demonstrate this, but they're only one part of an extremely rich oeuvre. With *A Touch of Sin*, Jia manages the miracle of venturing into a more directly representational cinema—a cinema that, classically, *shows* action—all without losing his capacity to capture an infinite variety of incidental details.

An exceptional talent is necessary to assemble the protagonists' deeds and gestures, shots of pure documentary contemplation—a landscape, two old women eating in a corner, the everyday life of the streets; mundane items that have no role in the narrative—and other more mysterious shots such as the disturbing appearance of animals, including unforgettable serpents, the bearers of mysterious powers. As for the horse, he foreshadows the extreme violence that the young woman in the Sichuan brothel will suffer, while also evoking Nietzsche's tragic mental collapse in Turin when he tried to protect a horse from being whipped. In *A Touch of Sin* the inclusion of what may seem like banal or trivial incidents lends the film greater substance and invokes a spirituality that, although invisible, binds together elements so disparate that they might seem diametrically opposed.

Structurally *A Touch of Sin* resembles both a river and a network. With a thrilling richness, the film's momentum irresistibly carries its internal movements. A single viewing is insufficient to grasp it all, and, undoubtedly, a

Western viewer won't be able to instantly perceive all of its meanings. It's in gently but firmly reviving this circular and upward movement that the film ends with a theatrical performance condemning corruption. Xiaoyu, the heroine from the third episode, is there in the audience, while the gigantic wheel of China's vast history, made up of an infinite multitude of individuals, keeps on turning.

* * *

How Jia Moved Mountains
Mountains May Depart (2015)

AT THAT TIME in a small town in central China, lived a charming young woman, played by Zhao Tao, and her two friends, both of whom are in love with her. The century—and the millennium—were about to change. The world's most populated country was going to move, at breakneck speed, from being a vast, under-developed land, to a near first world power.

In the small town, the beginning of the 21st century is celebrated with firecrackers and dancing to the Pet Shop Boys' "Go West," a cover of the Village People's hit.[17] In just a matter of weeks one of the suitors, a mine worker, sees himself replaced by his rival, the successful manager of a gas station, and an aspiring capitalist who is able to acquire great wealth with dizzying speed. It's he whom the beautiful Tao (Zhao Tao) chooses; he who blows up ice on the Yellow River with dynamite; he who haphazardly drives a bright red Audi; and offers to his sweetheart a puppy and the promise of material comfort. Tao's father, a gentle and wise man from another era, says nothing. The lucky guy buys the mine where his former friend worked and then fires him. The worker leaves town, and it was as if what could never be broken—the bond between childhood friends who share each others' trials and successes—is displaced beyond return. This is just the beginning.

---

17. The popular song "Go West" is by the American disco group, Village People, and was featured on their fourth album in 1979; the song became a hit again in 1993 when the British synth-pop duo Pet Shop Boys covered it. [Tr.]

Starting like a contemporary folk tale, the film expresses itself in a stylized, physical way, evoking the material reality of the country's momentous changes. And it will be a fable, one both desperate and sentimental, where the greatest Chinese filmmaker reinvents his narrative art. This film is entirely consistent with his previous work and yet explores new stylistic registers.

Mountains May Depart is a narrative told in three episodes, set in three time periods: 2000, 2014, and 2025. It demonstrates a startling freedom of expression, made clear by the shift in aspect ratio that accompanies each time period, and by the use of different visual elements, including moments that are out-of-focus, visions half-way between dreams, and a kind of *hyperrealism*. Over these three periods the film shows us the trajectory of Tao's life, fifteen years ago, today, and in fifteen years: what becomes of her husband, their son, the rejected suitor, and the woman he marries. This will be a trip with several speeds, like the trains, high-speed and local, that criss-cross a landscape that, despite undergoing accelerated social transformation, is unchanging. The film's narrative also allows for a close-up view of China's stratified society and its mind-boggling inequalities. Although part of *Mountains May Depart* is set in the future, it's not a science-fiction film. Instead, by setting the film in three distinct periods, Jia is able to interrogate the present from the vantage point of where it has been in the past, and where he believes it will be headed in the future.

Mountains May Depart is a work of great depth and great disquiet. It questions the fate of the core values that are the basis of human relations, all in the context of the staggering transformation of China's economy and ways of life. It also questions the blatant and vibrant contradictions between two distinct conceptions of life. Punctuating the chronological progression of the three episodes are the different forms of transport used by the protagonists: car, scooter, train, truck, bike, plane, streetcar, helicopter. The cyclical time of the Chinese tradition also comes into play here with the recurrence of figures and motifs from one era to the next.

Covering the brutal disintegration and reorganization of a thousands-year-old society that hasn't fully disappeared—that concerns a billion-and-a-half people in China (and of course other parts of the world)—Jia proves a real genius in his capacity for covering these overwhelmingly complex challenges with just the simplest of means: a set of keys, a dish of dumplings, a beloved dog.

Mountains May Depart is a family melodrama, one which mobilizes the resources of classical drama like never before in Jia's work. It has a new engagement with *fiction*, and with *romance*. This is helped immeasurably by Zhao Tao's moving performance, her sensitivity to the changes in time highlighting her acting talents like never before. Until *Mountains May Depart*—in all her films since *Platform*—the quality of Zhao Tao's performance largely pertains to her *being*, to the intensity and the accuracy of her *presence*. Without abandoning this, her performance is enriched here by *doing*, by a new investment in *fiction*.

With this film, Jia hones his reflection on the dichotomy between personal freedom and belonging, in the face of heightened pressures and temptations. He also seems to be obliquely addressing his own situation as an internationally acclaimed *auteur* who walks a tightrope by following his own vision, and filming his compatriots as he sees them. Jia does this by further expanding his artistic palette, as he did earlier with *A Touch of Sin* when he drew upon the stylistic qualities of thriller and martial arts' films. The film is moving, occasionally very funny, and offers an interrogation on what survives or changes over time, for better or worse. *Mountains May Depart* conveys Jia's ongoing concerns, and his unwavering evolution as artist and citizen.

* * *

A Heroine of the Century
Ash Is Purest White (2018)

IT BEGINS LIKE a film by Martin Scorsese or Takeshi Kitano, set in a world of gangsters that has the rules of a highly organized society with "godfathers," allegiances, honor codes, rivalries, machismo, rituals, betrayals, business sense and explosions of violence. This universe, known elsewhere as "mafia" or "yakuza," is called "triads" in China. In this world of men, Qiao (Zhao Tao), the girlfriend of gang leader Bin (Liao Fan), occupies a unique place from the outset: she's neither at the center—a position usually reserved for men—nor on the fringes: she is, after all, the boss's moll. Even before she commits a transgressive act—one which resonates like a thunderbolt against social norms and the gangsters' strict code—she hints at possible ruptures in this deeply conservative environment. *Ash Is Purest White* is her story.

The film's original title in Chinese, meaning the "Men and Women of Rivers and Lakes," evokes the setting of the *wuxia*, novels of chivalry whose heroes live on the edge of society. Those *wuxia* heroes, both men and women, were honorable bandits forced by injustice to break from the social order. More recently "the world of rivers and lakes" has since become synonymous with the underworld, a mob that exaggerates its own code of morality, transgresses public order, and acts like a bunch of violent, greedy, and dishonest scoundrels.

But not Qiao. An outlier, she's a romantic heroine truly worthy of the old-fashioned mythical world of rivers and lakes. She has a dual loyalty: to the principles of an honor code and to the man she loves, or at least once loved. It's these virtues that are put to the test by the long journey that the film recounts, a journey covering two decades, from 2001 to today. From one end of China to the other, Qiao faces hardship, betrayal, and disappointment. Her adventure isn't only individual, and fictional, but also the epic story of a country, a continent, an empire, whose way of life is changing, and along with it the lives of its billion-and-a-half inhabitants, and global equilibrium. It's the tale of the Chinese people who have collectively made this "long march."

Ash Is Purest White is yet another chapter in Jia's two-decades-long project of dramatizing his country's recent history. Ever since *Xiaowu* he's been narrating China's entry into the third millennium. *Ash Is Purest White* signals a momentum, a complexity—even a cinematic homage—that's unprecedented in his work, giving it an exceptional place in his filmography. And also an exceptional place in world cinema: what other film, what other filmmaker today, addresses nothing less than the current history of a civilization?

A homage towards cinema? In an impressively free association, the genres of gangster films and musicals, science fiction and documentary, burlesque and melodrama, are here combined to accompany, from 2001 to 2018, the story of Qiao, and the history of contemporary China. The film also pays homage, in a veritable gesture of love, to the woman and actor

Zhao Tao, increasingly central in Jia's work. Trained as a dancer and actor, she has steadily developed her resources from film to film, and here offers a peerless performance. Zhao's slightest movement—walking into a bar or onto a station platform—is enough to trigger ten stories. Even just sitting down, the only woman in a crowd of tough men, is sufficient for a light and vibration to flood the screen with contradictory, disturbing, and moving forces. Her face offering its nakedness to the camera is enough to suggest a fight, a defeat, a betrayal, a victory to be accomplished.

This is the opposite of the boisterous "performances" too often consecrated by awards and statuettes. Zhao's elegant intensity, her sense of tempo and movement, and her restraint and nuance, take the very idea of acting to unusual heights. That *Ash Is Purest White* was overlooked in the list of prizewinners at the 2018 Cannes Film Festival was a mistake, a serious mistake, and the kind that juries at major festivals, alas, frequently make. This error can be explained by the fact that, very deliberately, the filmmaker is playing less openly here with the codes of modern cinema. The passage through different genres, through emotion and psychology, have prevented some festival goers, including many critics, from perceiving the immense ambition and complexity of a film that also aims to be seen as widely as possible by the Chinese public. But that Zhao Tao did not receive the acting award is an absolute and inexplicable injustice.

Exceptional in terms of dramatic power and elegant finesse, Zhao energizes and propels *Ash Is Purest White*. Her presence in all of Jia's films since the beginning of the 21st century—her physical evolution and the transformations in her acting—chronicles the story of an entire society. Yet the narrative's duration transcends individual experience and stokes a suggestive richness encompassing China's last two decades. The film begins and ends in Datong, the great mining city in Jia's native Shanxi where he shot the short film *In Public*. The central part of *Ash Is Purest White* is set in the Three Gorges region in Hubei, in South Central China, where Jia made *Still Life*, a film that marked a turning point in his oeuvre. This new film does not simply retrace the same topography. Using or reusing shots filmed over the previous eighteen years, Jia highlights a variety of formats and image qualities that offer physical evidence of time's passing, and that further the significance of the three different formats employed in *Mountains May De-*

part. Thus the references and memories—incarnated by the presence of Zhao Tao, visualized by the changes in the image, haunted by the memories of previous films—contribute to illuminate, through the genres of film noir and romance, China's extreme transformations.

Ash Is Purest White underscores the uniqueness of Jia's work and epitomizes one of the mysterious, foundational truths of cinema at its best. On the one hand, every film draws upon both fiction and documentary. And, on the other, at the height of a film's power, more fictional elements signify an increasing proximity to documentary filmmaking. In other words, fiction isn't separate from reality but an abstraction or distillation of reality. All of Jia's films—here to an unprecedented degree—describe a reality that's moving, efficient, and always unexpected through its concatenation of fictional twists and turns: romantic adventures and passionate love affairs, fights and murders, travels, encounters, and even extraterrestrials. The social, technical and cultural upheavals experienced by this land of gargantuan proportions—a country that's physically traveled by the film and its heroine from North to South and to the Far West, but also traveled through its songs, dances, clothes, food and dreams—feed a cinematic fresco of unusual ambition.

Ash Is Purest White is the story of a woman who loved a man better than he was capable of loving her. It's also the story of a continent that, when changing centuries, changed the world.

* * *

So Close to Their Land
Swimming Out Till the Sea Turns Blue (2020)

STRAIGHT AWAY WE feel this film's presence, and that of its *auteur* too.[18] Jia's distinctive way of filming anonymous faces, encountered by chance, is immediately recognizable. They evoke the passengers on the bus of *In Public*,

---

18. This very personal presence of the filmmaker isn't a bit affected by the fact that, for the second time in his career (after collaborating with the female poet Zhang Yongming for *24 City*) he has a co-writer for the script, Wan Jiahuan. She was previously credited as producer in other films by Jia, and served as the Executive Director of his film festival in Pingyao.

the peasants at the dead worker's funeral in *Dong*, the villagers waiting to attend a show in *Platform*. For this new film the filmmaker has turned his camera on the elderly. The screen is filled with wrinkled faces and tanned skins, people whose bodies show physical evidence of their long lives. But we sense something else here as well: the sensation of time itself and the passage of *History*, the violent winds of events that have swept hundreds of millions of individuals into a storm. These are truly extraordinary images with an unparalleled cinematic power. On the one hand, they evoke the metaphorical solemnity of ancient or religious statuary while also remaining contemporary, without any fanfare or lyricism. And herein lies the crux of this film, which recounts the history of modern China since 1949. It's a story told through the individual experiences of men and women, and is inscribed on their skin, as well as in their faces and gestures. Materialized in bodies and lives, these memories are also present in literary texts, since this story is told through the lives of four writers and their work.

The opening scene of *Platform*, which shows peasants waiting in front of a village map painted on a wall, was shot in Shanxi near Fenyang, in a locale whose name means the "Village of the Jia family" (no direct connection to the director). This earlier shot reappears in *Swimming Out Till the Sea Turns Blue* and is followed by a recent image of the same place that shows tourists taking selfies in front of a contemporary map of the same village. The montage of these two shots crystallizes the passing of time and the change in era. It so happens that in 2019 this locality, the Jia Family Village, created a literary festival, where many writers of both sexes were invited, apparently under the auspices of Jia Zhangke. The filmmaker offers us snippets from their speeches, before launching into the film's main part, which is built around four authors whose lives testify to four successive periods in the history of the People's Republic of China.

The film is divided into eighteen chapters and, at this point, we are already in chapter five. Complex and playful, *Swimming Out…* circulates between key personalities—the four writers—and themes. Gradually Jia's overall project coalesces. It's more specific than just an evocation of the country's history, and more in sync with the filmmaker's overall approach: to depict the Chinese rural world's perception of this history. Jia identifies these rural areas as the heart of the country, its core, because of their demographic and historical weight, even if they're far from the centers of power—those places of cultural prestige or economic and technological success from where the history of China (and of other nations too) is usually told.

The film's main focus is the trajectory of four writers. Although their individual paths may vary, they feature one distinct commonality: they have all returned to their home village or town in the countryside to pursue their vocation. According to Jia,[19] this return home is very much in vogue among contemporary Chinese artists. The four writers around whom the film is centered are Ma Feng (1922–2004), Jia Pingwa (born in 1952), Yu Hua (born in 1960), and Liang Hong (born in 1973). The story of Ma Feng, a Shanxi native who lived in the Jia Family Village, is told by his daughter and those who knew him. A communist People's Liberation Army fighter and grassroots activist, he embodies the generation that accompanied the first decade of the Maoist regime in the countryside, both by helping to organize and educate the peasants, and by describing in his writings the tremendous upheaval that was taking place at the time. The three other writers, who are still very much alive, appear successively on the screen. They recount episodes that marked their lives and inspired their writings. Jia Pingwa lived through the chaos and violence of the Cultural Revolution (1966–1976), while Yu Hua embodies the Reform Age generation of the 1980s and 1990s, with its transition to an unbridled capitalism. An endearing and colorful character, Yu Hua is the only one of the four with a certain renown abroad, as his novels have been translated into some twenty languages. One of these novels, *To Live*, was adapted for the cinema by Zhang Yimou and screened at the Cannes Film Festival in 1994, where it was awarded the Grand Jury Prize.[20] The last of the four authors, Liang Hong, mainly writes essays describing the rural life of her home village and the lives of the migrants who left it—with the new millennium, inner migration developed exponentially with enormous social and human consequences. Each of these four authors is deeply rooted in a specific region: Shanxi for the first; the countryside near

---

19. As he explains in the very comprehensive interview included in the film's press kit at the Berlinale 2020.
20. In *ex aequo* with Nikita Mikhalkov's *Burnt by the Sun* (1994). [Tr.]

Xian, the capital of Shaanxi, for the second; the southern and coastal region of Zhejiang for Yu Hua; and the central province of Henan for Liang Hong.

In the interview accompanying the film's press kit, Jia describes *Swimming Out...* as the final installment of his trilogy on the arts in present-day China: after *Dong*, about painting, and *Useless*, about fashion design. Despite evoking this thematic grouping, he chose not to elaborate further on the connection. Stylistically, *Swimming Out...* clearly evokes *I Wish I Knew*, with its numerous filmed interviews recalling past events that, taken together, construct a comprehensive view of recent Chinese history. This time the filmmaker intersperses the shots from the country, where his subjects are, with urban scenes, and further includes a quote from each writer, calligraphed on the screen and read in voice-over by the author. *Swimming Out...* was originally to be titled "So Close to My Land," and proximity to places as well as people—faces filmed in the street or in the audience of a show—are clearly essential. The filmmaker clearly holds the work of these four writers in high esteem, but their writings aren't the film's *raison d'être*. *Swimming Out...* isn't a film about Chinese literature. It's rather a new way for Jia to examine his country's modern history, its tragedies as well as its advances. Once again, he affirms the perspective he's consistently adopted: that of the disenfranchised.

Under the guise of a simple documentary with interviews that follow a chronological structure, the film succeeds in creating a highly sophisticated narrative. It addresses three distinct audiences with different points of reference: educated Chinese, who are familiar with the works of these writers; the general Chinese public, who don't necessarily know these authors, but who have experienced, or whose parents or grandparents have experienced, situations comparable to those mentioned; and foreign viewers, who aren't familiar with the authors or their writings and have no direct relationship with this history.

Swimming Out Till the Sea Turns Blue—for once the original title in Chinese matches exactly its English translation—is probably Jia's least immediately accessible film to a non-Chinese audience. But whoever dives into it will witness the sometimes comic, often traumatic, experiences of the many individuals whose fates are evoked. And this is thanks to the irony of the film's title, which is said by Yu Hua, the author of *Brothers*. With his intense, facetious manner Yu recalls how, as a teenager, he decided to swim out until the sea turned blue—the sea that is often called "the Yellow Sea—and that, in doing so, he almost drowned, swept away by a powerful current (as powerful as the current of History). Obviously the sea was always blue, even if poetic license has described it as yellow. The risk he encountered is akin to Jia's activities of writing and directing, bridging the gap between the real and what is said, or the *written* and the *shown*. Here the ethics of artist and action are one, without borders.

interviews with Jia Zhangke

Jia Speaks

THE FOLLOWING INTERVIEW is the result of extensive editing. It's based on a series of conversations between Jean-Michel Frodon, Walter Salles (together or separately), and Jia Zhangke in November 2013. The exchanges took place in Jia's hometown of Fenyang, where he shot his two first films, and in the neighboring city Pingyao, where several scenes from *Platform* and *A Touch of Sin* were shot, and where Jia founded a Film Festival. The conversations were conducted on the train to Beijing from Jia's native province of Shanxi, in his production company's offices, in several public spaces including the theme park The World; or in Paris, at the Forum des Images, during the French release of *A Touch of Sin*. Some comments are from a public conversation Jia had with the professor Lin Xudong, who has collaborated on the editing of most of his films. This last conversation took place November 18, 2013 at the Central Academy of Fine Arts (CAFA) in Beijing, where Jia is a professor of Experimental Art.

You are very attached to the city and house where you grew up.

I lived the first fourteen years of my life in the same house, with my parents and my sister who is six years older than me, which is a lot. The different parts of the house are still there but their organization has changed. What remains are the thick walls—almost a meter in thickness. Before being transformed into residential quarters, the house was a prison.

When I was little, the color that most impressed me was green. I often banged into things running around, and each time I would see the color green. No matter what public space I found myself in—at school, in the post office, or in a hospital—there was always this same green on the walls. So, involuntarily, this has become my color, and it's present in all my films. For me, this color is representative of the 1970s and 1980s.

The buildings where I grew up are still there but they have been transformed: apartments didn't used to be separated the way they are today. Next to us there lived a military family, then a man who worked for a freight company, and in the back courtyard there were workers and peasants.

Everyone got along and we spent a lot of time together. The soldiers would come home in the evening with their army stories, the workers would speak about the factory, the peasants about their business, and my father about the school he worked in. In the evening, the courtyard would transform into a village square and people would chat and discuss politics while eating.

Was this courtyard an important place for you?

I was born in 1970. At that time kindergartens didn't yet exist and kids were like dogs on the loose, left to their own devices in the streets and courtyards. All the adults were at work. Both my parents worked and were usually absent. My father taught languages in a secondary school and my mother worked for a sugar and tobacco company as a salesperson in a state store. The courtyard was a closed world for us. In the winter the wind would blow a lot. I don't know if it's climate change or if it's because I was a child, but in my memory the wind really blew harder than it does today. Going into the courtyard I could hear the wind coming down from the mountains. It made quite a ruckus! It would make the electric wires vibrate so much that you would have thought people were crying! That wind would exacerbate my feelings of loneliness as I waited for my parents to come home and make dinner.

I would usually listen to the radio at the end of the day. The most mysterious program for me was the weather report, which introduced me to the names of many cities. When a cold snap was announced, it always started in the north, with the wind coming down as far as Shanxi. Every winter I would hear talk of Ulaanbaatar, up north in Mongolia. The wind would go through inner Mongolia before arriving in Shanxi. It took two days to get to Lüliang, then another two days to reach Fenyang. So for me, Ulaanbaatar was synonymous with wind, and seemed the coldest place in the world—it set me dreaming. Much later at university, I requested a visa for Mongolia so I could finally get to know the country of my fantasies. But ultimately I had to give up this idea. Since then, Ulaanbaatar has appeared in almost all of my films. In *Platform* some young people hear Ulaanbaatar mentioned on a radio weather report and joke about this city whose location they don't even know; in *The World* someone heads there, seeing it as the most extraordinary destination in the world. The word "Ulaanbaatar" has become synonymous with mystery and desire in my cinema. I myself have never actually been there.

Do you recall being very alone when you were little?

My parents were civil servants and would come home late because they would always have long meetings after work. Usually I was already asleep by the time they got back. But there was a woman whom I called my nanny—a widow with two grown sons—who looked after me. She would tell me lots of stories and traditional tales. It was like an alternative education. I didn't hear so many tales from my parents or the radio. She told me stories about gods, ghosts, animals; well-known stories like "The Legend of the White Serpent," where a man falls in love with a female serpent—a very sad story. In fact, it inspired a scene in *A Touch of Sin*, the one where Zhao Tao goes into a small van and finds herself before a blue serpent. According to the legend there were two serpent sisters—a blue one and a white one—so Zhao Tao is thus the white serpent. When my nanny told me this story, I would ask if a man could really fall in love with a serpent. By shooting *A Touch of Sin*, I came to understand the myth's meaning: it is about limits, insurmountable difficulties in life that not even love can overcome.

You have often said you owe a lot to your father. What did he give you that was important?

A love of books and literature. He taught me hundreds of classical poems. At a very young age, I could recite a great number of poems from the Tang and Song dynasties. But he never taught me music, which he taught my sister—he even forbade me to touch instruments! When I was little, I loved the electricity outages because there would be nothing to do. My father would read his students' best essays or teach violin to my sister. Although we didn't have much materially, our family always tried to maintain a literary and artistic life.

My father was a theater troupe director at his school. They performed often and I would follow them everywhere in Fenyang. I remember him staging the play, *The Wolf of Zhongshan*, the story of a wolf and a scholar in which swords were used. My father had an extra sword made and gave it to me. So I was familiar with the stage environment from a young age. I particularly liked the backstage areas and would spend most of my time watching the actors putting on make-up and getting ready for the performance. In *Platform* and in *The World*, I unconsciously showed my enthusiasm for these backstage areas. I really like all the preparation that happens before a show.

You describe a fairly happy childhood but the physical conditions were hard.

Very hard. Often, we were hungry. You never forget that! At that time in China there were shortages in everything, food in particular. In addition, what we did have was of bad quality. There was no wheat flour like today. We ate sorghum flour and corn flour but the caloric value was insufficient. We would make little breads and eat seven all at once. They'd fill us up for the moment, but then two hours later we would be hungry again. They also tasted bad. My sister, mother, and I still talk about the food shortage problems we had back then. Hunger made me really understand what poverty is.

Today China is the world's second economic power. Beijing, Shanghai, and Guangzhou display all the appearances of big modern cities and some Chinese people are very rich. Nevertheless, China remains largely a poor country, and the gap between the rich and the poor has significantly increased. Furthermore, centuries of poverty have generated a way of thinking, a perspective that hasn't really evolved, despite recent changes. When resources are limited people are pushed to always want more, to be greedy. It's a result of poverty. But, faced with this poverty that I'll never forget, individuals like my nanny embellished their existence and, in turn, showed me a real lifeforce. For example, she would cut out figurines from the newspaper and make puppets in front of the window to tell the story of the tiger who gets married, or that of the mouse with her little ones. These are traditional Chinese stories that were a way of educating me, making me understand the world beyond that of my parents and school.

Were you an unruly child?

Later, yes. I almost ended up a thug! At the time I was far from imagining a career as a film director. When I was in the third year of elementary school, some of my friends had already quit school. They roamed the streets instead, became pickpockets, and hung out with gangs. One morning, a number of arrested people passed me by: they were all tied with the same rope, and among them I recognized one of my classmates. This was during the "Strike Hard" campaign.[1] He was given seven years—seven years of prison—for a minor theft!

I always liked being with friends and also liked street life. In addition, I am small. It was in my interest to become strong and courageous; otherwise there's no place in life, especially for boys. That's more or less true everywhere, there's no doubt about it, and that hasn't changed much. Fenyang is made up of a myriad of alleys and in each alley there is a gang. If you don't belong to a gang you spend your time getting beaten up. It was the same at school. During the organized fights between gangs the youngest ones would supply the older boys with rocks. We were continually fighting. One day we attacked, the next we were attacked.

When I was a child the train didn't stop in Fenyang and, since people were poor, they didn't travel. Trains only really belonged to our imagination. They were something mysterious as we only saw them in films or on television. My father had been on a trip: he travelled by train to Shanghai and Suzhou to buy musical instruments for the school band. For a long time, for me and others living in the provinces, the train was synonymous with remoteness and the departure of the elders for elsewhere.

The first vehicle we see in Platform *is a bicycle. The image of an individual with outstretched arms on a bike has become a kind of symbol in your cinema.*

That shot was not in the screenplay. As children we often adopted that posture on a bike, imagining ourselves as birds with the ability to take off

---

1. The name of an official policy for intensifying repression, launched for the first time in 1983 (and resumed since then on several occasions).

and fly; the speed of the bike would reinforce this impression. In grammar school I learned how to ride a bike, a significant milestone that expanded the perimeter of my activities. Before that I only traveled on foot, and never left the neighborhood. With a bike I could venture into the surrounding areas to see what was happening in the brickyards and the military bases.

One day, with a group of friends, I decided to go to Xiaoyi to see the train. We left by bike full of excitement, on the way asking directions. We ended up noticing on the ground the tracks stretching into the distance towards the horizon. We stood there without saying a word, utterly silent, waiting. It was as if we were waiting for the arrival of a UFO! First, we heard the noise of the train, its shrill whistle. We were so excited!. Then, in the distance, we perceived a black form with a red star on the front. It was a freight train carrying coal. We watched it coming from far-off with the desire to stop it! We wanted it to slow down, but of course it continued on its way, without changing speed. Our eyes followed it until it disappeared at the other end of the tracks. This was the first time I saw a train.

There is almost the same scene in Platform.

And it's evoked again at the end of the film… thanks to the kettle I stole from a friend! A poet who lives in Beijing and regularly invites us to his place. One day, during dinner, I thought I heard a train whistle. But it was his new kettle, whistling like a train as the water came to a boil. I poached this kettle to use it in the film. At the end of *Platform*, after having criss-crossed routes and experienced great freedom—after having lived the events of 1989—Cui Mingliang, the character played by Wang Hongwei, returns home and reintegrates into his old social and familial system. Why does he decide to marry Yin Ruijuan, the character played by Zhao Tao? Why, after ten years, are they still together? I didn't want to provide an explanation. What counts is that the person who sang the rock song "Platform"—a young rebel like Cui Mingliang—ends up returning to the status quo in order to live like everyone else, to have lunch and take a nap in the sun. At that moment the whistle of the kettle is heard to indicate that although his daily routine never varies—day after day and year after year—his earlier life, the memory of his youth, still resonates deep within him.

The theme of life continuing despite everything is very present in your films.

I think that survival is the theme of all my films. Whatever we endure, we need to survive. Still today, the Chinese people are influenced by social and political changes, affected by new policies that influence a large part of the population. It's not the same violence that occurred during the difficult years of the Cultural Revolution, when everyone was affected, some more than others, by the constant strife that tore people apart: the never-ending meetings, the focus on class struggle, and the insecurity that resulted from it.

Did your parents suffer the direct implications of the Cultural Revolution?

Yes, particularly my father. My grandfather was a surgeon. Before the Liberation,[2] he worked as a doctor in Tianjin. Then, after having accumulated a nest egg, he returned to Fenyang and opened a small clinic. Over time, the clinic turned into a very small hospital. At a time when access to medical care was limited, my grandfather earned a good living that enabled him to buy land. So in addition to being a doctor and hospital director, he was also a landowner. When the Cultural Revolution broke out, my grandfather was already dead but my grandmother was not spared retribution. She was living with my parents. My father told me that one day some *Dazibao*[3] were plastered in front of our house, demanding that my grandmother leave the area that very day and return to the countryside. Despite her old age and the fact that her feet were bandaged, she had no choice. My father took my grandmother on his bike and took her to the country. Once there, she was forced to rehabilitate herself by sweeping the village streets every day. Then my uncle, my father's elder brother, was arrested and thrown in prison where he tried to kill himself. He survived with a maimed leg. His children, my five cousins—all older than me—had to interrupt their studies to go live in the country.

---

2. The official name for the creation of the new regime after Mao Zedong's victory in 1949.

3. Handwritten posters that were an important means of political struggle, expression, mobilization and possibly of denunciation supposedly at the initiative of the inhabitants themselves. The use of *Dazibao* was particularly intense during the Cultural Revolution.

Was your father also a victim of the Cultural Revolution?

His greatest dream was to study at university, but because of his "bourgeois" origins, he wasn't allowed to take the college entrance exam. He regretted this all his life. When I came of age, he insisted I take the college entrance exam; it was a kind of compensation for him. During his youth he had kept a diary; his notebooks were discovered during the Cultural Revolution. He expressed in them what made him suffer, discussing not being able to attend university due to his family origins, and how he was arrested and forced to dig air-raid shelters for his rehabilitation. He told me that when he returned home after having worked on the air-raid shelters, he burned all his notebooks. He burned everything he had written about his life.

Because of the Cultural Revolution, in my family as in many others, we got into the habit of making ourselves as unobtrusive as possible, of suppressing our feelings. I experienced firsthand the results of this. As a teenager I wanted to become a writer. Although my father had taught me literature from a very young age, he didn't want me to take writing too seriously. He took me aside and asked me to keep literature as a hobby, to instead to become a doctor or teacher. I said that I really liked literature, that I wanted to become a writer, and he responded: "It's too dangerous!"

You dedicated Platform *to him.*

The film covers the period from 1979 to 1990, which corresponds to my adolescence. My father didn't know much about those ten years of my life. Once the film was finished I dedicated it to him so he could see how I grew up. I returned home with a videocassette and showed it to him over the New Year's celebrations. The film is almost three hours long. My parents watched it to the end and my father said nothing—he went to bed. The next morning at breakfast, I gingerly asked him what he thought of the film. Without looking at me, he said while continuing to eat: "If this film had been shown before or during the Cultural Revolution you would certainly have been considered as a counter-revolutionary and imprisoned." He said nothing more but I was aware of his concern, and of the suffering he kept to himself.

It's worth noting that your films were banned at that time in China.

When I began shooting my first films—*Xiaowu*, *Platform*, and *Unknown Pleasures*—China had already greatly changed. But yes, although the country had become more open, my first three films were still refused a public release. They were "underground films." As a filmmaker living in Beijing, this denial of my freedom of expression was difficult, but the stress wasn't all that significant. During the same period, between 1998 and 2004, my father felt more pressure than I did. He was very worried about me—I was aware of this because he never spoke about my work, never asked me any questions.

In 2004 *The World* was granted a theatrical release and we organized a major exclusive preview in Taiyuan, the capital of the Shanxi province. Of course I invited my parents and by this time my father was less worried. Then I had the idea of bringing my parents to Beijing to live with me. I am the only son in my family and, according to Chinese custom, my parents should live with me as they're elderly. One day, at the beginning of 2006, when I had just finished shooting *Still Life* and was in the process of editing it, I received a telephone call from my sister who asked me to return home immediately from Shanghai. My father had a cancer that had rapidly progressed, and he died at the end of spring that same year. I feel his moments of happiness were few and far between and that I was above all a source of anxiety for him. I never had the chance to thank him. This is perhaps the nature of a father-son relationship.

After the Cultural Revolution, the general situation in China became less violent.

At the end of the 1970s, with the opening up of the economy and the reforms, society began to relax. It was the beginning of the era of the "Cultural Thaw" and, suddenly, the country's pent-up potential was anxious to express itself. Changes first took place in rural areas, as land that had been grouped together as the people's communes was redistributed to peasants. Production from these communes had been insufficient causing a grain shortage—I recall periods of real famine in my childhood. But, starting in the 1980s with the reforms and the implementation of fixed-price contracts, we no longer had famine; there was enough food to feed ourselves. This was a major change, immediately noticeable. Then came the new machines. I remember that when I was a child we often played with the teenagers. One day, at an intersection, we saw a mailman delivering telegrams on his motorbike. Watching him one of my older buddies said: "My greatest dream: to buy a motorbike!" Two or three years later, the streets were congested with motorbikes! The motorcycle had appeared in our lives. In school we were shown educational and scientific films about new technologies and the most recent inventions. One day, we saw a film about a Shanghai invention that was called a "Washing Machine." I was stunned! It never occurred to us that it would be possible to wash clothes except by hand. A few years later, families already had their own washing machines.

This period of improvement in material conditions was also characterized by changes in behavior, particularly in relationships between young men and women. Platform *expresses this.*

Yes, primarily thanks to the two female characters, Zhong Ping and Yin Ruijuan, who embody two different attitudes with regard to love. With Yin Ruijuan this is expressed in an internalized fashion. She's cautious and fairly conservative—the way women expressed their feelings in traditional China. In the 1980s bodies and feelings achieved greater freedom. Previously, open relationships were extremely rare and, during the Cultural Revolution, marriages were arranged. The goal was marriage and you could only have a fiancée or fiancé if he or she was presented by your parents or a family member. We had to leave our love life to the party and there was no private space. Feelings were dictated by habits and tradition, and also bound by the system, a certain discipline. This change is just as important as what happened on the material or cultural level.

How was this evolution reflected?

Stories about intimate relationships began to spread like wildfire, rumors that could be funny, but also grave, particularly those about young girls who got pregnant. These were tragedies, as it was almost impossible to imagine bringing these children into the world. I felt an enormous amount of admiration for the courage of these young women.

In *Platform*, I wanted the character of Zhong Ping to be in control of her body, unlike Yin Ruijuan. There's a scene where she goes with Zhang Jun to a clinic to have an abortion. Although we sense her personal suffering and a feeling of oppression, I was unsure how best to express it? Even if she sang what she wanted, she still couldn't adequately express her personal problems. So I settled on having her scream, without words and without knowing to whom the scream is addressed—it's her body that frees itself. Behind where the scene takes place there is a mountain range. Perhaps the mountains were also comforting to her, nature taking her to its bosom. I don't know why I wrote things like that. In any case, this was the emotional state that inspired this scene.[4]

These changes in daily life were accompanied by important changes on a cultural level.

Here, too, things were opening up. Pop music arrived and, little by little, television appeared in homes. Thanks to television we were able to have access to the outside world: we could watch programs from Hong Kong, Taiwan, and even Japan. A Brazilian telenovela, *Escrava Isaura* [*Isaura the Slave Girl*][5] was enormously popular—my mother loved it! The works of foreign philosophers began to appear, even in Fenyang; there were a lot of street vendors selling the works of Freud, Nietzsche, Schopenhauer and, later on, Sartre. In the 1980s philosophy was very much in vogue. I remember buying books of this kind while I was in high school. I didn't understand a thing but my enthusiasm was genuine. I bought a book by Nietzsche. I no longer remember which one, but it was substantive. I really didn't understand what he wrote but I do remember one phrase: "Life is like a wind that sometimes crosses the fields, sometimes a blank page." Life crossing a blank page!

---

4. About the filming of this scene, also read the interview with Zhang Yang, pp. 187–93.

5. Brazilian telenovela produced by Rede Globo, originally broadcast between October 11, 1976 and February 5, 1977. It's an adaptation of the eponymous novel by the 19th century abolitionist writer Bernardo Guimarães and tells the story of a *métisse* slave's search for happiness. It became one of the most popular telenovelas in the world and among the very first foreign TV shows allowed to be aired in China. [Tr.]

And of course there were the changes in music, which are so present in Platform.

Before the age of ten I never listened to pop music—we only heard revolutionary songs. Then street kids showed me how to listen to the Taiwanese radio, where other genres of music could be discovered. This was denounced by officials as "decadent sound," criticized for its languorousness, as it was the exact opposite of revolutionary music. But all young people appreciated this kind of music, mainly because love was its principal theme. That was a big change from "Workers, We Have the Strength" and "We Are the Builders of Communism" and "Union Makes Us Strong." Those hymns always said "we," while songs like Teresa Teng's "The Moon Represents My Heart," that were played on Taiwanese radio, dared to say "I." Six months or a year after discovering the radio, we saw teenagers a little older than us with Boomboxes, playing tapes smuggled in on the Zhejiang coast, especially Teresa Teng's love songs and Zhang Di's comic songs. Teenagers walked in the streets carrying these Boomboxes, and we followed them. Shortly afterwards, the government allowed pop music; it appeared on the radio and on television, and even singers from Hong Kong and Taiwan began to perform on the mainland. The authorities exploited this fad for the purposes of propaganda and, every year, there were one or two songs that everyone was encouraged to sing. For example, at the beginning of Deng Xiaoping's policy of reform and openness young people were encouraged to participate via a pop song entitled "We are the New Generation of the 1980s." Another one appeared to be a love song, but its true message was that Chinese society had to "follow its heart" to reform.

Thereafter we began to listen to rock. Cui Jian's song "Nothing to My Name," came out at that time. It's in *Platform*, along with European songs like "Dschinghis Khan" and "The Girl Under a Street Lamp," which I thought came from Hong Kong but that in fact were German. In one important scene, young people breakdanced to a song by Leslie Cheung called "Monica." Ultimately I had to cut the entire scene because the rights to the song were so expensive. We knew all the songs by heart, and many others coming from Japan and the United States: Hideki Saijo,[6] Michael Jackson, Wham!...

---

6. Hideki Saijo, Japanese singer most famous for the Japanese version of the Village People's

You use rock music as a political signal.

I did in *Platform* but I couldn't have done it before then. At the end of the 1980s, a little after the Tiananmen Square protests, we began to hear rock in Fenyang. It was music that came from big cities, from Beijing. "Platform" is the title of a song from this period. It has a rock influence, but is very melodic. My first real contact with rock was in the early 1990s. I began with Cui Jian's songs, followed by those of groups like Tang Dynasty and Black Panther. At the time I was twenty years old and I loved these songs. I remember one time, I attended a concert by Cui Jian at the Shanxi stadium in Taiyuan, the province capital. The concert was tremendous—his words touched many young people because of the revolt they expressed. I can still sing songs like "Let Me Go Wild in the Snow," and "A Piece of Red Cloth" in their entirety. But at the time those of us interested in rock music were still a minority. Even in Taiyuan there weren't that many who listened to this music. Those songs are part of my inner world; they belong to me.

You didn't use them in Xiaowu, *although other Chinese independent films from the period—*Beijing Bastards *(1993), for example—often did.*

For *Xiaowu* I filmed in a small inland city in order to show ordinary people, because I know them well and feel an affinity for them. My emotional world was—and still is—with them. I easily understand their feelings, even just from their gestures. When I look at them I sense their life because something in them is very familiar to me. But rock didn't exist in this world; these people did not listen to it. When artists create, they often impose their subjective vision on the characters. I didn't want to impose the rock music that I love on a small-time pickpocket, or a local police officer, or even less a *nouveau riche* fellow smuggling tobacco. You should not impose your own dreams onto your characters. I remember after a screening of *Xiaowu* at the Beijing Film Academy some students were angry with me: "Jia Zhangke, your film is too reserved. Why doesn't Xiaowu rebel?" But how can you expect him to rebel? By taking part in a demonstration? By shouting slogans

---

popular hit "YMCA" aka Young Man. [Tr.]

in the street? It's ridiculous. In the vast majority of cases the Chinese endure everything in silence. It's more important that cinema shows reality, that it tries to understand what people are going through. A character shouldn't do anything that's beyond their capacity or worldview, and a filmmaker shouldn't aim to be an omnipotent creator with a complete understanding of the world. That's an arrogant posture—no one is Superman! There is a place for my misgivings, my personality, and my real thoughts in a film. It's even a necessity, but that's not the same thing as imposing my point of view on a character, or pretending to have understood everything.

In Platform, *besides the songs, dance also plays an important role.*

Most of the dance scenes were improvised as I didn't want to choreograph them. For example, since everyone knew the song "Dschinghis Khan," I let the actors invent their own movements. I told Wang Hongwei to dance as he wished, but the others to dance the most disco as possible. Wang Hongwei could do what he wanted—jump and jostle everyone—and that's what he did. He's the only one who expresses this freedom—the exact opposite of Zhao Tao, who is more reserved. At that time only a few young people managed to dance like this, to free their bodies. In this way they're the elite of this small city: they manage to dance, to open their arms to a modern rhythm.

The 1980s marked a real turning point for the younger generation.

Yes. This decade was accompanied by an intense desire to express oneself. Among young people poetry was all the rage; everyone began writing poems and novels. We were also reading a lot: I devoured poets like Bei Dao, Gu Cheng, and Shu Ting. The changes of the 1980s greatly affected me. Particularly as they happened while I was growing up: in 1979 I was nine years old and in 1989, nineteen—childhood to adolescence. In 1989 I united with the student movement that broke out in the spring.

How did you experience that period?

We practically stopped going to class, and were glued to the news on TV. We really hoped for radical change. Even if I didn't fully understand the concepts of democracy and freedom, I thought that they were part of human nature—we all aspired to it. So when we saw students demand these things—especially when we saw students on a hunger strike fainting in Tiananmen Square—we were really moved! With our classmates we created a poetry circle. We were closest during this time, and would get together to watch television, listen to the radio, and share information. We would cross-check our information about what was going on in Beijing as Fenyang was so far away! Our professors were keeping an eye on us as our poetry circle was thought to be an "unstable element;" they were afraid that we would demonstrate in the streets of Fenyang. When the students began to demonstrate in Taiyuan, the provincial capital, we went to join them. I took the bus there with some classmates. On Yinzhe Street there was a huge procession, with some in tears, and others shouting slogans. My friends and I joined the crowd and followed it to City Hall. There was an enormous hope at that moment, but on June 4th the movement ended in defeat and we were lost—a very oppressive feeling.[7] For my generation this was a knockout blow, a terrible feeling of failure.

What were the consequences of this experience personally?

It sparked my creative impulse; a desire to express myself and tell my own stories. It seemed to me that our collective life experiences, with all their trials and tribulations, really deserved to be told. I didn't have a plan but from writing poetry I went on to storytelling through writing novels. I wanted to share my personal experiences and insight into the fate of others.

Although you didn't yet know you would become a filmmaker, films were already playing an important role in your life?

---

7. Starting on April 15, 1989 students led a peaceful uprising in Tiananmen Square calling for democracy and free speech. The protests ended on June 4, 1989 with the government's declaration of martial law and a bloody crackdown, the extent of which is still unknown. The Chinese government claims 200 deaths, while student leaders claim up to 3,400 deaths. [Tr.]

Yes, that was always the case. When I was small there were four movie theaters in Fenyang. Today, there is only one, but it's a multiplex that has an IMAX theater and karaoke. It has little in common with what I grew up with. In the 1990s the cinemas of my childhood closed one by one, as people preferred watching TV; they weren't interested in the films showing in theaters. One theater was transformed into a supermarket, another into a furniture store, a third into a warehouse... The multiplex is new, it was constructed in 2011.

During my childhood cinema was the only attraction in the neighborhood, and we went as a family every weekend. I remember the first film I saw: *Guerillas Sweep the Plain*,[8] a black and white film about a partisan leader in World War 2's Sino-Japanese conflict. I particularly remember the first scene: galloping on a white horse, a pistol in each hand, the officer passes through a village already in the hands of the Japanese, shooting at his enemies—it was full of movement! I cried out and bounced up and down in my seat. My father had to tell me to sit still because I was bothering people. That's my first film memory.

At the end of the 1970s, we could only see this sort of film: stories about war heroes and partisans—revolutionary films. There were also the "model operas" from the Cultural Revolution that were still shown: *The Red Detachment of Women*[9] and *The White-Haired Girl*.[10] As the country was just beginning to open up economically, we could also see foreign films that had been imported before the Cultural Revolution. That's how I was able to see *Bicycle Thieves* and *Rome 11 O'clock*,[11] as well as a lot of Yugoslav films, especially war films like *Walter Defends Sarajevo* and *The Last Bridge*.[12] I also

---

8. This 1943 war film was banned during the Cultural Revolution. *Guerillas Sweep the Plain* was part of the first contingent of films to be newly authorized in 1977.

9. The original ballet premiered in 1964. It became one of the Eight Model Operas that dominated the national stage during the Cultural Revolution. It's the ballet that was performed for President Richard Nixon during his visit to China in February 1972. [Tr.]

10. A Chinese opera and ballet, first performed in 1945. There was a film version made in 1950. [Tr.]

11. Two major works of Italian Neorealism directed by, respectively, Vittorio De Sica (1948) and Giuseppe De Santis (1952).

12. *Walter Defends Sarajevo* (1972) is a Yugoslav war film by Hajrudin Krvavac, which enjoyed

saw Indian films, particularly Bollywood musical comedies. There was one we really liked called *The Vagabond*.¹³ It's the story of the illegitimate son of a judge who is forced to live on the streets and becomes a thief. I liked the film's theme song, which was also called "The Vagabond." This is the film that's screening in *Platform* when Yin Ruijuan goes to the theater and her father makes her leave.

Later you were able to see different films.

Little by little, yes. Films from before 1949 were shown in the theaters. For example, *Tears of the Yangtze* and *Crows and Sparrows*,¹⁴ both of which showed the Shanghai of yesteryear. But it was from the mid-1980s onwards that film programming really became diversified, with new films released every three or four days. Among them were the films from the movement known as "Scar Literature," films that reflected on the Cultural Revolution. I remember seeing a film called *The Maple Tree* with my mother. I was too young to properly understand it at the time, but I think this film, which is an adaptation of a novella by Zheng Yi,¹⁵ remains the only accurate depiction of the violence of the Cultural Revolution, including between the different factions of the Red Guard. Zheng Yi is from Beijing—and the story is set there—but since he was sent for reeducation to Shanxi, and lived there a long time, we consider him a Shanxi author.

---

great success in China at the end of the 1970s. *The Last Bridge* (1954) is an Austro-Yugoslav co-production by Helmut Käutner, which also takes place during WW2 in Yugoslavia.

13. Film by and with Raj Kapoor (1951): the film made its director and actor enormously famous, and earned him the nickname of the "Indian Charlie Chaplin."

14. Cai Chusheng and Zheng Junli's *Tears of the Yangtze* (1947) and Zheng Junli's *Crows and Sparrows* (1949) are considered two masterpieces of classic Chinese cinema. They were made during the brief interval between WW2 and Mao Zedong's accession to power on October 1, 1949.

15. *The Maple Tree* was made in 1980 by Zheng Yi after his eponymous novella, which had a considerable success and was also adapted as a graphic novel. It tells the tragic story of two young persons in love in Beijing in the grip of the turmoil at the beginning of the Cultural Revolution, and who find themselves in two enemy factions.

Did you also begin to have access to mainstream films coming from abroad at that time?

It wasn't until 1984 and 1985 that we could see martial arts films from Hong Kong. The one that drove me crazy was *The Shaolin Temple*, Jet Li's first film.[16] After that, my friends and I all wanted to become Kung Fu masters! I did have the chance to learn a little because my nanny's second son was very good at Kung Fu; he'd learned martial arts with a famous Tai Chi master in Fenyang.

We didn't watch the majority of these films in a movie theater. Video rooms had begun to open everywhere in the mid-eighties, while I was still in secondary school. They had tables with TV monitors and VCRs that had been smuggled in from Hong Kong and Taiwan. This was how I discovered the exciting world of *wuxia*.[17] I saw many *wuxia* films, all kinds of Kung Fu films, and also gangster films, in particular those of King Hu, Chang Cheh, John Woo, and Tsui Hark. Also the first films of Ann Hui.[18] Sometimes amongst a bundle of *wuxia* videotapes there would be a porno film. That really excited us! We would all be silent, completely absorbed by the images. We never knew when we would see the next porno film. One day the owner of the theater said he had a surprise for us. We all thought it was a new porno film, but instead it was a propaganda animation about family planning! We were really disappointed. This is referenced in *Platform* when Wang Hongwei and the twins watch an animated sex education film.

What is your most memorable film viewing experience?

The film that meant the most to me was undoubtedly Wu Tianming's *Old Well*, which I saw at the end of the 1980s.[19] It was really different from other

---

16. Directed by Chang Hsin-yen in 1982.

17. The term denotes the stories of chivalry and martial arts in literature that has existed for centuries, as well as in cinema where it's called *wuxiapian*.

18. Ann Hui is the only filmmaker of the short-lived "Hong Kong New Wave" in the 1980s who succeeded in having a long career She's a major Chinese film *auteur* as well as one of the first important Chinese female directors.

19. *Old Well* (1986), with Zhang Yimou in the leading role, is adapted from the eponymous

films. I recognized on the screen a poverty that I knew intimately. But this wasn't the film that made me want to be a director. When I left Fenyang to study painting in Taiyuan, I saw Chen Kaige's *Yellow Earth*.[20] It's a film from 1984 but I only saw it about ten years later. When I did—then and there—I decided I wanted to be a filmmaker. But I've often told this story.

Going to the cinema deepened your film knowledge. But it's also a collective activity.

Yes of course, and for many the cinema was above all a space for amorous adventures, unlike video rooms, where you only watched the screen. In film theaters, the oldest among us would be very careful; pretending not to know each other, we would wait for the film to start to get close and take each other's hand. But not everyone took so many precautions. Many romances began in a movie theater. They were also places for us to see how we measured up to our peers. I remember that after seeing Lau Kar-leung's *The 36th Chamber of Shaolin*,[21] my friends and I fought with other boys in the street. Sometimes two groups of boys would fight in the movie theater, seeking in the film a pretext for a brawl—it was as if the fights had something sexual about them. And we got to know each other through these encounters. Sometimes we came out of the theater enemies and sometimes the brawls brought us closer together and we came out friends.

---

novel by Zheng Yi. It's the story of the search for a spring of water in an extremely poor village in Shanxi. Its filmmaker, Wu Tianming, is one of the principal figures of the "Fourth Generation." He was also the head of the Xian Film Studio, which made it possible for the first films of the Fifth Generation to be made, notably Chen Kaige's *Yellow Earth* and Zhang Yimou's *Red Sorghum* (1987).

20. Chen Kaige's 1984 film, considered as the first work of the Fifth Generation, takes place in 1939, during the Second Sino-Japanese War, and describes the relationships between a soldier of the revolutionary army sent to observe the local customs and record the traditional songs of peasants, and a young peasant woman who falls in love with him but who must obey ancestral laws. Shot in the hills of Shaanxi, a neighboring province of Shanxi, the film establishes the aesthetic of this movement that has come to signal the renewal of Chinese cinema after the end of the Cultural Revolution.

21. With Gordon Liu, 1978. It's one of the great classics of martial arts cinema.

You are still close with your group of friends from this period in your life.

Yes, it's a very strong connection. We played Mahjong, drank, and got into scraps together. We formed a soccer team, were in the same breakdance group, took part in the same poetry circle. When it was a question of fighting, we were always on the same side. We spent practically all our time together and grew up together. On weekends there would be a dozen of us roaming the streets on our bicycles. We were partners in crime and spent our adolescence together. These guys are the only people to really know how I grew up; they know my past and I know theirs. That creates a unique bond. Later I left for Beijing to study film, and most of them remained in Fenyang. But they're still my *brothers*, and I don't use this word lightly. We once carried out a ceremony to seal this fraternal union from different families: we knelt together, bowed, burned incense and prayed to Heaven and Earth. When I left for Beijing, they would go to my parents home to help out, in some ways assuming my filial role in my family.

So on your visits home you continued to see them?

It's been over twenty years since I left the Shanxi province for Beijing, but we have kept in touch by phone. Initially, unless I was filming, I would return to Fenyang twice a year: for the holiday in mid-autumn—which coincides with my mother's birthday—and New Year's. When my mother was still living in Fenyang, no matter where I was in the world, I would make a point to come home and wish her a happy birthday. And New Year's is the most important holiday in China. So on those trips I was able to spend time with my parents and my friends.

In 2006, after my father died, my mother came to live with me in Beijing. Since then, unless I shoot a film there, I only go to Shanxi once a year at New Year's. But, since *Unknown Pleasures*, I haven't shot there much, although I did film some scenes of *Useless* in the old quarter of Fenyang, and a part of *A Touch of Sin* too.[22] Every time I leave Fenyang, not knowing when

---

22. Subsequent to this interview, Jia began returning to Fenyang more frequently in order to oversee both the programming of an art-house complex, and the film festival, in the neighboring

I will see my friends again, it makes me sad. Fortunately there's the phone and texting, plus I speak to them on Weibo. It's our way of being together.

For the Chinese, where you are from, your native region, is very important. Every time I return home my friends and I get together to drink, play Mahjong, and talk about our lives. Most of my friends work for State-owned companies: the Office of Telecommunications, in distilleries… One of them opened his own clinic. There's a journalist, a farmer, a cop, a prosecutor, a judge, a bank accountant… Yesterday, we drank too much and sang our favorite song: "One Night in Beijing," about the wolves of the north. In fact it's a Taiwanese song but in high school we loved singing it as it seemed to be about us—we are the people of the North and we saw ourselves as real wolves! At the end of the song, we would all howl in unison like wolves, hurting our lungs! This morning the palms of my hands reeked of alcohol. Just now I made a phone call because one of my older friends fought with one of the younger ones and I wanted to know if there had been any damage. They told me: "Everything is fine. Nothing better than a good fight to maintain a friendship." It feels as though we're back in our high school days.

After high school you studied fine arts at Shanxi University in Taiyuan.

It was the only school where I could enroll because of my poor math scores. Also, my father encouraged me to go there.

Do you think that your training in fine arts has influenced your approach as a filmmaker?

Yes, my studies in visual arts have given me invaluable training. I was taught to observe the world differently. When you are drawing, you unconsciously become sensitive to questions of light, shape, and color. And, in studying the history of art, you acquire an understanding of, and appreciation for, other painters' work. Above all, practicing the fine arts honed my intuition for a painter's tools. You have to understand different materials in order

---

city of Pingyao, he created in 2017. In 2021 he announced the launching of a Film Academy in the province of Shanxi, with two major venues in the cities of Fenyang and Pingyao.

to study art, understand what defines each material. Oil painting and ink painting have nothing in common aesthetically. Ink borrows from water its uncertain character and has an abstract feeling, very different from the more concrete nature of oil painting. Studying the fine arts you become acquainted with different materials and their potential. You can explore ways of using them beyond their usual framework, expanding creative possibilities. Creating with water, sculpting with wax, or even with fat, opens up your perceptions. Then, when I came into contact with film at the Beijing Film Academy, I explored the aesthetic possibilities unique to the film medium, and found myself considering the innate characteristics of the image, its texture. This curiosity was awakened in me by studying art—for me it's a never-ending reflection.

When Akira Kurosawa received an honorary Oscar for his lifework, he said that he didn't deserve it as he didn't think he understood cinema, that he hadn't yet grasped its true essence. At least two lessons can be drawn from his words: firstly, no matter what art you practice, you need to try to know your medium, to find its beauty, its specificity. Secondly, you should not expect to find a definitive answer on this quest. Even a great master like Kurosawa thought that he never found the answer. From one generation to the next, artists seek—and try to understand—the possibilities of the artform they have devoted themselves to.

Despite the material differences when it comes to production, do you find commonalities between painting and cinema?

Of course. I devote a lot of time to this topic when I teach. When conceiving a cinematic image, you ask the same questions as you would in painting. The difference is that cinema has movement, which has its own singular characteristics. But certain conventions in painting can guide the process of film production. For example, when I am working on a dramatic composition I pay close attention to the Golden Ratio, which allows me to determine where to place a key moment in the story. There are many ancient principles of painting that can be used, but this would take more time to elaborate.

Could you have continued on the fine arts track?

At the time, the question didn't present itself like that. I wanted to go to Beijing and had heard it was possible to get into the Film Academy, but only in the literary division. I thought that the classes would be on screenwriting but, instead, they were on film theory. I applied and was accepted. In 1993, at a relatively-advanced age for a student, I left the provincial capital for the country's capital, which was a radical change! Suddenly, I could go to the theater, to rock concerts, and could hear my favorite poets reciting poetry in bars! Plus I had access to original works of art.

I remember when I was still studying Fine Arts in Taiyuan I took the train to Beijing with some classmates. At that time there wasn't yet a high-speed train, and it took all night to cross the high mountain ranges—eight or nine hours to reach Beijing, while today it would take only three-and-a-half hours. We went to Beijing to see the Rodin exhibition, the first exhibition of his sculptures and drawings to take place in China. It was a real adventure!

In the Film Academy's curriculum, there was some continuity with aspects of what I had learned studying the history of art at the School of Fine Arts. In Beijing, I concentrated on film theory and film history, and this helped me understand film as a medium of expression; how it was born and how it evolved through different eras. This knowledge formed an important background for my work, giving me a real foundation. At that time the teaching at the Film Academy was very lively. The latest theories—neo-historicism, structuralism, postmodernism—hadn't been fully understood but were already being taught to us. This was great as each theory's value was less in what it specifically said, and more in its power to open up new possibilities and perspectives for observing and apprehending the world.

Moving to Beijing represented a real change in your life and your relationship with others.

It was completely different. Fortunately, Wang Hongwei was already there. We met senior year in high school, and then again at the Film Academy in 1993 when we were in a film theory class together. In our second year we organized what we called the Youth Experimental Film Group. The core was made up of Wang Hongwei, Gu Zheng, and myself—plus students from other departments on a less frequent basis. Our group began really as a game. At the Academy there were a dozen of us who were friends and who loved contemporary cinema. Each one of us had a different method for getting hold of the latest films, and we formed this group in order to swap videotapes. For example, in 1993 or 1994, someone got hold of Jane Campion's *The Piano* and, as the others hadn't yet seen it, we passed the tape around. A few days later, someone else got Antonioni's *L'Avventura*, which we all watched. Some time later, one of us befriended Taiwanese students who had a number of Pasolini's films. We were really a group of cinephiles.

It was with these friends that you made your first shorts. What pushed you to begin making films?

At that time the Film Academy would screen two recent Chinese films each week.[23] They had an agreement with the Beijing Film Institute to borrow films whose commercial run had just ended, in order to show them to students. I found that these films didn't really reflect our lives.

There were mainly two types of films. Firstly, "entertainment" films, mostly action movies or films we called *gun fu*, which is a hybrid genre of crime and martial arts that takes place in a make-believe world. I didn't have a problem with these films. Everyone could see that they were made-up stories and some of them were entertaining. The second kind of films they would show were supposedly realist, but to me it was a filtered or deformed reality. For example, every year we would see films with the same story: a student about to finish his studies receives a proposition to work in a poor isolated village. Once it was Guizhou, then Shanxi, later Henan—but always the same story! It was in these films that supposedly depicted real life that there was no *reality*. They didn't show poverty, or depict the difficulties people encountered. Although they seemed to talk about reality it was an illusion. Seeing these kinds of films is what made me decide to make my own.

Were your first shorts conceived within the framework of the Youth Experimental Film Group?

---

23. See also the chapter "The Films of My Life," pp. 203–10.

Yes. They weren't exactly school films and weren't shot in the context of the curriculum, even if students from the Academy did work on them. Since I wasn't in the film directing department I wasn't supposed to make films.

In the Youth Experimental Film Group there were people who studied theory—like me—and others studying subjects including cinematography, sound, set design, and production. And it's in this context that our first short came about, a documentary entitled *One Day, in Beijing*. We used a Betacam camera that one of us borrowed from his father's newspaper company—I don't know why but they had a camera. We borrowed the sound equipment from the Film Academy. I went to Tiananmen Square and shot like crazy throughout the day. I showed the film and it became our first documentary. Unfortunately this film is lost. After moving several times I now don't know where it is.

I then wrote a screenplay titled *Xiaoshan Going Home*. At the time, in 1995, hordes of migrant workers were starting to leave the country to work in the big city. My main character was a young cook planning on going home for the Chinese New Year. He doesn't want to make the trip alone, so is looking for a travelling companion among his friends in Beijing. The film cost 20,000 yuans that was mostly my own money. At the time, like several other students in my department, I was writing short scripts commissioned by television. I wasn't allowed to sign my name to them, but did earn a small sum. This is how I was able to bankroll my three shorts. After *Xiaoshan Going Home* I made *Dudu*, but that's also lost.

How did you come to cast Wang Hongwei in the leading role? He wasn't a trained actor.

It's true. At the time he was writing a thesis on Tarkovsky! But I immediately thought of him because his gestures were so vivid. He had very expressive body language, and would gesticulate a lot when speaking. Sometimes while we were talking he would suddenly squat down or swing his arms, moving his whole body. Hongwei's body language is as eloquent as his voice. In my opinion he was much more interesting than the acting students who, after several years of training, wound up just looking like statues. If you were to put them on a street in Fenyang or a popular market in Beijing, they would immediately stand out as actors. Wang Hongwei was a much better option as I wanted the film to be very realistic—shot entirely on location with a handheld camera and with the dialogue in dialect. Wang Hongwei's acting was in sync with all of this. Still, at the time, everyone thought that choosing him for the film was a monumental mistake.

Wang and you also took a training course for actors.

We mainly studied film theory but did also have one acting course. We drove our professor mad! He hated our acting and, it must be said, we *were* lousy. One day, infuriated, he said: "Jia Zhangke, Wang Hongwei, and Gu Zheng, lie down on the floor and make believe you are dead. I want to see if you can manage that!" We stretched out on the floor without moving and the professor said: "Okay, you're stretched out on the floor without moving but where is the acting?" Oh, so we're not completely dead? Then we began to move. The professor said: "Your gestures are exaggerated; that's not it at all…" All that just made us lose confidence in our acting ability. But, from *Xiaowu* to now, Wang Hongwei has shown what he's capable of. He's an outstanding actor but he must be in sync with the film's style. I also think that we were helped by the fact that we came relatively late to the Film Academy. We both already had some life experience; more in any case than the other students we hung out with.

How did the screenplay for Xiaowu *come about?*

It originated in the anger and sadness I felt in response to the demolition of Fenyang. When I was home for the New Year, I had learned that there was a plan to destroy all the old streets. It was shocking to learn this and it occurred to me that in a few years all the places from my childhood would be gone.

Added to this was another thing that inspired me, something related to this. When I returned from Beijing, I realized that my friends were experiencing serious problems in their personal and professional lives. They spoke only of disputes and break-ups—with their parents, their friends, their wives or their girlfriends. I was shocked. Of course before there were problems, but never quite on this scale. I soon discovered that the economic changes in the country were behind their personal conflicts—money had become the regulator of human relationships.

Another factor was the unbelievable proliferation of karaoke rooms. There was a place in Fenyang called the Fenzhou Market that previously had shops on two levels. Local specialties were sold there such as brandy, Chinese dates, millet seeds, and also household items. When I went home in 1997 all these stores—or nearly all—had been transformed into karaoke rooms, with young women working there who sang with the clients, and sometimes even went out with them. This had become the job for a great number of young women, like Meimei, the film's heroine. The boutiques often had exotic names—Dream of Paris, Vienna, New York—that expressed a yearning for other cultures. Many men fell in love with these young women, destroying their personal relationships. In 1997 I was told several stories about this— how families had been affected, and so on. As soon as I got back to Beijing I started work on the screenplay based on all of this.

Did you know the main story right away?

Yes, I knew immediately that the film would be built around a central character; that everything would be filtered through him. It was similar to painting a portrait. I was haunted by the image of a boy of my age from the streets of Fenyang, an incarnation of all my friends. When I first had this idea it was based on several elements: the changes he was experiencing; his rapport with his parents, with his girlfriend, and with his friends. And also his appearance: while writing the screenplay, I was thinking all the time about his physical appearance and had imagined him poorly dressed in the kind of Western-style outfit we would wear in the 1990s. An outfit too big for him with the label visible on one of the sleeves. He also wore a pullover knitted by his mother.

How did the shoot go?

In March I returned to Fenyang to scout locations. The demolition had already begun and we couldn't find the places we wanted and had to change the locations. I would also change the dialogue constantly as the shoot was largely improvised. This was possible as I knew all the performers well. Besides Wang Hongwei the other cast members were friends from Fenyang or members of my family.

We were still students and *Xiaowu* was done before we graduated. The technical crew was mainly made up of students from the Film Academy. The same crew I formed for my first shorts—we were tied together by a strong friendship. The production conditions were very difficult. Being surrounded by friends was crucial as, without financial backing, we could only count on our own resources. The cameraman and the sound engineer borrowed the equipment they needed from the Beijing Film Academy. We had no production budget and no one received a salary. My crew members reached into their own pockets so I could make my film. It was our shared love of cinema that made things possible, bringing us together and allowing us to be a very tight-knit crew. From the first shorts, I knew that that was how I wished to make films. Ever since, even as production conditions have improved and my crews filled out, I have maintained this spirit.

You ultimately managed to find the locations you needed?

I adapted to the situation at hand. I am pleased with the karaoke place where Meimei works. I searched for a long time and ended up finding a space that I like a lot. It was very confined with no natural light. But there was a small door and behind it, a courtyard, with a kitchen, a coal depot and a room where someone lived. In front, we had the karaoke room—a special place—separated from the living space by just a simple door. The setting was very realistic. And the street provided great opportunities for the sequence where Xiaowu takes a walk with Meimei. I purposely hired an actress taller than Wang Hongwei. Their difference in height conveys his constant feeling of inferiority, and in order to reinforce this she wore heels. Shortly before shooting I noticed that the difference of height between them—about ten centimeters—was the same as the measurement between the street and the sidewalk. This inspired the moment when she says ironically: "I shouldn't have worn high heels. I'm already taller than you," and Xiaowu, offended, moves up onto the sidewalk and finds himself at approximately the same height as her. Noticing his change in attitude, she suggests he go up even higher on the walkway. Wang Hongwei climbs the stairs and walks up high while Meimei continues walking below. This use of space reflects Xiaowu's lack of self-esteem and his sensitivity. By climbing the stairs he shows Meimei his need to assert himself. I tried to film all the movement in a single frame but it didn't look good. So the shot begins below with Meimei and continues on him as he climbs the stairs up to the top. When he re-enters in the frame in the background, we see Shanghai Night, the karaoke room.

Was all the dialogue improvised?

There was written dialogue but we kept changing it during the shoot. In order to adapt to the situation around us, we would make changes all the time. From this point of view, not much has changed in how I make films. But in most of my films the progression of the narrative does follow the script. Before filming begins I speak with the actors and explain that, although they must conform overall to the details of the plot, they're free to choose the manner and exact words with which they convey the details. Wang Hongwei and Zhao Tao are similar in that their acting is different in each take. Every time they offer different replies and different gestures. The only thing that doesn't change is their position in the frame, which has been determined during rehearsals.

From your first films, you often film in long takes. This has remained a regular artistic choice. What is its meaning?

I am always surprised when people think that I do long takes because it's easier. On the contrary a long take demands a lot of technical know-how and preparation. I like long takes because, first of all, they're true-to-life. Our memories and impressions are fragmentary; when they come to our minds, it's as if we've edited them as we would in cinema. Films usually create this kind of temporality, where certain aspects of life are omitted or intensified. In contrast, the long take gives a feeling of real time. With film, for example, I can take a punch that lasts for less than a second and make it last ten seconds. I can film it from several angles and edit it together in ten different shots. But I personally prefer the feeling of reality that comes with a complete moment in real time.

Of course I am not the first filmmaker in China to use long takes. When Chinese cinema began to modernize at the end of the 1970s, a number of directors began to value its use. Ironically the films from the revolutionary period were very Hollywood; in fact, they mixed the Hollywood and Soviet models. But, after the 1970s, many Chinese filmmakers used long takes because they bring equality. Making a film by aggressively putting together many shots represents a violent imposition of one's point of view, assigning viewers a passive role. In contrast, the long take signifies a more democratic relationship with the public. The viewer can decide to look where they choose and real time can be experienced without interruption or distortion. It offers both justice and equality.

Even though you didn't closely follow it, did you write a complete script for Xiaowu?

No, as I didn't yet know how to finish the story. I had written a slapdash ending where Xiaowu was arrested and then taken by the police across a busy street and into the crowd. It was something like the ending of many Italian Neorealist films. I knew this wasn't satisfactory and was only a temporary solution. While preparing the film, and up until the start of shooting, I was thinking about how to finish it.

The idea for the ending came to me from observing the reaction of people on the street during the shoot. Nowadays, hardly anyone stops to look at my shoots, but in 1997 in Fenyang we were surrounded by a crowd as soon as we unpacked the camera. As most of the shoot was outside on location, this happened constantly. So it occurred to me that when the police seize Xiaowu, why not let the crowd stare at him? The camera could shift from Xiaowu's point of view to the perspective of those surrounding him. Then I remembered something else: one of my childhood friends was a cop who was fired after he left a handcuffed suspect in the street to go and take care of a personal problem. That's how I got the idea to handcuff Xiaowu to a pole. We shot this final scene without knowing what people's reaction would be. We had only one can of filmstock left, just enough to do three takes of the scene. We didn't control what happened with the bystanders.

At the end of three takes, it was the end of the roll—really the end of the film! So passersby contributed without even knowing it. Of course, they said things different to what we hear from them in the film, like "Look, there is someone with handcuffs in the street." People also said things like: "They're shooting a film," or "Shanxi TV is shooting a serial." That gave us some problems during the sound edit![24]

Xiaowu was invited to international festivals, beginning with the Berlin Forum in February 1998.[25] *Did you anticipate this while filming?*

When I was making *Xiaowu*, I knew that the film would not be shown in China, and that foreign film festivals were its only chance. Thanks to the international attention the Fifth Generation had received, I knew that this opportunity existed; those filmmakers had led the way. But I never imagined that from this first film there would be such a strong response, and that I would end up traveling so much. When the film was invited to Berlin we flew to Hamburg, then took a bus for Rotterdam to make the subtitles, then a train to Brussels, later a car for Paris, and then another plane to Berlin. For someone who had only ever imagined traveling, it was a dream come true!

Was it your first trip to the West, or even outside of China?

As a university student I made my first trip abroad to Malaysia, a country largely imbued with Chinese culture. So this was very different. On the flight to Germany all the passengers were sleeping except me. I was very excited, very happy, and very anxious, particularly since I didn't speak English. I was also curious to see a capitalist country. But I was mostly excited that I was visiting "the world of cinema." At university, some professors—particular Xie Fei[26]—took advantage of their travels abroad to bring back films to show

---

24. See also the interview with the film's sound engineer, Zhang Yang, pp. 187–93.
25. A parallel section of the Berlin Film Festival, the International Forum of New Cinema is known as a major place for revealing new talents.
26. One of the principal figures of China's Fifth Generation of filmmakers, Xie Fei is best known

us. That's how I discovered Abbas Kiarostami, Krzysztof Kieślowski, Tsai Ming-liang,[27] and many others. By going to Berlin I felt I was leaving to go to *their* "country."

The invitation to Berlin must have been exciting news.

Yes, but I was also worried. My film openly broke with the films of my predecessors, the Fifth Generation. I liked their first films, particularly *Yellow Earth*, but found them removed from my reality. The invitation to Berlin scared me as I knew Westerners liked the Fifth Generation's films, and feared that my film would seem incomprehensible or uninteresting to them.

Did you get the impression Xiaowu *was understood by Western viewers? Were you surprised by their reactions?*

The first reactions of foreign critics reassured me. And the exchanges with the public after screenings confirmed it—people understood my film. I had been focused on what separated us but then I realized that what's essential are the similarities. Everyone can understand the human relationships that *Xiaowu* talks about—between friends, in the family, between a man and a woman, etc. When I was making the film, my goals were vague. I liked the streets and people so wanted to film them, and to take note of how they were changing. I was very attracted to non-professional actors as they have a vitality rarely found in professionals. When I met Western viewers, I saw that they interpreted and discussed this method in aesthetic terms, they were right. I understood then that what I had done instinctively—in order to stick to reality as much as possible—was also a specific stylistic choice grounded in my story and my own references. Western viewers taught me to look at my country in a new way, to look at it from an outside perspective.

---

as the director of *A Girl from Hunan* (1986) and *Women from the Lake of Scented Souls* (1993). The former was one of the first mainland Chinese films screened in the US, while the latter won the Golden Bear at the Berlin Film Festival. Xie Fie was an important mentor to the subsequent generation of filmmakers.

27. See the chapter titled, "The Films of My Life," starting on page 203.

Finding oneself so far from home can change one's perception of what one knows. Was that later conveyed in your films?

In Berlin something happened that I don't often talk about. Some friends suggested I go to an evening of Taiwanese cinema. I was happy to attend as I was very much a fan of the films of Hou Hsiao-hsien and Edward Yang. As soon as I got there I noticed a Taiwanese flag on each table, and I panicked. My upbringing was telling me it would be dangerous to be there.[28] In the end I did go in and join my friends. This might seem negligible to you, but for me it was a major break. It made me reflect a lot on what it means to belong to a country—a system of representation produced by political parties and ideologies—and on the capacity to construct one's own point of view. From there was born the desire for a film in which being defined by political boundaries could disappear. I later satisfied this desire with *I Wish I Knew*.

Did the positive international reception of Xiaowu *facilitate the production of* Platform?

In Berlin I noticed a Japanese man who followed me everywhere. But, as I didn't speak English, I couldn't communicate with him. After a few days, Yu Lik-wai—who does speak English—arrived from Hong Kong to join me. Now I was able to communicate with the man, who was Shôzô Ichiyama, and who has been the co-producer of all my films until now. He told me Takeshi Kitano had created a company to co-produce young Asian directors, and asked if that was of interest to me. You bet it was!

---

28. As a result of the second phase of the Chinese Civil War (1945–1949), China was split into two present-day, self-governing entities: the People's Republic of China (PRC; commonly known as China) and the Republic of China (ROC; commonly known as Taiwan). For more than two decades the Beijing governments have been intent on recuperating Taiwan through a combination of economic inducement, diplomacy, and the threat of force. In the years 2008–2016 the Chinese believed they were making progress towards this goal when the Taiwanese president Ma Ying-jeou signaled an openness to reunification. Beijing regards Taiwan as a breakaway province that will eventually be recuperated. In 2020 Tsai Ing-wen won a second term as president of Taiwan: she favors the country's eventual independence from the mainland. [Tr.]

Immediately I thought of *Platform* as it was already written. I just didn't have the funding to make it, which is why I had made *Xiaowu*. Thanks to the support of this company—Office Kitano—it was then possible to make *Platform*.

Also in Berlin I met Annette Ferrasson and Philippe Chevassu, a French couple with the distribution company Connaissance du cinéma. Right after the screening they came to see me and were enthusiastic that my film would have distribution in France. Berlin proved to me that I could exist as a filmmaker without needing to depend on the Chinese system.

Did the film's positive reception in Berlin have any effect in China?

When I received the prize at the Berlin Forum, some Chinese journalists working in Germany did write reviews. That was the beginning of recognition in China as people began asking: who is this Jia Zhangke? What is this film that no one's heard of? Thanks to the audiovisual attachée within the Cultural Service Department of the French Embassy,[29] I met Lin Xudong who asked me for a DVD of the film, and then suggested organizing some private screenings in China.[30] When I presented the film for the first time to a Chinese audience—at the Lycée Français in Beijing—I had to translate the dialogue into a microphone as the film is in the Shanxi dialect which no one in Beijing understands. Personalities from the intelligentsia came to these screenings—including Zhang Yimou, Cui Jian, Liu Xiaodong[31]—and some favorable reviews appeared. There were screenings from the end of February to November 1998.

---

29. At the time, Isabelle Glachant was the audiovisual attachée at the French Embassy. She played a pivotal role in the encounters between contemporary Chinese and French filmmakers.

30. Also see the interview with Lin Xudong, who will become Jia's editor and close advisor, pp. 194–99.

31. Zhang Yimou was one of the principal filmmakers of the Fifth Generation before becoming China's most highly ranked official filmmaker. Cui Jian, China's greatest rock star, is the most popular artistic personality of the "Tiananmen Generation." Liu Xiaodong, a prominent painter, is the subject of *Dong*, which Jia shot in 2005.

Just in Beijing?

No, of course not. All over China. In June, I went to show it in Shanghai during the International Film Festival. Not in the festival itself, obviously. With a university professor's help we organized a secret screening. Several classmates from the Beijing Film Academy, who worked for the Shanghai studios and the festival, sent messages to guests to inform them that *Xiaowu* was screening that evening at the university. There was quite a crowd. After the screening I met a Japanese journalist from *Asahi Shimbun* who was posted in Shanghai and, ever since then, he's interviewed me once a year. Two years ago he published a thick book of these interviews titled *Jia Zhangke Speaks about Jia Zhangke*. I also showed the film in Yunnan and, of course, Shanxi. Whenever an opportunity presented itself for me to travel with the film I took it. I liked that it was acquiring fans.

But the response to Xiaowu *wasn't always positive...*

In November I received a call from an official who summoned me for an interview at the National Film Bureau. I remember the meeting very well. His first question was: "Where did you park your car?" He couldn't believe that I didn't have one and kept saying that all filmmakers were rich and had cars. Then he asked me if I knew why I was there and I answered no. He told me that I had broken the law in making *Xiaowu* without state approval to make or show the film. I said that it wasn't a commercial film but my final school project—a student film. Plus, I had filmed it on 16 mm, which was not allowed for films meant for theatrical distribution. He went on to outline the regulations that I had violated, which is how I learned what they were. They were published nowhere with only those who worked in the studios knowing and respecting them. At that time the authorities forced the Beijing Film Academy to add a course for students to learn the existing regulations.

The conversation with the official lasted a long time. In a friendly manner he gave me advice, like a benevolent elder. As I got up to leave he said that I should thank him. So I did, and he said: "But why are you thanking me?" I said it was because he'd spent a lot of time with me and been very courteous. He then said: "No, that's not why you should thank me. If I hadn't called you, the people from national security would have and, with them, things would have gone very differently." That made me very angry.

So the meeting wasn't so benevolent after all. There were consequences...

The following January I received an official document with three points: I had shot a film illegally; I had shown it in festivals illegally; and I had sold it abroad illegally. As a result I was prohibited from making films for an unspecified length of time. I felt as if I had been given a life sentence. In addition I was fined, but the amount was not specified. I wasn't the only one to have these problems: after screening their films at the Rotterdam Film Festival seven Chinese directors—including Tian Zhuangzhuang, Wang Xiaoshuai, Zhang Yuan—faced a similar situation. The authorities sought to break independent filmmakers by crushing them with fines. Later I was told that I had to pay 50,000 yuans, an enormous sum for me. I contacted the person-in-charge at the National Film Bureau, and told him that I had just finished film school and didn't have a penny. He agreed that it was a lot of money and said he would try to reduce it. A few days later he called me: "Can you pay thirty thousand?" I said of course I couldn't. He re-negotiated the sum and, in the end, I paid 20,000 yuans, which was still a lot of money for me. I thought that I shouldn't have paid anything as the National Film Bureau isn't the police and, although they do have an ability to exercise financial pressure, it's limited. But I thought that by paying the fine I was paving the way to start filming again.

This incident was very instructive to me. I realized that there was a difference between the system, which is profoundly toxic, and the people who work there, who are more or less open, ready to ask questions, and find solutions. In fact, they're people like us. Since then I have ceaselessly conferred with them in order to push things forward, even in small steps. Over the years several of these film officials have become friends.

Did that facilitate things from then on?

When I was preparing *Platform* I made contact with the Beijing Film Studio, thinking that if I could reach an agreement with them I would be able to have the shooting ban lifted. The Beijing Film Studio liked the project a lot and even proposed Tian Zhuangzhuang as Executive Producer. China was then experiencing an exponential economic development and the general atmosphere was optimistic. Everything seemed possible and it felt like things that had been banned a few months before would no longer be so. I sent the screenplay to the National Film Bureau, together with a letter of recommendation from the Vice-President of the Beijing Film Studio, wherein he guaranteed that the film posed no political problem, and would be of an exceptional artistic quality. With that, I was very confident and left to look for locations in Shanxi. But I then got a call from the Studio saying I had to return immediately. The project had been rejected for two reasons. The first: it was out of the question that the ban would be lifted; and the second: the National Film Bureau deemed that I was too young to talk about the period 1980–1990 when the film is set. They said I needed to wait another ten years to be able to recount those years. I thought about it for a long time and concluded that I nonetheless wanted to make the film. I took a bus that ran all night through the mountains and reflected on my anger and frustration, telling myself that never again would I ask for authorization; that I would make my films independently, even if it meant remaining on the margins.

Thereafter, film after film, you increasingly won international recognition. Often filmmakers who find themselves in this situation of making films primarily for foreign audiences and the international festival circuit are criticized. Have you received such criticism?

The directors of the Fifth Generation were often criticized for this, in particular Chen Kaige and Zhang Yimou. When *Red Sorghum* won the Silver Bear in Berlin it sparked a controversy in China with a lot of people saying that such films shouldn't be shown abroad. Ten or twelve years later, when I began making films, the problem was not so acute. Each one of my films was attacked by the Chinese press up until *A Touch of Sin*, but not because they targeted a foreign audience, but rather because of an incomprehension regarding my artistic choices. Already, at the time of *Xiaowu*, critics wrote that anybody could make a film in that style, since all you needed was to leave a camera running in the street. This is the kind of criticism that I often receive.

The yearning to travel and see faraway places is at the heart of Platform.

In the beginning I was motivated by a nostalgia for the 1980s, for my youth: the upheaval tied to the reforms—on a material and spiritual level—and the end of the period that was ultimately marked by the Tiananmen tragedy. It was also a nostalgia for the music of the time, and for the adolescent explosion of desire. It was all these feelings that pushed me to make the film about an artistic troupe, to use their itinerant lifestyle to convey my impressions and memories of the period. The travelling troupe also allowed for the introduction of a dynamic—a tension—between an attachment to the world of my childhood and the desire to leave, to go elsewhere. As a teenager I longed to leave home because Fenyang was so isolated and opportunities for traveling were rare. In high school I was able to go to Yulin, on the other side of the Yellow River with my breakdance group—at the time, this was the farthest destination I could imagine in this big world! What then could Ulaanbaatar be like?

My first real trip took place at the end of high school. My father had decided I should study at the School of Fine Arts in Taiyuan. Taiyuan is only a hundred kilometers from Fenyang but it *is* the capital of the Shanxi province. In Taiyuan there is a train station, an airport, and a Fine Arts museum, whereas Fenyang has none of those things. Moving there was sufficiently different from Fenyang for it to be very exciting! I then realized that there was something else missing in Fenyang: a foreign language bookstore. The one in Taiyuan had a cabinet full of books imported from abroad. That's where I first saw reproductions of Van Gogh, Cézanne, Renoir, Picasso, Millet—they had all kinds of books. Aesthetically speaking, this definitely widened my horizons! At the time in China, although we had access to translations of the classics of Western literature, we had practically no access to books on Western painting, aside from a small number of painting albums. I don't know why the manager of this store permitted customers to leaf through such precious works. He was an exceptional pedagogue, allowing people like me to discover art. In talking about all this we have strayed from discussing the screenplay for *Platform*, but it's fed by all these experiences, this desire for discovery…

The film was shot in conditions very different from Xiaowu.

Totally. I found myself with a large crew—several people for the image, sound, sets, etc.—and didn't know how to manage them. The shoot was also complicated because it involved a lot of travel. We needed a real wizard in the production department to coordinate everything! We ended up learning on the job and spent our time going from Fenyang to Pingyao and back in search of locations. A lot of mistakes were made. However, it shouldn't be assumed that we were doing any old thing. We were learning what it meant to oversee a budget, to give an accounting of our expenditures, and to eliminate a scene because there was no more money. In short, we were becoming professionals.

It was on Platform *that your core film crew of collaborators with whom you consistently work was formed: director of photography Yu Lik-wai, sound engineer Zhang Yang, and actor Wang Hongwei—who had all worked on* Xiaowu—*plus editor and advisor Lin Xudong, and actors Zhao Tao and Han Sanming.*

Yes, that's when our collaboration really took shape. Since then, as soon as I have my first glimmers of inspiration I share them with Lin Xudong, Yu Lik-wai, and Zhang Yang. I discuss my ideas with them over dinner or tea and get their feedback, which helps me move ahead. At each stage of conception on a project they're the first to know my thoughts. By the time I begin writing the screenplay they already know what the film is about. The script is more a kind of clarification meant for production to allow for greater precision with the actors.

Incidentally, an essential step for me is that of location scouting. Initially I scout locations on my own, traveling as a tourist to places that I sense could serve as locations. I then go back to those places as soon as possible with Yu Lik-wai, Zhang Yang, and the set designer. So our conversations about a project often occur while we are location scouting. We discuss the plot and sometimes I share with them my ideas for the overall *mise-en-scène*. Yu Lik-wai adds what he has to say from his point of view as a cinematographer, and we also address the sound design. For example, for *Platform*, we went to Pingyao and Fenyang, and together wondered how best to reproduce a place from the end of 1970s with all its characteristics: the feeling of desolation, the difficult material conditions, and the surrounding stagnation. During the shoot itself I talk very little with the crew. As much of the finetuning is done ahead of time, my time is freed up to focus on the actors.

In Platform *there is one actor and character with the same name: Han Sanming. He reappears in your later films, always as a secondary character.*

Sanming here plays the protagonist's cousin—and he's really *my* cousin! His family lived in a mountain village and, when I was small, I would often go there. Sanming and I would play together as we are practically the same age. His personal history is very close to that of his character in *Platform*: straight after dropping out of school he worked in a number of iron and coal mines in different places in the region. I had lost contact with him at school. Later, when I was at the Beijing Film Academy, I would often visit my aunt—his mother—with my mother and sister. Sanming was then shy and would speak little, but did smile at me all the time. He always stayed in a corner, but our visits made him happy. He told me he was working in a coal mine which I knew was fairly well paid, although extremely dangerous. While writing the script for *Platform* I decided that the first stop of the traveling show after Fenyang would be in a coal mine. Based on this idea my mother suggested I call Sanming and offer him the role.

There is one enduring memory from the shoot. When Cui Mingliang, Wang Hongwei's character, is going to visit his aunt in the village, he meets Sanming, who tells him that he's found work in a coal factory. I wanted a prop that would reveal Sanming's identity—that he was a miner—but we didn't have one. So I asked Sanming if he had a helmet, imagining one with a flashlight on the front of it, like the image of miners that we have from movies and TV. He went to get his work helmet: it was made from the branches of a willow tree with no flashlight, and looked really fragile. How can you guarantee someone's safety with that?

In this and your other films Han Sanming has a special presence. He doesn't resemble the other actors.

It's above all a question of rhythm. In 1999, when I was shooting *Platform*, changes were occurring all over China. The rhythm of life was speeding up and we had the impression that everyone was in a hurry. Those of us making the film felt this, and of course the characters, who are carried forward by a youthful energy. In the midst of all that, I was struck by Sanming's very slow rhythm, his way of walking, talking, and reacting. In comparison to him we all appeared on edge. Later, when I did *Still Life*, I asked him to keep this tranquility in his performance. Even if he no longer works as a miner, he hasn't really changed.

At the time of Platform, *how did all these societal transformations affect your work?*

They certainly increased the tension but that's normal. To make a film a director draws on previous experiences, while also letting go of them. That's part and parcel of the job. When working I ask myself what are the usual techniques that help me as a filmmaker? And which techniques need to be discarded to discover something new? On the one hand, there is a need to accumulate and on the other to eliminate. You have to maintain a kind of void in order to receive inspiration. When one is in control of the situation, and knows and understands all that one does, the emotion decreases.

Platform *was selected in competition for the Venice Film Festival, which is even more prestigious than the Berlin Forum. It met with great success at foreign festivals, even more than* Xiaowu. *It was also distributed commercially in several Western countries. Did you have the feeling of reaching a new stage in your career?*

Certainly, but it didn't happen that simply. In 2000, I left for the Venice Festival accompanied by Shôzô Ichiyama. I was thirty years old and *Platform* was the first of my films in competition at a major international festival. Before arriving I was calm and peaceful; I didn't know much and had no idea what the main competition would be like. The red carpet was completely foreign to me and I didn't understand the importance of the awards. There was all this hectic hustle and bustle that we thought amusing once the screening was over. The film received a large number of positive reviews from very different sources and this aroused my desire to win.

The morning of the award ceremony many newspapers, and even the festival's gazette, wagered that *Platform* would be the big winner of the evening. So I began thinking about and celebrating our success with Ichiyama. But, around noon, he came to tell me that we would not be winning anything. I took it badly. It was a tough blow! Deeply disappointed, I went to sit alone by the sea and heal my ego. I really felt a dirty trick had been played on me. And I felt really sorry for Ichiyama, that I had disappointed him and Office Kitano. Later, Ichiyama came to join me. We were both sitting by the sea and I apologized to him. He became angry and shouted: "What are you talking about?! We only missed an award at Venice, that's all. It's a very good film! Why talk about failure?" He told me that a film's life isn't limited to just one evening, that I need to trust in its ability to last. At the time I didn't really understand this as I was too sad. But later, *Platform* was screened and distributed worldwide—people were talking about it and the film really had a great trajectory. Then, ten years later, the Toronto Film Festival contacted me to say it had made their List of the Ten Best Films from the early 2000s. When that happened I thought about Ichiyama and what he had said to me on the beach in Venice.

In China, although it was banned, it was seen by many on bootleg DVDs.

At first, I was really surprised by this, as it was usually only foreign films that were bootlegged. The first time I saw a pirated DVD of one of my films, I was in a store and asked what new films they had. The owner said to me: "This afternoon I am going to get a really great film by the filmmaker Jia Zhangke, called *Platform*. Does that interest you? If you come back around 2 or 3 pm, I should have it." So I went back later and there was a pile of brand new DVDs of *Platform*.[32] It's a bit like losing a child—you look everywhere

---

32. In *Unknown Pleasures*, Wang Hongwei's character asks (without luck) a seller of pirated DVDs for copies of *Xiaowu*, *Platform*, and Yu Lik-wai's film as director, *Love Will Tear Us Apart*.

for them and then, finally, they show up in an unexpected place. It's a very strange feeling. But it's thanks to bootleg DVDs that so many people have been able to see certain films.

At this time critics began writing about my films on the internet, which further increased their notoriety. Digital technology was in the process of demolishing the entire system of official control. I remember once the National Film Bureau assembled banned filmmakers, and I said to them: "You should no longer try to prevent directors from expressing themselves because technology won't allow it. With digital technology, we can shoot very easily; films are circulating on bootleg DVDs and viewers are talking about them on the internet." Of course it was still impossible to see these films in theaters. China doesn't have art-house cinemas, just state-run distribution. The only alternative that exists are screenings in museums and art galleries. For example we regularly screen films in the 798 Art Zone in Beijing.[33]

There is also the possibility—something that has existed since your earliest films—of underground screenings in cafés.

Yes this has existed since the end of the 1990s and still continues today. I like to show my films in all kinds of places. In cafés, the atmosphere is special. The crowd tends to be small but they're real cinephiles who discuss the films after the screenings. These intimate showings allow a small group of individuals to get together and have real discussions, to debate the social and political issues that cinema deals with. That said, the conditions in alternative spaces like cafés aren't always favorable technically.

I remember, in 2001, a Beijing café wanted to screen *Platform* and I offered to come for a discussion with the audience. The café publicized the event which was planned for 2:30 in the afternoon. When I got there I realized that the café had transparent walls—it was a glass box! The film was screened but with the daylight pouring in you couldn't see anything. Everyone was busy trying to mask the light—we looked for black fabric to

---

33. The 798 Art Zone is a Beijing neighborhood devoted to contemporary art, with many galleries, cafes, discussion forums and touristic boutiques.

line the walls! Once this problem was more or less solved, it began to rain and water began seeping into the café. The screening went ahead but under terrible conditions. I was sad that my films couldn't be shown in real film theaters; a real screening with proper seats and good technical equipment. I felt the same sadness painters must feel when confronted with poor reproductions of one of their works.

Bootleg DVDs and alternative screenings were possible thanks to the arrival of digital technology, which also changed the conditions of production. You began shooting digitally from your next film, In Public.

Yes. Although this film did come about thanks to this technology, it's due even more to my nomadic lifestyle at that time. I was frequently traveling, especially all over China. This was to show my films but also just to travel. There was one trip that I particularly liked to do: I would take the bus in Beijing to Taiyuan, then another to Fenyang that dropped me off just in front of my family house. I would spend the night, then take another bus to continue on the road, beyond the Yellow River and as far as Yulin, before continuing on toward Mongolia. A long trip!

Once I was on the bus when suddenly it stopped to let on a pregnant woman and her husband. The bus continued on its way, and I noticed that a pickpocket was stealing from the sleeping passengers. A little later the bus stopped again to let on travelers who were laden with gifts. They got off at the next station, going to a wedding or a birthday. Traveling produces so many unexpected encounters with all kinds of people! We can imagine their lives.

I remember one day after I had just begun my studies at the Film Academy in Beijing, I spotted one of my friends from Taiyuan outside the cafeteria. I was very surprised, because at the time getting to Beijing meant a twelve-hour train journey. I invited him to lunch and asked him why he was in Beijing: "I just wanted to share a meal with you," he said. He had traveled overnight by train just to have lunch with me for two hours and then was going to take the return train back that night. I had imagined he didn't know what he was doing, when in fact he had come just to see a friend!

I also remember how once, while waiting for a train, I saw a traveler sleeping in the waiting room with his hands tightly clasping his bag. I almost cried at this exhausted fellow who still kept up his guard to protect his bag. That's a good reflection of life's stresses. Traveling allows you to notice and understand details like this that animate people. It's like a magnifying glass that reveals the subtle framework of life. I made *In Public* to take advantage of these observations and transform into film my feelings, without the added pretext of a story.

How did you go about making In Public?

I took my camera and left for Datong. Once there I was on the lookout in bus stations, train stations and suburban bus stops, waiting for individuals to come towards me. But I didn't intend to speak to them. I simply wanted to stand to the side and watch. It was as if I were silently welcoming and accompanying them.

My idea was simple: to use the camera to capture strangers. On the one hand, the project was very concrete because it involved specific individuals. On the other, it was very abstract, because the time for such encounters was extremely limited. I regard these encounters with strangers on public transport, or in public spaces, as a kind of ceremony: when, bathed in the lights of the setting sun, travelers laden with bags are getting ready for their departure, it's like a ritual. Coming near these people—people who are crushed by daily life and are visibly struggling in its never-ending race—and just taking note of their existence, is sacred in my eyes. There in that sea of humanity you find what is most precious in life. Just focusing attention on each of these faces allows the discovery of so many varied individuals, each with their own dignity. I have a deep gratitude for the camera: without it, I wouldn't be able to capture the life around me, and would be alone with my feelings. The camera allows me to bring this reality to life on the screen. Otherwise, it would just be a fleeting personal impression.

Of course digital technology makes shooting easier. It allows for shooting freely in surroundings where earlier I could not. I shot *In Public* with a small Sony digital camera; so small that people aren't intimidated by it. They thought I was something like a surveyor doing field surveys. When on the bus with my camera, they thought that I was just playing with a toy. This little camera immediately has an intimate relationship with people, and they're not hostile to it; it can freely wander among them. That said, I am convinced that from the moment a director agrees to get close to people, to live among them without rejecting them, no matter what kind of camera is being used—even an enormous Panavision—he will succeed. Everything depends on the filmmaker's attitude, his ability to remain in proximity with people, especially when dealing with strangers.

And of course traveling also spurs the imagination. When I see travelers coming and going on a train, bus, or boat, I always imagine their journey. For example, I see a man with a bag and imagine that he's perhaps sick and going to a doctor's appointment, or he's just gotten out of prison and is going home. Or perhaps his family is in need and he's going to look for work. Perhaps he hasn't found anything in one place and is going to try his luck elsewhere. It's precisely because I don't know who he is, and don't know what's happened to him, that I am able to imagine these different scenarios. Some of them later appear in my fiction films.

You travel a lot under special conditions tied to your profession. But traveling has become banal nowadays for many in China.

Yes, it's an enormous change. Previously Chinese people were physically tied to their land. But with China's economy opening up, they began to work elsewhere, seeking new lives in other provinces. Little by little, many became city dwellers, bidding farewell to a certain way of life. Such a loss is almost universal. So this need to travel affects not just a filmmaker like myself, but all the migrant workers who invade the Guangdong region for employment. They too are leaving their home region for faraway locations. Chinese society has become a vast swell of humanity on the move. People migrate from the interior toward the big cities, from the West toward the East Coast, from North to South; everyone moves with the idea of finding a better life. But, like me, most people hold their native region dear in their hearts. Maybe people even love it better because they left—in any case, they understand it better. When I left my region and was sufficiently removed from it to spend time in Beijing, Paris, or New York, I began to think differently about it. I began to better understand my country and the relationships between people, society, my parents, my classmates, and the poverty of my province. If today I can recognize myself as a native of the Shanxi region, it's because I left it.

Why did you choose the city of Datong to shoot In Public*?*

I felt I needed a change. Since childhood I had spent a lot of time watching people in the streets of Fenyang. At the same time, I didn't want to go into too large a city, where the contact with other human beings can be overwhelming. When I shot the film in 2001, I wanted to plunge myself into a place that was different to Beijing and similar to Fenyang. In Datong, which was once an important industrial and mining center, there were a lot of industrial buildings dating from the 1950s, and collective apartments for workers—aging architecture and public spaces that had undergone many unexpected changes. For example, the train station has now become a billiard hall, with its waiting room transformed into a dance hall. The place itself, and the alterations it has undergone, tell a story.

Could we say that the documentary In Public *gave birth to the fiction* Unknown Pleasures*? Both were shot in Datong.*

Yes, absolutely. The places of *In Public* gave birth to the characters of *Unknown Pleasures*. It's as if *In Public* began a dialogue with the city that I wanted to continue. In some ways *Unknown Pleasures* is the equivalent of *Platform* for the next generation: it testifies to a deadlock—an impasse—in which an entire generation of young people found themselves. At least those who didn't benefit from the country's economic transformation, which is the vast majority. Even if its hopes had been broken, the generation of the 1980s had had the chance to move—it soared toward a different future. These young people just went around in circles.

This is conveyed effectively in the scene where some youths try to leave the city on motorbike—to leave for another world—but find themselves stuck.

This scene gave rise to a lot of discussion and I was told it was unnecessarily long. Of course I could have edited the sequence more efficiently, but chose not to. When filming the shot I was overtaken by emotion and just left the camera running. During editing I decided to trust this instinct, without worrying about the result visually or its overall effect on the narrative. I was thinking more about the connection between this film and my own life as the shot for me embodies a personal memory, a memory that could also be meaningful for others. Some consider this long take unbearable and an error in the *mise-en-scène*, but for me it reveals the deep and sincere emotion that I felt while working on the film. Say, for instance, we were talking about a literary work—instead of a film—where a sentence is the equivalent of a shot, and one of the sentences holds a similar effective power but was grammatically incorrect—I would still insist on keeping it.

With The World, *your cinema enters into a new phase, broadening its horizons to new locales.*

I wanted to film more generally the direct impact of China's transformation. After I left Shanxi for Beijing, life in China really accelerated. There was a feeling of permanent emergency, with no possibility of slowing things down. It started to feel as if day and night had become indistinguishable. Even the perception of the different seasons was affected. I no longer noticed time passing. These changes were all driven by the stranglehold of capital on our way of life. The focus was only on profit, and life felt like a permanent race against the clock. Even art had to be sped up! The storyline had to be quick! In such an environment we lose our ability to live in harmony with nature, and to live with others. We become cogs in an economic mechanism undergoing lightning transformations and have to adjust to this galloping pace of life. What we gain in speed is offset by the loss of our former, slower, way of life.

In 2003, in response to the enormous migratory flux, cities were expropriating property en masse for urban programs. This was accompanied by a staggering real estate speculation. Seeing advertisements in Beijing, I was startled by the names of these new developments. All these new constructions were given the names of faraway capitalist and developed countries; things like "The Gardens of Rome," "The Forest of Vancouver," or "Venice." This showed how much people desire to live another life, how much they have lost confidence in a way of life supposed to be theirs. All these impressions—even physical sensations—gave me the intense desire to make the film. But I didn't yet know how to address it: Should it be the story of a filmmaker? I didn't know. Then one day when we were on our way to Hong Kong, Zhao Tao told me of her experiences working at the "Window on the World" Park in Shenzhen.[34] Suddenly inspiration came to me! It should be set in a place like that park, a virtual space where people *appear* to live freely. I wanted something about the way economics, with the arrival in China of Western chains like McDonald's and Starbucks, feeds our illusions about freedom. Beijing has become heavily Americanized giving the *impression* we are in communion with the world.

At that time I was travelling regularly. I remember once when I was on the way to the airport in Bangkok, and saw a line of shops that I knew well from China. They even had the exact same advertisements as in Beijing! That's when I understood to what extent "globalization" meant both "standardization" and "Americanization." The Beijing World Park provided me with a location that epitomized all this.

In *The World* I also drew on my personal experience as, at the beginning of the 1990s, I had taken my parents on a visit to the Beijing theme park when it had just opened. This was before I had travelled abroad. By the time I did have the means to travel abroad, and to take my parents with me, my father had passed away. But I was able to take my mother to Hong Kong, and my sister took her to Japan. In preparing *The World*, I recalled my own impressions as a visitor, as well as those of my parents; what we had felt while China was in a boom economy.

In the film, the main characters work in the park but there are also their friends from Shanxi who work on a construction site, and also visitors to the park.

I wanted to create an interaction between the world of the park and the world outside. The film reveals different types of alienation. For example, the visitors who come to the park and see a fake Eiffel Tower or a fake White House are given the illusion of a trip around the world; the feeling

---

34. Read also Zhao Tao's interview, pp. 169–76.

they're moving in an open and free space. This contrasts with the feeling of confinement the park employees feel. The park's visitors don't realize the extent to which those that live in the park are prisoners in the artificial décor of a globalized world. They attend these artificial shows without thinking of those who, day after day, have to repeat the same gestures, changing costumes and "countries" several times in the course of the day. They cannot escape, or even change, their monotonous routines.

During the location scouting I returned to the park with Zhao Tao. She found most of her former colleagues were still working there, often doing the exact same job as before. You could call it a life sentence! Of course, the exploited workers on construction sites are also very far from finding the better world they left their homes for. I wanted to emphasize that traveling is an act in itself, never mind that it's in search of a better life or to go discover another world. A trip has meaning only if it allows one's own life to be transformed. For human relationships to evolve there has to be motion, a real movement, which has nothing to do with either distance or exoticism. To go twenty kilometers to see a friend may constitute real movement, while simulating a trip to Paris in a Beijing suburb is a sad illusion.

Added to this distorted relationship with the real world is the entirely new relationship generated by the virtual, the new means of communication.

Smart phones were only just beginning when I was planning *The World*. Since then, more and more people, especially the young, have begun to live in two distinct worlds: the real world and the world of the Internet, the virtual world. These are two different but related worlds. Young people are infatuated with the virtual world—the world of video games and the Internet—because they're dissatisfied with the real world. For me this virtual world is remarkably similar to The World theme park: both offer an alternate space for life, where you pass borders, moving freely from one country to another. Both of these—the virtual world and the theme park—constitute two responses to a feeling of confinement. But what gets lost is accountability. For example, before if we had something to say to someone we would have to address them directly, in person. Today SMS messages allow for things that are difficult to express—words that you don't dare articulate—to be sent without having to worry about a physical confrontation. They allow for life's problems to be dodged rather than confronted. I don't think this is an improvement.

The park that we see in the film is an amalgam.

It's true. We shot some scenes in the Beijing Park and others in the Shenzhen Park, depending on what we needed. The two parks are different: the reproductions of famous buildings are bigger in Beijing, but Shenzhen offers some monuments Beijing doesn't have—the Eiffel Tower is in both parks. In Shenzhen the buildings are better imitations, more meticulous.

For me, the famous monuments and buildings have another connotation: they make me think of films. For instance the Trevi Fountain reminds me of *La Dolce Vita*, the Eiffel Tower of *The 400 Blows*, Manhattan's Twin Towers of *Taxi Driver*... This isn't surprising since these places are very much like movie sets. I like this aspect a lot, as long as you don't allow yourself to be fooled by the illusion. This is why I have so often filmed the backstage of shows. In fact, most of the action in *The World* takes place backstage.

There are other simulations in the film too. For example, the airplane that passes over the construction site at the end was added in post production. It was impossible to film this shot in reality as planes aren't authorized to fly over Beijing.

The ending is strange. It opens up in a way not foreshadowed in the film.

When I was writing the screenplay I wasn't sure if the film should end in the park or outside. Finally I decided to close ambiguously: it's not clear if what we see is real or a hallucination. I didn't want to end on an upbeat note, with a happy ending for the protagonists, as this didn't seem realistic. But neither did I want to end on a doomsday note. The truth is I have no idea what will happen and the film's ending reflects this uncertainty. The young man says to his girlfriend: "We're not dead. This isn't the end. Everything is just beginning."

For The World *you had gained enough recognition to reach an agreement with the Shanghai Film Studio. This makes it your first "official" film and, as a result, it was distributed in Chinese theaters. Is this why you sought such an agreement?*

As a state-run enterprise, the Shanghai Film Studio has a bargaining power with the Film Bureau that I alone could never have. At the time, I was still an "underground" filmmaker, but I wanted my films to have a theatrical release. So, yes, the reconciliation with the Shanghai Film Group was strategic. It was possible thanks to Ren Zhonglun, who was running it then. Before becoming a filmmaker, he was a film critic and had been the leading editor of a Shanghai film journal. So he knew a lot about film and was a real cinephile, which is rare among those with power in the film world. When I finished the screenplay for *The World* I sent it to him; he liked it a lot so we met. We're on the same wavelength and as film people we talk the same language. Right away he was confident in the possibility of reaching an agreement with the Film Bureau and we went there together. Indeed the project was accepted. At the time the Film Bureau was undergoing a major reorganization: the emergence of a viable film industry encouraged the Bureau to abandon its prior ideological outlook in favor of profit. I benefited from a favorable climate on both sides. On the one hand the Shanghai Film Studio, on the other the Film Bureau.

The World *was theatrically released. How was it received?*

Reactions were mixed. In China only a minority liked it. In general, viewers had a hard time understanding it and found they couldn't enter into the story. The film's positive reception abroad fueled lots of discussions. I wasn't really surprised by the reactions of critics and the public in China, as I knew the story's complexity would confuse many. Its depiction of the everyday reality of people within the theme park, and its emphasis on the contrast between reality and representation, required a certain perspective foreign to most of the viewers. It's understandable if you think about what they usually watch. During the shoot I was aware of this challenge.

With this in mind, were you not tempted to make the film more accessible to a larger public?

No. I am unable to do this. I can only work with what I am, with my ideas, my way of seeing the world; what to me feels like the right way to make a film. It doesn't make sense to want to change my education, my personality, my way of experiencing feelings and emotions. I don't want to think strategically, basing my choices on types of viewers. When you make a film you are looking to interact with human beings and shouldn't divide people up: between Beijing natives and immigrants, Chinese and foreigners, Easterners and Westerners. We in China can easily assimilate ancient Greek literature and Neorealist Italian films, German art and Japanese art. Why shouldn't we produce works to be appreciated by all? Art that isn't limited geographically. For me there is no such thing as a human being from such-and-such a place. There are only *human beings*.

Often your films are born from real life circumstances; something that happens to you or an event you react to. Isn't that also the case with Still Life, *which you filmed on the site of the construction of the Three Gorges Dam?*

Yes, but indirectly. *Prima facie* I didn't intend to film the Three Gorges Dam. For several years, it was the region where all of China and the foreign media focused their attention, because of its economic, ecological—and above all human—consequences: the dam was going to force millions of people to leave their homes and numerous cities were going to disappear under water. We heard so much about it in the news that I didn't want to address the issue myself, as it seemed to be already overexploited. I wasn't sure what I could add to the topic.

But then my friend the painter Liu Xiaodong went there to paint, and I joined him to make the documentary *Dong*. As soon as I got there I was impressed by the site. The area of the Three Gorges had been transformed into something completely phantasmagorical, with these endless piles of rubble, like the ghosts of thousands of buildings. It was as if the place had suffered a nuclear attack or an extraterrestrial invasion. So it was really the look and ambience of the place that led me to make the film.

Although you do conjure up some science fiction images in this hallucinatory setting, your attention is mainly focused on the human beings of this area.

The problem in such a space was to find a point of view, a way of getting close. What was my perspective as a filmmaker going to be? Should I adopt a position of familiarity with this place, or should I maintain the perspective of a newcomer? Only the second option was really possible. This is a marked change from the insider's perspective of my previous films, even *The World* where I shared common ground with certain characters, and especially thanks to Zhao Tao's experience. This was completely different. That's why I chose two fictional protagonists who come from elsewhere, like myself, who are able to act like guides to the world of the film. At the Three Gorges site we discovered those who were living there: individuals expelled and stuck in endless conflicts in order to safeguard their rights, the construction site managers, and most of all of the demolition workers. They were the ones whom Liu Xiaodong was painting and they interested me the most—it was because of them that I wanted to make the film in the first place.

I have always been interested in individuals and their social relationships. But with this film, I was also attracted to the natural beauty of these people: bare-chested workers dripping with sweat under the blazing sun as they demolished buildings with their bare hands—they exuded life. Liu Xiaodong sought to capture this quality in his paintings. Think about it: these workers who had taken part in the construction of the city were now demolishing it. What a tragedy! The place, and the discovery of these men, is what convinced me to make a fiction film.

Did you write the film all at once?

I was in the middle of shooting the documentary with Liu Xiaodong when I had this desire—or rather this need—to make a fiction film. My imagination was taking off but I had no time to write as the city of Fengjie was already in the process of being destroyed. I was very anxious as I thought the city was going to disappear before I got a chance to film it! My assistant and I would work on the script every night until late. At 9 a.m. I would perform what we had written. I performed the whole film like that, from the first to the last scene. Then we printed the script and we went off to shoot, although I did make more changes on set.

There are two dimensions in Still Life: *one that's social and political, tied to the actual construction of the Three Gorges Dam. But there is also a metaphysical dimension that both exalts humankind's place in a superhuman environment, and underscores its absurdity and pathos.*

I think the film manages to capture, in real time, something of the changes China was going through, with an ever increasing anxiety regarding the effect they're having on humankind, an anxiety that people will disappear and memories will fade. When it comes to the location—a location that carries a universal memory that I wanted to capture on film—I think I did succeed in finding something. When it comes to the people, I have deep regrets as I feel that I failed to truly capture their life-force and beauty, or pay justice to what they suffer.

You approach the individuals who live in these conditions through the lens of fiction. This is made possible by combining professional actors—or at least people that have become professional actors through their work with you such as Zhao Tao and Han Sanming—with non-professionals who are playing themselves.

The actors, especially the non-professionals, manage very well when playing situations that correspond to their own lives. When it comes to more dramatic moments the results are often mediocre, despite repeated attempts. At first this drove me crazy! Is it the actors' fault? Is it because they don't understand my screenplay? Are they ill at ease? Do they have problems at home? Why don't they enter into their roles? Then, I discovered a rule: when an actor begins to seriously struggle with their performance, the first thing I should do is check the screenplay. Inevitably there is something in the writing that rings false, that's not credible. An actor who doesn't believe in what they're doing cannot act. So now whenever I have a problem with an actor's performance, I modify the script. It's useless to fight it. It's almost certain that the problem comes from the script and that the gap between reality and what I've written is too great.

The actors must also contribute, as I don't like it when they stick too closely to my text. I always tell them that I've written dialogue that they should translate into their own language. Generally we rehearse a little on set and, when I hear the actors' suggestions, I tend to realize that their words have a far greater significance than what I've written. When combining non-professional actors with professionals, the first thing to do is to reassure the professionals. When acting with non-professionals, they often experience a mental block. Their experience tells them it's a matter of two different systems of acting. They think that they will never have the natural feel of non-professional actors, a naturalness that they know I seek. I do, however, strive to conserve the theatrical *je ne sais quoi* that professionals contribute. So I have them perform in the foreground as a warm-up exercise to put them at ease and make them understand their role in creating something other than a brute transcription of reality. They're creating a different reality via film.

For example, in *24 City*, Joan Chen was always asking me how she could erase any trace of theatricality from her performance.[35] I told her that I wanted to work with her precisely because I needed some of her acting style in the film. Together we had to discover real situations where she could make use of her own idiosyncrasies. I spoke to her about her body because professional actors tend to pay close attention to their bodies, primarily with the intention of ensuring their physical beauty. If the on-screen objective is that the result of the work of the professional actors is absolutely the same as that of the non-professionals, why call upon them? You might as well only use non-professionals.

The example of Han Sanming, who plays the main male role in Still Life, *is a little special. To a certain extent he's an actor as he appears in different roles in all your films since* Platform. *But, at the same time, his roles aren't as varied as, for example, those of Zhao Tao and Wang Hongwei.*

---

35. Shot after *Still Life*, *24 City* is primarily a documentary, but among the many people who appear, four are played by professional actors, including the Chinese American actor Joan Chen. See also pp. 60 and 138.

There are two important points for me. The first is the name Sanming. Zhao Tao has different parts: in *Platform*, she's Yin Ruijuan, an actor in an artistic troupe; in *Unknown Pleasures* she's Qiaoqiao, an amateur model; in *The World*, she's a dancer in The World park called Zhao Xiaotao. In *Still Life*, she's Shenhong and in *A Touch of Sin*, Xiaoyu. In contrast, Sanming always appears in my films under his own name. Han Sanming *himself* is a regular character in my films.

The second point is his dress. Once, when I was still at the Beijing Film Academy, I visited my aunt and Sanming was wearing a *Zhongshan* jacket[36] with the blue overalls of Chinese workers. When I was in high school he already wore this uniform. This costume has also become a visual leitmotif in my films. In *Platform*, Han Sanming has just gotten a job in the coal mine, signing a life or death contract. In *The World*, he arrives in Beijing from his hometown in Shanxi to take care of the funeral for Er Guniang, a childhood friend of his who has died on the construction site. In *Still Life*, he's the main character, and again has left mining work in Shanxi, this time to look for his wife and daughter. And in *A Touch of Sin*, he's still Sanming who, in Fenyang, prepares to bring new workers onto the Three Gorges site. It could be that he'll make money and be able to buy his wife from the owner of the boat and take her back with him. He's a character I don't want to change.

At the end of Still Life *we see him leave with this tightrope walker who traverses the devastated landscape on a wire. The end resembles a dream—it's not really a conclusion, more like an ellipsis.*

The end of my films is very important, and is always difficult to find. I work a lot on this while writing, all the while knowing that it's very likely that what I choose will not be the actual ending; during the shoot I am always looking for a better solution. A film is like a living body which grows and evolves and my job is to sense where it's headed. Little by little, as the work progresses, the universe of the film appears and I begin to understand what

---

36. Also known as the Mao jacket. [Tr.]

it will look like on screen, to perceive what the atmosphere will be. One key factor, which cannot be foreseen before the shoot, comes from the actors' suggestions.

You might think that through this process I am *creating* a new ending, but I prefer to think I am *discovering* the true ending. It's the process that tells me how to conclude. Often I will all of a sudden realize that what I just shot is the ending. This is especially true with my documentaries. For example: while making *Dong*, after shooting for a day or two in Bangkok, I wandered off one evening after we had dinner at a restaurant. With my camera in hand I went into a market. There was a blindman singing while walking and I followed him with my camera, filming him continuously. Hearing his song, I felt that our walk was like a river. The market stalls were the riverbanks and the people I passed like boats on the water. I followed and filmed this boat in front of me—this blindman who was singing—with the feeling that we were drifting, the camera bobbing along to the rhythm of the water. I thought of the Yangtze, the Mekong,[37] and then realized I had the end of my film. But this was only after I had filmed the work scenes with the painter and all the rest.

The characters in all your films are ordinary people. But in 24 City *it's difficult to distinguish between real workers playing themselves and film stars playing characters from everyday life.*

24 City is a film that means a lot to me. It allowed me to experiment in different ways with *mise-en-scène*. I had been wanting to film the life of workers since the 1990s, when, as the country transitioned from a centrally planned economy to a socialist market economy, factories were closed and people forced to change jobs. Many workers found themselves marginalized after having held a central role in society. So, from that time, there were no more *workers* as such in China. Why? Because their life had previously been tightly linked to the factory they worked for. Their education, the education

---

37. The Yangtze River is the longest river in Asia, and the Three Gorges Dam is built on its course. The Mekong is a trans-boundary river in Southeast Asia and the seventh longest in Asia. It flows in Thailand (but not in Bangkok) where the last part of *Dong* was shot. [Tr.]

of their children, their hobbies, their social welfare, their retirement, their relationships with neighbors and friends—*everything* was tied to the factory. In changing jobs, workers became mere employees, with no emotional bond to their place of work, and so began to move from factory to factory. In *24 City*, you can see this change: the workers lose not only their job but their world. This comes up again in the fourth episode of *A Touch of Sin*. The boy who works in the electronics factory isn't thought of as a *worker*, he's just an *employee*. His relationship with the machines, and contractual relationship with the factory, has no roots. Everything is unstable.

By deciding to show this transformation in *24 City*, I discovered something key about China's economy. Why were factories being demolished? Because they inhabited land in the center of the city, enormous amounts of land that real estate agencies can turn a huge profit on. The change in the country's economic model directly led to the demolition of these factories. So I came to understand the true power of the real estate business in the Chinese economy, and how it has influenced numerous sectors, including the film industry.

What is the rapport between the two?

Real estate speculation causes many of the film industry's ailments. Most movie theaters are located in commercial centers and built by real estate firms who charge extremely high rents; as a result the theaters' net profit is meager. The difficulty of making a profit—exacerbated by renting and not owning the venue—means exhibitors have to choose films that'll make the most money in the least amount of time. So films that depend on word-of-mouth to reach an audience really have no chance as no long-term strategy or in-depth work is possible. But the real estate market affects not only filmmaking, but also civil engineering, steel, coal, and other sectors. Because of this, I initially thought the real estate project *24 City* would be the film's protagonist. It was fortunate that I shot *24 City* in 2008: it captured the economic model affecting the lives of millions of Chinese at exactly that moment. I think this is why it seems like a documentary.

But I also want to talk about the idea of an "Everyman." It's easy to classify a film character as an ordinary individual—a thief in a small city or an actor with a traveling show who lives in an isolated place with no resources. But I don't like the designation of "Everyman" because it presupposes the existence of someone special or important. Who is this "important person"? At the time of the centrally planned economy the workers of *24 City* were important: they had the best salaries, a social standing, and dignity. But with the introduction of the market economy, they have been marginalized, and their lives have become harder.

So who exactly has suffered from these changes? I don't think it's an "Everyman." Such a person doesn't exist. There are just specific individuals. Most Chinese resemble the people in my films: an academic, a lawyer, a banker, workers, or farmers are always equal in nature. You could call my characters those without power, the anti-bigwigs. They have no control over society's wealth, and are at the mercy of life. I consider myself one of them. I'm not interested in knowing if someone is a bigwig or an ordinary person. We all live in the shadow of authority and power. You live your life, you try to fight, to find a way to express your internal voice. Xiaowu expresses his inner voice by singing a romantic song he's ashamed of in his bathroom. By performing in very isolated regions, the young people in *Platform* might seem aimless, but doing so gives them a freedom to avoid censorship and express themselves by singing their favorite songs.

We all have a routine, with moments of inactivity, and all kinds of different relationships with people. This is the life we are living, it's our real world. Why create an artificially dramatic world when making a film? In Chinese films from the 1920s and 1930s, daily life was often depicted. Films like Yuan Muzhi's *Street Angel*, Wu Yonggang's *The Goddess*, and Fei Mu's *Spring in a Small Town*. These films show elements of people's lives and their problems.[38] After 1949, we saw what the invention of an "ideal world" led to in films. Revolutionary imagery fabricated myths and our real lives disappeared from the cinema. Human foibles, spontaneous physical action—even language—was modified. Suddenly regional accents disappeared.

---

38. *Street Angel* is a left-wing film set in Shanghai from 1937. The 1934 silent film, *The Goddess*, featuring Ruang Lingyu, one of the most prominent stars in China before her suicide in 1935, marked Wu Yonggang's directorial debut. Fei Mu's *Spring in a Small Town* (1948) is widely recognized as a masterpiece of the pre-revolutionary era. In 2005 the Hong Kong Film Awards Association declared it the greatest Chinese film ever made. [Tr.]

There was no longer a homeland or a cultural identity and everyone spoke like a radio announcer.

You mentioned that 24 City *"seems like a documentary." Isn't it one?*

I wouldn't say so. From its origins cinema is at the crossroads of two possible approaches. On the one hand, it's a means to record the natural state of people: their expressions, their movements, their bodies, even their weight. How can cinema express weight? The invention of sound cinema brought the feeling of weight, of volume. For example, without sound, a train that passes on a screen resembles a gust of wind—you don't have the feeling of its weight. With the advent of sound, the pressure of the train on the tracks— the noise of iron crushed by the train's mass—gives us the feeling of its weight. The cinema is able to recapture the natural state or essence of things.

On the other hand, cinema is also theater's heir. Méliès introduced the tradition of illusion and of drama. But my films are closer to a documentary aesthetic. Cinema reveals to us what we often overlook: the human beauty that's in front of us every day. When the face of an actual worker or a familiar place is shown on screen it brings a feeling of astonishment, of rediscovering life. By making use of what exists in the natural setting, it becomes possible to capture and preserve its beauty.[39] But a documentary aesthetic isn't a mechanical register. It demands a deep understanding of reality—filming alone is insufficient. And to execute this a large dose of imagination is needed. You have to ceaselessly give it shape, make choices, recompose, during the shoot as well as during editing. It may seem paradoxical but a documentary approach is fiction; it requires imagination, a vast imagination born from a profound knowledge of life. The closer one is to reality—to real, natural space—the more imagination is needed. In this sense, the emphasis placed on daily life in Chinese films before 1949 was above all an aesthetic choice. As André Bazin said: realism in art can only be obtained through artifice.

---

39. Jia here clearly evokes Rossellini's famous dictum: "Things are there... Why manipulate them?" [Tr.]

Despite their obvious independence from each other, there are certain echoes reverberating like secret links between your films.

One day I would like to have a retrospective of my films in Beijing. First I would show *Platform*, which covers 1979–1989; then *Xiaowu*, on China in the 1990s; *Unknown Pleasures*, on China of the 2000s; and afterwards *The World*, on the years 2002–2003; *Still Life*… up until *A Touch of Sin* (2013). These films, made at two-year intervals, are closely related: regrouped, they illustrate my personal point of view on the changes in China from the end of the 1970s until today.

For me it's not a question of individual films but of a large series that's still ongoing. Sometimes I consider the idea of characters from an old film appearing in the world of a new film. In *Platform*, the characters dream of an outside world—what would they have thought in seeing *The World*? Or: if Xiaowu knew of the characters' misfortunes in *A Touch of Sin*, what would he think? Undoubtedly, he would be dumbfounded. It's true that there are these links, and with *A Touch of Sin* I reinforced them by returning to places I had previously filmed. I showed the wall of *Platform*, the textile factories of *Useless*, the boat on the Yangtze of *Still Life*, all filmed in the same way. The same mountains, the same river, the same earth, the same boat, and, as Sanming reappears, even some of the same people. Reusing the same locations means we are confronted with the same places, the same people, but their situation has changed and they're faced with new challenges.

I really like this repetition of settings. And I really enjoyed moving the crew around for the shoot of *A Touch of Sin*, because the characters themselves are in flux. Incidentally, the idea for the film came to me on a trip. I still don't know how to drive. I did want to learn but all my friends, starting with Zhao Tao and Yu Lik-wai, talked me out of it, saying that, as I am so often lost in my thoughts, it would be too dangerous. But thanks to my driver, Xiaoma, I can still travel. Last year I asked him to take me to Datong, which is 300 miles from Beijing, and where I shot both *In Public* and *Unknown Pleasures*. I like this city. On the way I listened to music and gave free rein to my thoughts, thinking about my screenplay. Xiaoma dropped me at a hotel in Datong and then left. I stayed for more than a week working on the script.

At mealtimes, I would come down to the first floor to eat. Then, I would go back upstairs to continue writing. Once I was finished, Xiaoma came back to get me.

A Touch of Sin is a story on the move: from the Shanxi province in the North to Guangdong[40] way down in the South, criss-crossing all of China. At every step along the way, a new world is discovered with new stories, new landscapes, new people. The characters were itinerant and we too, when filming, were also itinerant. If I borrow the vocabulary from *wuxia* novels,[41] I would say that we were all descendants of the "world of lakes and rivers," because our work and our concerns took place on a journey, a trip. Together, the film's different locations form a fairly complete map of China. Shanxi represents the vast China of the North that lives off of farming—the region still lags economically. Chongqinq, which is a densely populated city on the Yangtze, supplies workers to the coastal regions as well as Guangdong. Hubei is a central region where, despite the immense aggression of the Three Gorges dam, some of the natural sites are still preserved. We are able to see what the Chinese people of earlier times saw: the landscapes of traditional paintings. The studio sets of martial arts films in Hong Kong are always trying to reconstruct what can be seen naturally in Hubei. Guangdong is the China of the South where the climate is temperate all year round and rainfall is frequent, in contrast to the great cold of the North. For me, this makes a complete map of China.

Together your films provide a precise portrait of the gigantic changes that your country has undergone in the last twenty years.

I was aware early on that we were rapidly experiencing enormous changes, which lent an ephemeral aspect to all of our lives. I knew I needed to pay close attention to what was happening. Such changes are swift and sometimes subtle; if you aren't paying attention a lot can be missed. So my goal was to

---

40. Guangdong is a coastal province of southeast China, bordering Hong Kong and Macau. Its capital, Guangzhou (formerly Canton), sits within its industrial Pearl River Delta region. [Tr.]

41. See note 17 on page 100. In the "world of lakes and rivers" thrive the wandering knights, the heroes of the *wuxia* novels.

make films that quickly responded to this period of critical change. I didn't want to just lament after ten years that nothing would be like before, or be nostalgic for a world that had disappeared fifty years earlier. Faced with momentous change, I wondered if I could react in the moment, like a painter with sketchpad and pencil.

In painting or drawing, it's relatively simple to do this. Even in music and literature, because the tools of these mediums are easy to use. But cinema is faced with distinct obstacles stemming from its industrial nature. Production times are long and, along with the creative work, there is much necessary organization to be done. The screenplay has to be written and the financing secured. After a great deal of negotiation, investments are found and a contract signed. Then the film needs to be cast, the locations chosen, the shoot, and post-production. This whole process tends to take a year-and-a-half to two years. Does such a model allow for a sensitive response to our time?

Ever since *Xiaowu* I have tried to have quick reactions. At that time I was working on a short film called "Tender is the Night"[42] about a couple who had been together for some time, but never spent a night together. Then, one day, the man is lent an apartment. It would have been a story of this couple during one night—it was about encounters, and about sex too. I liked the screenplay a lot. But after having written it, I returned home to Fenyang and learned that the city where I had lived for more than twenty years was going to be demolished. I immediately abandoned "Tender is the Night" to make a film as rapidly as possible, one that attempted to understand the problems people were facing. I spent three weeks on the screenplay and began shooting immediately afterwards. Since then, I've never stopped.

In addition to there being subterranean links between your films, you also create incongruous relationships within the same film.

As a student in the 1990s, I was interested in new movements from abroad such as structuralism and postmodernism. Although my interest in them was largely superficial, they gave me new perspectives on society and human

---

42. The title echoes the F. Scott Fitzgerald's eponymous novel (1934) and derives from John Keats' poem "Ode to a Nightingale." [Tr.]

behavior, and helped me forge structural relationships in my films. Narrative is of course important, but what is more important to me are the relations created by the formal structure.

For example, in *Dong*, I attributed a lot of importance to the fact that Liu Xiaodong took me to the Three Gorges' region, and then to Bangkok. Although far away from each other, and very different, these two places have in common the presence of water, and are united in Liu's paintings—many echoes and rich associations. In *Useless*, there are many associations between the garment factory in Lishui county near Guangzhou, the Paris fashion show, and the tailors in the Shanxi mining region. If I had only spoken about the Shanxi tailors or the Paris fashion shows or the Lishui factory, I wouldn't have been able to make my point; it's in tying these three places together that an internal logic is revealed, like a food chain. The interrelationship between these regions, these social classes, and these professions needed to be brought to light. For example, how did the Shanxi tailors come to lose so many of their clients? Why, in such an isolated city, does the cost of raw material to make a suit far exceed the cost of a factory-made suit? The Lishui factory impacts the tailors of the Shanxi mining region, while the fashion designer working on a collection for the Paris shows is on the breaking point between the rapidly disappearing artisanal work and the Lishui garment factory. I believe it's very important to highlight, in a single film, the hidden structure interconnecting all these things, which don't initially seem related.

There is a similar structure in the more fictional A Touch of Sin, *inspired by several particularly violent news stories that occurred in China.*

First, there is the violence itself. I was shocked by the violent outbursts in our society. I then realized that I was ignorant of the very process of violence. Why do ordinary people resort to such behavior? How is it that victims so often become torturers in turn, inflicting suffering on weaker individuals? How do normal people, people with ordinary lives that could be my own, wind up committing such acts? This isn't a mythological revenge story, but a real tragedy committed by real people. Would I likely do the same thing under the same circumstances? The film arose in response to these questions, as filmmaking is the only way I have of making sense of the world. In Fenyang, my friends often say to me: "Jia Zhangke, you are too serious! Why do you always make such heavy films?" Initially I wasn't bothered by this question. But more recently, I have begun to think about it. The truth is that when I have at my disposal the human and material means to make a film, I don't want to waste it. I have to focus on what is most essential. This is no doubt why, since *Xiaowu*, my one and only subject is observing the evolution of society. The rest doesn't matter to me. No doubt this comes from experiencing poverty when I was young: it wouldn't occur to me to waste human and material resources on a trivial issue.

The topic is critical?

Yes, in the sense that I can't devote myself to a film whose topic doesn't seem important to me. But the topic itself is insufficient; you have to also find the best way to tackle it. Take *Dong*, *Useless*, and *In Public*: it seems to me that their very structure aids in comprehending reality. Of course, some viewers say that they don't understand my films, and I understand this perfectly. In fact they understand very well but become blocked because they know there is more than what they see, that the structure of the film itself carries a meaning that they don't have the resources to work out. Often, during post-screening discussions, I stand up to my critics and answer: "You will only understand my films when you understand their form."

When you are making a film—documentary or fiction—the mode of thinking differs very little. What is important is what one has to say and the means you adopt to say it. Several times I've been a jury member in festivals where jurors are opposed to evaluating documentary and fiction together. But for me this opposition is uninteresting. The reflection that emerges from the film, the approach to *mise-en-scène*, is essentially the same in both cases.

Although you prioritize the shoot, you do also write screenplays. What are they like?

I don't always use the same method. Some of them—in particular the screenplays for *Xiaowu* and *Still Life*—were composed incrementally from an outline. They were written in a hurry. Other screenplays—like *Platform* and *A Touch of Sin*—are more literary. I dislike the American style of shooting script that includes directions like "close-up" or "360° shot"; I think that this kind of thing doesn't help one's imagination. Why do this when you will be on set? Why not write a more traditional literary work—like a novel—full of details? Details provide the collaborators—whether it's the actors, the cameraman, the sound engineer or the set designer—a more precise understanding of the atmosphere and the feelings of the characters that the director or the screenwriter expects. If I have one suggestion for anyone who wants to become a screenwriter, it would be to pay attention to literature, because the process of cinematographic production, with storyboards and *mise-en-scène*, is the work of a director after the screenplay has been developed. It's not the responsibility of the screenwriter. Their job is to propose an idea and to convey it—via the screenplay—to those who will ultimately make the film.

When I write a script, I become pretty obsessive. I pay very close attention to the validity of phrases, to their musicality and their precision, not just their meaning. At the Beijing Film Academy, we learned that this is a waste of time because in the end the screenplay will be transformed into an audio-visual film. But this isn't my opinion: when you refine your sentences, when you examine them one by one, you become more and more precise in the conception of the context and the interior world of the characters. If you watch me on set, you'll see that I never have sheets of paper in my hand, because by then, thanks to the work done during the writing stage, everything is perfectly clear to me.

With A Touch of Sin, *in order to tackle the complex subject of contemporary China's growing violence, you had to invent a new form.*

A new form for me, because it's different from everything I had done previously. But in reality this form is part of a tradition. It's a tradition that comes from tales, from what in China we call the *shuoshu*, an oral narrative that I really liked in my childhood. It's a popular art, the life stories of our ancestors that have been passed down from generation to generation. Still today, *shuoshu* are listened to on the radio. Since *Still Life*, I have come to see myself as more and more of a *shuoshu* artist—my vision of my profession has changed.

After identifying the four stories that were going to make up *A Touch of Sin*, I was struck by their similarities with popular novels from the classical period, especially novels about chivalry like *Water Margin*.[43] Similarly, in that novel, people resort to violence when faced with unbearable social situations. *Water Margin* has inspired countless adaptations for the theater and opera, adaptations that are still performed today; proof that it's still relevant. I love to imagine that one day, in fifty or a hundred years, someone might film a new version of *A Touch of Sin*.

Classic martial arts movies are also among my references. These films are the continuation of *shuoshu* tales, novels, and plays. The first two heroes of *A Touch of Sin*, played by Jiang Wu and Wang Baoqiang, are directly inspired by Lu Zhishen and Wu Song, two of *Water Margin*'s heroes; the appearance of Zhao Tao is based on the heroine of King Hu's *A Touch of Zen*,[44] played by Hsu Feng—and to which the international title of course pays homage[45]—while the appearance of Luo Lanshan, who plays the main character in the fourth episode, is based on the heroes from Chang Cheh's films.

A Touch of Sin includes an important number of action scenes. This is new for you.

I watched a lot of *wuxia*. There are a stack of them at the office. I wanted to draw from their style, but avoid imitating or complying too much with it. When I first met, in Shenzhen, with the fight choreographer—a real expert—I told him he would have to create two scenes with guns, another with a knife, and one with a fatal fall. He answered that this would be easy, assuming I wanted action scenes akin to those in the films of John Woo or Johnnie To. He showed me highly stylized action scenes he had directed with people flying up in the air shooting or being shot. I told him: "Sorry I

---

43. One of four great classical novels of Chinese literature, *Water Margin* (aka *Outlaws of the Marsh*), is based on an oral tradition, collected by Shi Naian in the 14th century. It relates the individual and collective adventures of 800 outlaws who rebelled against the oppression and corruption of senior officials and dignitaries from the imperial court. This story, a major reference for *wuxia*, and its characters, remain well known today in China.

44. *A Touch of Zen* is a 1971 *wuxia* film, co-edited, written and directed by King Hu. In 1975, it won the Technical Grand Prize at the Cannes Film Festival. [Tr.]

45. The literal translation of the film's title is *Heroine Woman*. [Tr.]

would like a scene where the person who has been shot falls to the ground and doesn't move." His response: "This will be more difficult. If you want the person to fly into the air after being shot, the technicians can do it easily with a suspension wire. But to achieve this sudden, realistic, and heavy fall to the ground, without protective measures and without hurting the actors, is more difficult." It was a real headache for him but he ended up finding the right solutions.

You take advantage of new technologies but you're also wary of them?

There are several ways to make use of technology. I am always mindful of technical advances because, whether we like it or not, they influence cinematic style. From the silent era to the arrival of sound, from black and white to color, each new technology has brought innovations to film aesthetics. A filmmaker should always be interested in new technology, but being interested shouldn't mean performing visual stunts every time there's a new piece of equipment. Technology can however help in finding aesthetic solutions. When you're struggling to capture an intense realism, technology can sometimes help.

Even in the more overtly fictional A Touch of Sin, *you remain loyal to a certain realism. Is this the reason why you favor filming on location?*

Reality deeply inspires me, even when I'm using eccentric ideas like the science fiction scenes in *Still Life*. I always try to shoot on location even if it limits me with regard to camera movements and lighting. Real-world settings possess a certain beauty. They're a great source of inspiration and have a real texture. They contain traces left by time and human activity, as well as certain unexpected details. This level of charm, beauty, and emotion can't be artificially created, and is extremely important for the actors. I find that actors are very receptive to the charms of a real location that they can have a real dialogue with. They believe in the identity of their characters and in what is freed from their imagination over time. For example, if we were to film actors seated in this room, they would immediately feel its authenticity. If actors are on a studio set, however well constructed, the ambiance of the place will never allow them to completely forget they're in an artificial setting. They will feel this lack of authenticity.

Does this mean you don't alter real locations?

No. Of course I do. My goal is to create the truest and most credible setting, one that will elicit real emotions from the actors and my camera. But not all natural decors have the same potential. I often say to my set designer: "We have to find a place with a soul." That said, my vision isn't completely naturalistic: I am never satisfied with just filming what I see. What matters above all is the story's veracity in relation to who the character is and their circumstances.

How exactly do you change your locations?

For Dahai, the main character in the first episode of *A Touch of Sin*, we chose a house that was suitable for someone like him.[46] Later we then changed it to reflect his precise character. When Dahai quarrels with others, he always says: "There's a reason I studied law!" The set designer arranged law books on his bed, as it had to be clear this man reads a lot of legal works to help preserve his rights. We also placed a large torch light—a remnant from the collective society—on his nightstand. This implies he may have been a manager in his village, possibly on the night watch. All the furniture in his house dates from the 1970s and even his army overcoat seems outdated. For Dahai the world stopped a long time ago. All this is in keeping with the fact he has a weapon hidden in his closet. But I don't like highlighting such props; they have to belong naturally to the setting and participate in the overall complexity of information delivered to us. If the audience detects them, so much the better. And if not, these elements will still have contributed to creating a convincing environment.

But I imagine this cramped interior didn't help the shooting conditions.

---

46. This part of the interview took place on the film set in Fenyang.

Yes the space was very tight, but I still felt good there. Before the shoot I had a long discussion with Yu Lik-wai as I wanted to maintain many of my usual methods for filming—long takes etc.—while also knowing that the film would be cut more in the style of genre cinema. Everything had to be very mobile, as the film's modus operandi is that the characters are constantly moving. Then Yu Lik-wai made a very good suggestion: "Why don't we try the Steadicam, even though you hate it?"[47] It's true that I don't like it and had always refused to use it in the past. This is because, for me, it distorts our relationship with space. But in this particular case he was right. The Steadicam brought a feeling of mobility and, in that restricted space, was able to capture many details.

So the space conveys an authenticity.

Not only. It can also suggest other things. For example, the courtyard in front of Dahai's house dates from at least the Qing dynasty;[48] it's steeped in history. I love the feeling of disaster and defeat the space conveys. It also has vestiges of a bygone prosperity, such as the rounded door Dahai emerges through carrying his gun wrapped in a towel. The architectural style from an earlier era remains, but it's in decline as if the space has been forgotten. This decay and this forgetfulness evoke Dahai's situation, that he's not kept pace with social changes, not even in his village. Also, the image of him passing through this door evokes an old photo from the years 1890 to 1900, during the Boxer Rebellion that took place at the end of the Qing dynasty.[49] Photos of this revolt show men as impetuous as Jiang Wu, men of the same caliber. They're armed and symbolize impulsive violence and dissent. Dahai's rapport

---

47. An apparatus for filming where the camera is equipped with a gyroscope and attached to the cameraman by a harness, allowing for smooth filming, without any instability, including when walking, running, etc. See the interview with Yu Lik-wai on page 176.

48. The last dynasty of Chinese emperors, dominated by the Manchus. The Qing reigned from 1644 to the declaration of the Chinese Republic in 1912. In this context, Jia is referring to buildings from the end of the 19th century.

49. Powerful popular uprising initiated by the secret society of the Boxers. The bloody uprising was anti-imperialist, anti-foreign, and anti-Christian and took place towards the end of the Qing dynasty, in 1899–1901.

with this space directly brings to mind this China of yesteryear. The houses with their thick walls and this sort of door are characteristic of this bygone era. They transport me to my childhood memories. When I was little, we were still surrounded by buildings from the Qing dynasty, and from the Ming period too.[50] Aside from the electric poles and television antennae, I lived in the same environment as the Chinese of a much earlier time.

Again the film's ending is unexpected: Zhao Tao reappears in Shanxi, where the first episode took place.

As always, I was wondering from the start how to best end the film. Of the four people from the news stories I adapted, the only one who survived is Xiaoyu, the character played by Zhao Tao. She was declared not guilty and released. So I wanted the film to end with her. What was her life like afterwards? I imagine she left her native region, that she changed her name and chose to settle down in a place where no one knew her. This is common for *wuxia* personalities: after having made headlines they often return to normal life under a false identity. I like the idea that one of these avengers is amongst the people that surround us. So I imagined that she ends up back in Shanxi where her destiny could cross paths with the widow of the murdered boss from the first story. Two women: Xiaoyu with her own tragic life story, and Jiao's wife suffering the tragedy of her husband's murder. The other important element is the city's surrounding wall: it evokes an earlier time, and traditional operas from the Ming dynasty.

With the crowd of villagers Zhao Tao takes part in an opera. It's titled *Yu Tangchun* and tells the story of a woman who has been wrongly accused. At the end the judge asks her repeatedly if she's guilty. I particularly like Zhao Tao's performance in this scene. Unconsciously she lowers her head as if acknowledging her guilt. Then, little by little, she lifts her head up and gazes with an expression of anger and distress. For me, this look of revolt is really directed at the judge.

I also had another idea for the ending: In the middle of the crowd a man shouts out. When the judge is repeating, "May the guilty party be punished

---

50. The Ming dynasty lasted from 1368 to 1644 and was succeeded by the Qing dynasty.

on the spot!" I imagined a young person, reckless as I was at twenty, shouting in the direction of the stage: "May you, the judge, be punished!" I liked this ending a lot but once I saw it during editing, I understood that it was too simplistic. I want the spectator to refrain from deciding in advance who is guilty, and to instead try to understand the violence, the human feelings and difficulties of life that can lead to it. *A Touch of Sin* should push us to question ourselves. It's *all of us* who have created this society, have allowed it to become what it is today. So I opted for a different ending as I felt this one, although very strong, was too simplistic in regards to human nature.

Would you say that your films are looking to make an argument?

In my opinion films should never be made to prove a point. A film's purpose isn't to hold forth on one subject or another, and it's value isn't in the conclusions it draws. Instead, it should be for telling a character's story. Of course my perspective and individual experience will color the telling of the story, and will inevitably result in a new understanding of the character and the film's overall meaning. But I've always thought that the beauty of film lies in description, not in argument.

Sometimes I am said to be a director with a critical outlook, but I don't believe filmmakers should use their films to judge life or their characters. What's important is to describe the characters' situation, their daily lives and their relationship to others. A lot of people in China asked me why I was defending criminals in *A Touch of Sin*. But a movie theater isn't a courthouse. With films we must learn to understand others. From a legal standpoint a man may be a criminal—it's up to the judge to enforce the law—but we can also listen to him, try to understand what could have pushed him to commit an act forbidden by law and morality. This is a collective issue that concerns us all. If we can't comprehend the forces that lead to crime, and only take refuge behind legal or moral convictions, we'll never understand human nature.

Implicit in your approach is a desire to share your films with the public-at-large. Even though your first films were banned, you give the impression—unlike many filmmakers—that you wouldn't be content to make films just for yourself. You wish to share your thoughts with others.

From the beginning I have wanted my films to be widely available, ideally in theaters. My attitude is pragmatic. Some filmmakers find this approach limiting and prefer total freedom. But I have always wanted full access to the public. I can reach an audience through DVDs and the internet, but this is insufficient for me as I believe cinema's true potential can only really be achieved in a movie theater. It's also the only way of truly belonging to the world of Chinese cinema and avoiding marginalization. A filmmaker whose films don't reach the public or critics will lose touch with reality and the work will suffer. A film's vision—its ideas—are meaningless if they're not shared. In order to belong to both the real world and the world of Chinese cinema the link of the movie theater is necessary.

This is why I've long wanted to create a small movie theater where I could present films I like, and offer good screening conditions for young independent filmmakers. It would also be a forum for discussion, a place where filmmakers and critics could interact with the public. I would organize retrospectives and show great films from the past. In Beijing it's hard to find somewhere like this. A friend of mine is in the process of building a private museum and I suggested he build a small screening room with a hundred seats. But it's far from the city center and is difficult to reach. We'll see. Ideally it would be possible to create a series of movie theaters like this throughout the country, but this idea remains out of reach for the moment.

Your approach is in sync with your position in general: while keeping your independence, you remain in touch with both the public and the professional world in China.

Early in my career I vowed never to give up my independence, nor to be marginalized. I have been able to maintain this position mainly because of foreign partnerships, starting with Office Kitano, my partner since *Platform*.[51] Ichiyama and his collaborators grant me complete freedom and their unwavering support allows me to secure additional financing for

---

51. Office Kitano closed in 2018 after its founder and leading figure, the producer, director, actor, and TV performer Takeshi Kitano left it. Shôzô Ichiyama continues to co-produce Jia's films as an independent producer.

my projects with other partners. Their support is the lynchpin for all my productions. They know full well that my films aren't going to amass huge fortunes, particularly in the short run, and are okay with this, although everyone must be very careful with expenses. In China today you can find investors easily but they tend to want a big payback right away. The strategy of Ichiyama and Office Kitano is different, which inspires confidence, honesty, and hard work.

The partnership with Office Kitano was forged when you created, early in your career, your own production company: Xstream Pictures.

I didn't create my company right away as it would have been complicated in China at that time. After a Hong Kong screening of my short *Xiaoshan Going Home*, I met Yu Lik-wai. He already had a small production company, Hutong Films—with another friend Li Kit-ming[52]—and produced my first films as it was easier to raise funds in Hong Kong. In 2004, when I was authorized to make films for release in China, it was necessary to create Xstream Pictures, which I finally did with Yu Lik-wai in 2006. The mission of Xstream Pictures was to produce both of our films, since he wanted to make films in China. At the time, more and more private investors were becoming interested in cinema and we thought we could help other filmmakers by producing them. So, in order to produce other filmmakers' first or second films, we created a subsidiary called Tian Yi, which means, "Extra Wings." Due to a lack of funds or technical know-how, many young filmmakers are forced to work alone under terrible conditions. We intend to help these filmmakers and encourage, in the long run, the emergence of an independent cinema. The idea is to provide filmmakers the proper means to make their films and to have them benefit from my connections in the industry by finding distribution. Screenings in bars and alternative festivals is a start, but it's not enough. And it pays nothing. You can't make a living from it.

What are the concrete results of this initiative?

---

52. See also the interview with Yu Lik-wai, pp. 177–86.

We have managed to produce four films. Han Jie's *Hello Mr. Tree* (2011), Song Fang's *Memories Look at Me* (2012), Quan Ling's *Forgetting to Know You* (2013), and *Fidaï* (2012) by the French director Damien Ounouri. They're all films made under correct conditions that can be theatrically released. Since 2003 the system of censorship has evolved. Before, you would present your film and would receive a document saying that the film was approved or refused, or that you had to make such and such a change. Now it's actually possible to discuss and even to defend a project. Despite this, young filmmakers often engage in self-censorship, or just choose to work in an underground manner. It's absurd. If they have something to say, it must be heard.

For example, Han Jie was convinced that his screenplay for *Hello Mr. Tree* would never be accepted, and was getting ready to shoot it outside of the system. So I went to defend it before the China Film Administration.[53] The film does have a critical message: it's set in a mining area and deals with young people's problems, environmental issues, water shortages and rural exile. Nevertheless, the project was accepted.

We quickly discovered that the biggest difficulty was not censorship but the fact that investors, although ready to invest money in my films—thanks to my reputation they knew that they would get visibility, even if not big financial rewards—were unwilling to work with young unknowns. Negotiations were difficult; the investors would frown when learning the funds were for a filmmaker named Han Jie or Quan Ling. This is why I decided Xstream Pictures should participate in the risk-taking and that from now on, regardless of the budget, we would provide a third of the overall financing, with the rest coming from outside investors. Xstream is no longer just a production company but also an investment company, which reassures the financiers.

---

53. The China Film Administration, or CFA, was a component of the State Administration of Radio, Film, and Television (SARFT) meant to review films for their content, and to determine whether, when, or how a film is released. The SARFT was suppressed in 2018 and replaced by a dedicated department of the Communist Party Propaganda Office. The result has been an increased tightening of regulations. [Tr.]

Did your company have the means for such investments?

No, of course not. From then onwards, I have been engaged in more commercial activities. Shooting commercials has become very important. We have succeeded in establishing long term collaborations with certain clients: banks, insurance companies, brands of Western drinks, cars, etc. But cash flow does remain a problem. For example, Han Jie needed to raise money for *Hello Mr. Tree* quickly so he could shoot at a specific time of year, but we didn't have the funds. By chance, at that time I was invited by an insurance company to give lectures in different places in China; ten all together, one city per day. I had to speak about youth, growing up, the importance of having a goal in life. The compensation was more than comfortable, and the beginning of Han Jie's shoot was financed by these talks.

Do you enjoy making commercials?

It's completely different from my work as a filmmaker. Commercials are a service to be provided, exercises with precise requirements that must be met. As we are getting more and more requests, I am able to choose based on the fee—since the goal is to develop financing opportunities—and also depending on my values. There are clients for whom I will never work. Furthermore, it brings me an understanding of certain realities. For example, I have acquired financial knowledge from making an ad for a bank, or an understanding of modern agriculture in making an ad for a pesticide, or an awareness of the luxury sector when it's an ad for a watch, or car culture when it's an ad for a car. It's all enlightening.

Do you worry that directing commercials will influence your style?

First of all, I have no desire to create a unified style. For each of my films I am looking for the most suitable approach for the theme. The commercial work I do is completely different: advertising is devoted to what one sees, to what one shows; while in cinema the most beautiful is what you don't see, the abstract or intangible. As a film unfolds, the spectator takes into account all the things outside of the film itself, the physical parameters of the screen. The films that I like always have, in one way or another, this kind of beauty. Cinema conveys poetry: it's capable of revealing the invisible poetry that occurs in life itself; the lights, the colors, the bitter experiences of humans, their exchange of words, the state of the sky. Sometimes, it's a material poetry based on technical decisions: a camera movement or the musicality of a change in shot can conjure up this poetry.

Do you also experience this "invisible poetry" in life?

Yes, but for that you have to find a pregnant pause in the course of things. It's not easy. Sometimes I fear such moments have disappeared from my life, as my attention is always on work. Lately I have been forcing myself to take more time off. It's only by cultivating solitude—in being really alone—that you can nourish your passion, allow things to mature, and see ideas surface.

[*The sound of firecrackers is heard in the distance.*] I love these sounds! When I hear firecrackers, I imagine that someone is getting married, that a couple are entering into a new phase in their life. It's possible to imagine that off in the distance, where the noise is coming from, people are united in a great ceremony. Two or three hundred people sharing a meal—that's life! When I return to Fenyang or the region, my imagination overflows under the influence of these kinds of sensations, this almost unconscious perception that all around me life is pulsating. In my youth I would imagine someone like me far away who expressed his heavy heart by screaming. The wind would carry his cry to me and I would listen. This is why I like the wind so much.

Do you sometimes dream of what you are filming?

Yes, that happens. And sometimes my dreams wind up in my films. The serpents in *A Touch of Sin* appeared in my dreams during the writing of the screenplay. Just yesterday, I dreamed I was in a European city, in a transit hub like FedEx. There was a large room crammed full of film reels from all over the world. An employee held out a can to me that I opened. Inside was Bertolucci's *The Last Emperor*. I had the impression all these films were being sold on the cheap, decided to buy it, and suddenly heard myself ask if there was a copy with Chinese subtitles. I unwound the film and, noticing interruptions, tried to remember what the missing passages were. Then I woke up and couldn't get back to sleep. This may be the opening shot in my next film! I understand the dream's meaning: in cinema, there is a frame and what is outside of this frame is a richer world, and an immense source for the imaginary.

On *Mountains May Depart*

AFTER THE PUBLICATION of the first edition of this book in Brazil, Jia Zhangke presented *Mountains May Depart* at the Cannes Film Festival in 2015, resulting in a new interview. It would have been artificial to incorporate this into the preceding long interview, so it's here reproduced separately.

What is the genealogy of Mountains May Depart?

The film matured over a long period of time, and comes in part from sequences that were filmed during the shoots of my earlier films. Since 2001, when I got my first digital camera, Yu Lik-wai and I have traveled a lot, filming at random. We have shot many images without knowing what we would do with them; images that weren't exactly tests, more like notes. Four years ago we did more or less the same thing with a new digital camera, the Arri Alexa, which has been a gamechanger for filmmakers and cinematographers because of its increased functionality. It was the juxtaposition of these two sets of images, shot ten years apart, that gave me the idea for the film. I was struck by how far away the images from 2001 seemed, as if from a vanished world. I found myself wondering what I was like back then, and if it was possible to reconnect with the person I was so long ago—ten years, which seems enormous.

The changes weren't only technological. You also had changed during this period.

Yes I was of course a different man back then. Today I'm forty-five years old and have a life experience I lacked back then. I found it interesting to imagine myself in the future, based on my current trajectory. When you're young you don't think about old age; when you get married you don't think about divorce; when your parents are alive you can't imagine them being gone; when you're in good health you don't think about illness. But when you reach a certain age, you think not only about the present but also about the future. The subject of *Mountains May Depart* is the relationship of feelings to time; feelings can only really be understood with the passing of time.

For that you also needed to go into the future?

If you only concern yourself with the present, you'll lack perspective. Positioning oneself from a point of view of a possible future is a way of observing the present differently, and understanding it better. Having lived my whole life in China, I am very aware of the lightning transformations that the country has known; in economic matters, but also in regard to individuals. Our entire way of life has been turned upside down, with the intrusion of money at the center of everything.

You also tried to depict time itself?

The film hinges on a comparison between the stages of life and the landscapes that pass by us, hence the importance of the idea of travel in the film—the car, the train, the helicopter, etc. There is constant movement, and yet at the same time the stability and repetition of daily life; activities such as eating: she made Dim Sum, she is making Dim Sum, and she will make Dim Sum…

The film travels in effect through multiple landscapes, but there is also a home base— Fenyang—where Zhao Tao's character lives.

That's where I was born, where I grew up, and where I shot my two first films—*Xiaowu* and *Platform*—and part of *A Touch of Sin*. It's an emotional anchor for me. My friends and some of my family are there, but it's also an aesthetic and social anchor as, for me, Fenyang represents the experience of the average person in China. This region is also very attached to a concept central to the film, one that's represented by the Chinese characters *Qing Yi*, which refer to the strong sense of loyalty one can have to those closest to you—your family, the person you love, your friends. This idea—which is similar to what in Europe during the Middle Ages was called the oath of fealty—is central to the novels of Chinese chivalry. In Chinese mythology it's embodied by Guan Gong,[1] the god of war. His traditional symbol is a

---

1. Also known as Guan Yu, this mythological character is named after a famous general (160-220) of the ancient times. [Tr.]

long halberd with a red feather, and this object appears in each part of my film. The person carrying it wanders aimlessly, as if not understanding the concept of fealty.

You're nostalgic for deeper and longer lasting relationships between people.

Yes, but not only between people, also with places, and especially with memories. In the daily life of the Chinese people I see a profound loss of relationships of mutual commitment, and this affects memory. Even if a relationship between individuals ends, there shouldn't be any reason not to continue respecting what was shared. If you abandon that, everything can come undone, even "the mountains may depart."

Is this also the title in Mandarin?

The Chinese title literally means "old friends are like the mountain and the river"—they're unchanging. The wording in English is the reverse of the Chinese title, but it conveys the same idea, the same question.

The shift to an ever larger format—going from 1.33 to 1.85 then to 'Scope— conveys as much a loss of bearings as an opening up.

When filming I followed the constraints of the different techniques, with the techniques themselves corresponding to the various scenes. The scenes in the night club and with the coal lorry stuck on the road were shot at the time in 1.33 so I wanted to keep them in that format. With the Alexa and the wider ratio of 1.85, the whole relationship to space changes, not only the size of the frame. This changes again with images in 'Scope, for which we used anamorphic lenses which distort the space, even if it's not obvious.

Why did you choose Australia for the future part?

The majority of Chinese who emigrate go to the United States or to Canada—especially on the West Coast—but Australia seemed to me much further away. It's in the other hemisphere; when it's winter in China it's summer over there, when it's very hot in Australia it's snowing in Shanxi. The international success of *A Touch of Sin* led me to travel to many countries and I became interested in Chinese immigration, particularly immigrants from Shanxi. I am especially interested in the fate of young people and their relationship with their parents. In many locations—Los Angeles, Vancouver, Toronto, New York—I saw ruptures in language with profound consequences. In many immigrant Chinese families only one of the two parents can speak English, which is the only language their children speak. So there is one parent with whom the child cannot talk at all. It's an enormous upheaval.

In the third part of the film entire sequences are in English, a language that you're not completely fluent in.

For me that's not a problem. I know the meaning of what the actors are saying since I wrote it, and then it's just a question of rhythm. Under these circumstances it's not difficult for me to direct scenes in English.

Two songs play an important role in the film: the Pet Shop Boys' "Go West" and a Cantonese variety song.

The Pet Shop Boys' song was extremely popular in China in the 1990s, when I was at university and discotheques were opening all over the country. In nightclubs and at parties, "Go West" was the song that was always played at the end of the nights—it brought everyone together in a collective dance. We didn't question too much what the West signified; it could be California (which for us is East) or Australia, like with the characters in the film.

The Cantonese song is "Run without Care," by Sally Yeh. She's a star of *Cantopop*, but the song itself isn't well known. I like her a lot and listen to her often. Pop music has always interested me, and has helped me to understand life. Those songs are a good testimony to collective life as they describe society. Recently I am struck by the absence in newer pop songs of strong feelings, of a faithful commitment toward someone or something— earlier this was very present. I've even published an article on this topic. There are still love songs but they're more concerned with trivialities. In contrast, "Run without Care" says that even if a breakup is imminent what was shared in the relationship will not disappear.

Often your films feature images that don't develop the story but that do enrich it indirectly, like the shot of a caged tiger in Mountains May Depart. *Where does this image come from?*

I felt sorry for this tiger. I felt as sad for him as I did for the human beings—the characters—in the film. When I travel to China's small cities, I often visit animals at the zoos. Seeing them moves me deeply.

Zhao Tao has been present in your films since Platform. *In* Mountains May Depart *there is a new development, a new way of acting. Did you ask her to perform differently?*

I didn't ask her anything. It was all her doing and she really surprised me. Since we're married and have worked together for so many years we know each other very well, but with this film I discovered aspects of her that I hadn't seen before, an inner world unknown to me. Early in pre-production she asked me if I could give her some guidelines on the character. I gave her only two words: "explosive" for the first part, and "ocean" for the second. From there, she worked hard, filling several notebooks with thoughts about her character; everything that I intentionally hadn't made explicit in the screenplay so as to leave a lot of room for improvisation during the shoot. She composed a real literary creation. For example, she sought to explain to herself how this woman could have accepted her son leaving with her husband. She took a lot of initiative. For example, in the final scene she's wearing my mother's clothes. This was her idea. She also worked on the physical movements for each period, helped by her experience as a dancer.

Who are the other actors?

Zhang Yi who plays the husband has appeared in a lot of television, and is well known in China. I saw him in Peter Chan's *Dearest*, which was in Venice in 2014 and really liked his performance. Liang Jingdong, who plays the other man, was in *Platform*, but hadn't acted in a long time. The son, Dollar, is played by Dong Zijian, who comes from the Central Academy of Drama.[2] And Sylvia Chang, of course, is the star of dozens of films by Li Han-hsiang, Ann Hui, Tsui Hark, Edward Yang, Johnnie To, Mike Newell, Ang Lee, Tian Zhuangzhuang, et al. She's also a filmmaker, but I needed above all a good Chinese actress who is fluent in English.

The Shanghai Film Group co-produced this film, despite the problems you encountered with A Touch of Sin, *which has still not been released in China. Was it difficult working with them again?*

No, the Shanghai Film Group liked the screenplay and were willing to join me. With this film I hoped that they could recuperate the money they had lost because of the ban on *A Touch of Sin*. That ban was decided at the last minute, after they had already incurred significant costs for the film's release. Among the co-producers, besides my company XStream and Office Kitano—an unfailing ally for the past fifteen years—we also received support from Nathanaël Karmitz, the head of the French company mk2, thanks to the recent agreements of French-Chinese co-production.

Has the film been authorized for release in China?

Yes, theoretically there won't be a problem.

---

2. The Central Academy of Drama in Beijing is a prestigious drama school in China. [Tr.]

interviews with Jia's collaborators

Interview with Zhao Tao, Actor

ZHAO TAO HAS acted in all of Jia Zhangke's films since *Platform*. They married in January 2012.

How did your collaboration with Jia begin?

I could never have anticipated what happened to me. It was 1998 and I had just graduated from the Beijing Dance Academy. I was teaching dance at the teachers' training school in Taiyuan, the capital of the Shanxi province. One day in October—I remember many of the trees in the school's courtyard had already lost their leaves—I passed a group of men as I was going to the dance room. They all had a funny look about them: they had either shaved heads or long hair or a beard. I thought that they were headed to the Fine Arts department, but in fact they went to my department, and I followed them. Once inside, the head of the dance department told me that they were going to shoot a film and were looking for actors amongst my students. I was okay with this. I didn't tell my students that a casting was taking place, and hoped they would be in top form. After about an hour-and-a-half, an assistant came to tell me that the director wanted to work with me. *Work with me?*

This experience reminded me of a school in Beijing, where often so-called directors would attend our classes. Once outside, they would suddenly appear between cars or behind bushes and tell us they wanted to photograph us. Often classmates did let themselves be photographed, only to have these "directors" disappear never to be heard from again. As a result, the day I was chosen, and found myself face-to-face with Jia and his crew, I thought the same thing would happen and that there would be no follow-up. So I accepted perfunctorily without thinking.

But there was *a follow-up.*

I never would have thought that in January 2000 an Assistant Director would show up and tell me that the shoot was going to begin soon. That was when I began to really believe it!

How did you prepare for this part in Platform?

Jia gave me a lot of music, but none of it inspired me. For the scene where I perform the Spanish dance, I had to listen several times to a particular song, and I rehearsed it under Jia's direction. When the filming began, he asked me to forget what we had done. "And do what?" Answer: "No need to dance. You just wiggle a little." *Wiggle?* What?! I'm a professional dancer! I was furious he asked me to play an amateur. But, in the end, I wiggled just as he asked.

Is dancing in front of a camera a different experience?

As soon as the camera started rolling, I would begin to dance to the music, while at the same time respecting the director's requests: namely to move slowly at the beginning and progressively build to a real dance. As a professional, I focused on my mastery of the rhythm. Although, for me, there were only really two seconds in the scene in which I could reveal my abilities as a professional dancer—the rest was just movements dictated by the moment. But people do really like this scene. It's the one that moves them the most. And now I also appreciate it.

Although you dance in Platform, *you are above all an actor playing a part. How did you work with Jia?*

From the start he gave me and the other actors a thick screenplay. I read it attentively, covering it with notes. But then, one week later, he told us to get rid of it, so as to free us up to do more creative work. I had to get used to arriving each morning on set without knowing exactly what I was going to do. Upon arrival, we would sit with Jia and soak up the atmosphere of the place. Looking back, if I was able to perform with ease, it's because I was buoyed by his confidence.

Was he open to others' ideas?

He didn't criticize my impromptu suggestions. He would support them and encourage me: "Not bad! Not bad!" Human beings need encouragement. He gave me confidence and the feeling that I was performing well. As a result I was able to give my imagination free rein, providing suggestions for each take.

Was this relationship specific to your early years or has it continued on the shoots of your subsequent films?

It became our way of collaborating. On set I often convey my ideas to Jia by acting out the scene in different ways. He can then judge which he thinks works best. I offer my creative input and he as the director decides what to use.

To a large extent, The World *was inspired by your personal experience.*

When I was still a student in Taiyuan, my school had a collaborative program with the theme park Window on the World in Shenzhen. Much like the Beijing World Park, it features copies of famous buildings, in which lavish dance performances are staged. One year before graduating, I did an internship there. This was the first time I had ever left my hometown of Taiyuan in the Shanxi province—and I was in Shenzhen, one of the most open and developed cities of the time![1] What struck me the most when I

---

1. From 1979 onwards, the city of Shenzhen, near Guangzhou in southern China, became a

arrived was all the real, fresh flowers as, in Taiyuan, we only knew plastic flowers. I would often touch the petals of these real flowers—it made me happy. But after a month in the park I discovered the monotony of working there. We would get up at 8 a.m., do our exercises, rehearse and then, at 10 a.m., go to the location of the performance. At noon, we came back for lunch and then at 1:00 resumed the shows until 8:30 in the evening. It was the same routine every day: we ate the same thing, we walked the same paths, we were always with the same friends discussing the same things, and we performed the same shows. After a couple of months I thought I was going to lose my mind!

So you shared these experiences with Jia?

One day, on the way to Hong Kong, our train passed by Shenzhen and I noticed the Eiffel Tower in the Window on the World park. Seeing it bought back many memories and I began to share them with Jia. I told him my adolescent stories, my flirtations, my hopes, and how the dancers who appear to be living the good life were, in reality, very lonely once they returned to their rooms.

At the time, Jia didn't have much of a reaction, but the following year, he told me he wanted to shoot the stories I had told him and that the film would be called *The World*.

So you were performing your own story?

Yes, especially since a part of the shoot took place in Shenzhen. While there I met up with many of the teachers from my internship, and also many former classmates who were still working there. It broke my heart seeing that, after seven or eight years, they were still leading exactly the same life. I was there to act out what for them was real—the contrast was brutal.

---

laboratory for the shift to a socialist market economy. Declared a "special economic zone," it experienced staggering development, both a forerunner and a caricature of what the Chinese megacities would become in the 1980s.

In The World, *your character has a bond with Anna, a Russian dancer. Did that really happen?*

This relationship was Jia's idea. The Russian dancer was one of the dancers at the theme park at the time of filming. Although fictional, this relationship between me and the Anna character was still very strong. When we eat together in the film, we don't have a common language: she's speaking Russian and me Mandarin. We don't understand each other, but I'm still able to sense what she's talking about, and she, in turn, feels what animates me. In reality, when performing with the actor, Alla Cherbakova, a strange connection did unite us. For our last scene, where I find her in the bathroom, Jia wanted us to express our feelings for each other openly and spontaneously. In the first take, she said to me: "Tao, Tao, are you okay?" I was so moved she said my real name, and not that of my character, that I burst into tears.[2] I think that, in that moment, I felt the pain of women like Anna, without distinguishing her from Alla. The lives of these women are entirely constrained—their passports are taken from them and they really have no rights. The conditions were of course very different for us. Alla had no idea I would be so moved in this scene—but then neither did I! We fell into each other's arms and burst out sobbing. Once the scene was edited, it became clear how moving it was.

What was the shoot of Still Life *like?*

There were just two weeks between the time we were hired and the start of the shoot. Most of the dialogue and the actions were decided on the spot, during improvisations.

---

2. The English subtitles of *The World* obscure Zhao's point here for those not fluent in Chinese. Xueli Wang has elucidated her comment for me: "The full name of Zhao's character in *The World* is Zhao Xiaotao (赵小桃). This is the name she tells the Russian dancer Anna when they first meet. Other characters in the film address Zhao's character as either 'Xiaotao' or 'Tao jie' ('elder sister' Tao—a common, familiar way for Chinese people to address each other). Her character's name is indeed different from her real name (赵涛). The English subtitles translate her name as just Tao, for simplicity's sake no doubt." [Tr.]

How did you prepare for the part?

As I had never been to a place like Fengjie, I spent a week roaming the city's streets before we started rehearsing. I wanted to see what it was like for the men and women who lived there. I would spend my days crouching, nibbling on watermelon seeds with a drink in my hand, watching people coming and going. I wanted to understand what was unique to this place.

In your opinion, who is your character Shenhong?

She comes to Fengjie from a distant province in the hope of finding her husband, Bin. She's come to tell him in person she wants a divorce, and once she's done that she turns on her heels and leaves. I remember well the scene where I dance with Bin at the river's edge just before our separation. That day, it was very hot and I spent a lot of time teaching him how to dance. During the second take, while we were dancing, I really felt Shenhong's pain, and that of women like her, who know perfectly well their husbands no longer love them, and yet nevertheless must continue on in their marriage. I think that only those who have lived such an experience really understand the kind of pain that is. I was overcome with emotion, but Jia told me not to cry as my character isn't someone who easily shows her feelings. I waited for the moment after each take, when I could move away from the camera and allow myself to cry. I had to release the emotion! Shenhong is a woman who greatly saddens me. On the other hand, she's a strong woman who confronts her marital situation and finds confidence in her life. She allowed me to feel what one endures in the face of humiliation.

It's a very special role, with very little dialogue.

Yes, that was Jia's idea from the beginning. I found not being able to express my feelings with words very difficult. Most of the time in the film I am walking. In fact, apart from walking, my only action was sipping water because of the intense heat. I had only my body, my internal state, and my feelings. I needed to be sufficiently inhabited by emotion so that the viewer could experience this woman's feelings. The role was much more difficult than my previous roles in *Platform*, *Unknown Pleasures*, and *The World*. I had to walk amongst passersby, and there is nothing more difficult for an actor than to be in the midst of a crowd, still ensuring the viewer understands that you're the center of attention, and all the while erasing the slightest trace of your performance.

In a way, your performance in I Wish I Knew *pushes this idea still further.*

I didn't know how Jia would use my walking around the city, nor how he was thinking about structuring the film, but I did know that I was playing a fictional character. For me she was a ghost, a wandering soul from the past roaming the streets of Shanghai, a modern city. I would move through the crowd—some of whom would react to me—usually in silence, without responding to those around me.

What did Jia ask from you for this character?

He wanted me to comb the city in silence. To go through every nook and cranny of Shanghai, so as to highlight the city's modernity. Initially there were also fictional elements to the character's life but ultimately he decided not to keep those. When I saw how he had used the footage of me to punctuate the film and connect the different interviews, I felt he had made the right choice.

Your role in A Touch of Sin *is very different from what you had done up until then.*

My previous characters were ordinary women. Whereas Xiaoyu, my character in the film, is someone that resorts to violence in response to the brutality of the two men who dishonor her. I really enjoyed playing this character. She allowed me to grab a knife and kill a man who has humiliated me—all fictional of course!

The scene in which Wang Hongwei hits you with the banknotes must have been difficult to shoot.

It was a painful moment. Jia told me to stare right back at Wang Hongwei while he was hitting me; to not back down. He wanted me to stress my gaze, expressing this woman's strong determination. In reality, I was completely stunned by Wang Hongwei's blows. Weeks later, during the Cannes festival, half my head was still aching. So, when it was time to kill Hongwei, I was happy to do it! But to reach this state, the scene had to last a long time. Jia told me a dozen blows should suffice to capture the scene, but, in filming, I realized that even if I was able to express Xiaoyu's humiliation, the actor Zhao Tao had not yet reached the point needed to pull out a knife. This scene lasts only about ten minutes but we spent about six hours shooting it, as we had to do multiple takes. Finally, when I took out the knife I was no longer just the character of Xiaoyu. I was an old-fashioned avenger, like in chivalrous novels. I invested a lot of my personal feelings about personal dignity into the role.

Interview with Yu Lik-wai, Cinematographer

RENOWNED CINEMATOGRAPHER Yu Lik-wai, born in Hong Kong in 1966, is also a producer and filmmaker who directed the feature-length films *Love Will Tear Us Apart* (1999), *All Tomorrow's Parties* (2003), and *Plastic City* (2008).

How did you get started in the cinema?

I began my studies rather late, at the age of twenty-five. I trained as a director of photography at INSAS in Brussels.[3] After graduation, I returned home to Hong Kong to look for work as an assistant. At the time, in 1994, the film industry in Hong Kong was doing very poorly; a lot of technicians were unemployed, and I could only find work on soft-core movies or melodramas,

---

3. INSAS (Institut national supérieur des arts du spectacle), located in Brussels, is one of the most prestigious film schools in the world.

quick productions shot over just two weeks. As a cinematographer I couldn't make enough money to live on, so I found additional work as a photographer for a film journal; but was still struggling to get by. Fortunately, in 1996, I received a subsidy from the Organisation internationale de la Francophonie and a grant from the Hong Kong Arts Development Council to make a documentary, *Neon Goddesses*, that was co-produced by the Centre de l'audiovisuel in Brussels. The film received prizes at the Hong Kong Festival of Short Films and at Yamagata.[4] By then, I had already begun writing the screenplay for my first feature film, *Love Will Tear Us Apart*.

How did you meet Jia?

I met him in 1996, when we both attended the Hong Kong Festival of Short Films. He was showing *Xiaoshan Going Home*, which won the prize for best fiction film, and I showed *Neon Goddesses*, which received the prize for best documentary. At our first meeting, we talked a lot about our own projects and our vision for an independent Chinese cinema. He spoke to me about the screenplay for *Platform* and invited me to accompany him to Shanxi on a preliminary location scout for it. We then decided the project was too onerous for a first feature film, so he quickly wrote a new screenplay, which was *Xiaowu*.

What brought you together?

Two things made me want to work with him. First, we have the same taste in cinema—we almost always agree about films. An artistic affinity like this is very important to work well together. Second, we are both very pragmatic. We detest endless discussions and impossible projects that waste time, and spend a lot of time thinking about how best to realize our projects. Jia is very flexible and is able to adapt to reality. The fact that he put *Platform* on the backburner in order to make *Xiaowu* is a very good example of this.

---

4. The Hong Kong Independent Short Film and Video Awards. Yamagata in Japan is the main documentary film festival in Asia.

In addition to working with him as cinematographer, you are also the co-founder of his production company, Xstream Pictures.

Before Xstream, I had created a small production company called Hutong in 1996 with a friend from Hong Kong, Li Kit-ming. Hutong co-produced my documentary with the Belgians, and then co-produced Jia's first two films—*Xiaowu* and *Platform*—as well as my two first feature films, *Love Will Tear Us Apart* and *All Tomorrow's Parties*. Hutong was incorporated under Hong Kong law, which greatly helped facilitate co-production with Japan and France.[5] The fact that the company had a Hong Kong identity also gave us some protection. Our situation was very fragile because all four films were made in China without state authorization; they were underground films. Li Kit-ming is the executive producer of these four films, but in 2003 he had to leave the company. So Jia and I then set up Xstream Pictures. Xstream coincided with Jia beginning to make films that were authorized by the Chinese authorities.

What was the shoot of Xiaowu *like? It was your first film together.*

The pre-production lasted a long time. We were both recent graduates; we had the luxury of taking our time and doing a lot of pre-planning. We would discuss and prepare the shoot over a drink or a good meal. Talking things out like this allowed us to examine issues from all angles and solve most of the problems in advance. Little by little, we learned to work collaboratively. Since then, the preparation of films we work on together is always done in this somewhat informal manner, without a strict schedule.

How did you select the format for filming?

The choice of format was initially dictated by the options available to us. At the time of *Xiaowu* we had very little money and so really had no choice; it had to be Super 16 mm. But this format also corresponded aesthetically to

---

5. *Platform* was co-produced by the Japanese company, Office Kitano, and the French partner, Joël Farges.

the project as we wanted to make a film with a documentary feel. A small 16 mm camera was ideal for this. Subsequently, our choices were more deliberate. For example, for *Platform*, Jia specifically wanted us to shoot in 35 mm.

Why was that?

Jia had very clear intentions. He believed that shooting the first part of the film on 35 mm and with static shots would convey the general paralysis and rigidity of Chinese society prior to the reforms—it's as if the camera were recording the populace's actions within a single painting. Afterwards, as the film entered the reform era, Jia progressively allowed certain camera movements and the use of tracking shots.

Was the mise-en-scène of Platform *precisely planned in advance?*

Yes, but that didn't prevent Jia from inventing on the spot. One of my favorite moments is the film's opening shot. A group of peasants are waiting in the lobby of the theater for the performance to begin. Jia and I thought for a while about all the different ways to stage this: how should the extras move in the space? Initially it didn't occur to us to just let them move about freely in the lobby, talking among themselves. But this is what we ultimately did and it was the best solution. It enabled the space to function almost like an actor; every space has its own logic, which determines how people inhabit it.

For example, if I enter this room, I am going to put myself next to the glass door. Others might like to sit in a chair. It's very mysterious but it reveals someone's inclinations, their temperament, and behavioral logic. The methods employed in documentary to obtain a desired effect, sometimes deliver their share of mysteries and marvels. You can spend hours searching for the best use of a space, having the actors pose in different configurations, but to no avail. Then suddenly out of the blue inspiration comes and you have an idea. I'll never forget this shot in the theater. To light it I used just a single bulb—visible in the frame—hanging from the ceiling. It was in perfect harmony with the location.

Were there also rules and guiding principles for Platform's *mise-en-scène?*

I remember that Jia wanted a static camera and, in the establishing shots, people to appear relatively small in the frame. I think he had in mind the relationship between the individual and the collective—the ratio that existed at the time between individuality and collectivity. As the film progresses, people start to put themselves forward and show their individuality. As a result, the proportions naturally change.

Platform *is the only film Jia shot on 35 mm. Afterwards, you switched to digital.*

This was a choice that was in large part dictated by the working conditions of the time. Our relationship with the authorities remained difficult and we were still making underground films without authorization. In this context, digital technology was an enormous help. If we had shot on celluloid, especially 35 mm, the authorities would have exerted more control over us during filming, and distribution, even in alternative venues, would not have been possible. So the choice of digital technology was really obvious.

As a cinematographer how did you experience this shift in technology?

My first experience with digital technology made me realize the extent to which it was going to modify the director's work, as well as my own. Jia improvised a lot more and was able to wait for the right opportunity. We heard "cut" a lot less often on set. Jia would usually keep the camera filming, in case something interesting would appear. In this way, digital technology has an undeniable advantage for the handling of certain subjects. As a cameraman, I saw very quickly that a digital recording had little in common with celluloid, that it doesn't have the quality and nuances of analog. Once the choice of digital technology has been made, comparisons with traditional formats should stop. Digital technology possesses its own aesthetic qualities and brings its own possibilities, including in the color grading. What digital technology offers has nothing to do with the aesthetics of a traditional celluloid film.

With The World, *you again innovated by employing a 'Scope format.*

It was a big change for us. From *Xiaowu* to *Unknown Pleasures*, we had always shot in 1.66 or 1.85. I experimented in new ways to achieve Jia's vision. As a lot is expressed by the exterior sets, we decided on the 'Scope format as it would show more.

I should also add that with *The World* we had more money and more time than with the previous films. So I was able to set up a lot of complex camera movements and tracking shots, shifting point of view often within the same shot. Looking back, I would say that, in this film, Jia and I raised too many issues. We fretted too much over how the camera should move, and the overall staging of scenes. As a result the simplicity of our earlier films was lost. In my opinion, *The World* was a transitional experience, and the complexity of the project was beneficial to Jia. This idea of the contemporary was very important to him at the time, including the contemporaneity of images with characters in the throes of this new technology. He wanted everything to be spectacular: the images as well as the stage shows. But in hindsight I think it's too much. There's no continuity with the previous films nor the following ones. Jia was groping for something new—he was deeply invested in exploring this notion of the contemporary—but I feel we weren't able to fully grasp it.

Even though I find your judgement of The World *harsh,* Still Life *is definitely more obviously in sync with the previous films. It also points towards what was to come.*

On *Still Life* Jia tricked me! He told me we were going to shoot a documentary, *Dong*, and asked me what material to use. I suggested the mini DV as it was the most practical and economical. He had said there wasn't really any money for the film. So we took this small camera—I think it was a Sony Hi8—and went to make our documentary. After a week, he said he wanted to take advantage of the situation and to use his documentary background to make a fiction film. The screenplay was written very quickly. After just a few days he gave me a first draft. *Disaster!* How do I shoot a fiction film with the Sony Hi8? It's an amateur camera with very limited capabilities—for instance you can't focus in a tracking shot. We got off to a bad start! But in the end we decided to go ahead and use it.

As it turned out, this little camera with all its limitations gave us a great amount of latitude. We were shooting in neighborhoods where destruction was imminent and that had neither water nor electricity. There was nothing. Shooting conditions were tough as the layout of these places was changing from one day to the next. Unable to control the environment, we could only note the daily changes, like the rise of water or the destruction of an apartment building. In retrospect that little camera really helped us.

Did Jia define a particular aesthetic for this film?

Yes, he had a very specific vision in mind that was fairly complex. On the one hand, he wanted it to have a rough documentary feel and, on the other, he wanted to evoke the feeling of traditional Chinese landscape painting, as the region had been popular for painters.

Southwestern China is very humid: everything is covered in a veil of fog and the mountains never appear in sharp focus. This gives the impression that the landscape is in the clouds, just as in traditional paintings. Classical Chinese painting unfolds on scrolls with the eye slowly discovering the landscape in its entirety. Derived from this traditional scroll painting is a narrative model favored by the Chinese, one that employs multiple perspectives and points of view. Jia conceived *Still Life* consistent with this principle. He tells what is happening here, and then talks about this character, and then another one over there—the opening shot, a 360° pan filmed on a boat, shows this. I initially didn't know how to go about it. We were aboard the boat with many people, all of whom needed to be filmed. I suggested we use a bokeh effect in the transitions. In the end the shot has the effect of scroll painting, as the camera moves horizontally from one point to another, unrolling without a cut.

Although very different, I Wish I Knew, *from a few years later, also unravels harmoniously. It's composed of completely disconnected elements, one being the interviews with the different participants.*

I Wish I Knew was commissioned by the Shanghai World Expo. Jia did a lot of research as he wanted to do something more accomplished than a simple documentary work. He wanted a film with its own distinct aesthetic, and told me about Antonioni's 1972 film *Chung Kuo, Cina*, a dispassionate portrait of China that's stylistically experimental and innovative. Jia believed we could make a documentary as personal as that, but in our own way. Many scenes were shot as in a fiction film, such as the men who carry goods to the old warehouses. Of course there are also many elements that are straight from documentary, but everything was organized in advance, particularly the interviews. There were also reconstructions to show characters' frames of mind, their past, and their vision for the future. Jia succeeded in ensuring that each one looks back on their past and on their present, and then organized all these stories. In the film Zhao Tao is like a ghost who navigates space and time, a character from the present time who has the power to find herself in several places and times at once. This gives the film a magical, invocative aspect.

A Touch of Sin brings still more important changes. How did you respond on a technical level?

When Jia first came to me about *A Touch of Sin*, he only had a few pages of text summing up the different stories. Right away I thought about the 'Scope format as Jia wanted to make a contemporary *wuxia* film, an homage to King Hu. In the 1970s in Hong Kong and Taiwan, many *wuxia* were made, often with anamorphic lenses, which compressed and greatly distorted the image. I thought that we could bring the past alive by also using an anamorphic optical system for our film. Today in Asia, it's difficult to find anamorphic lenses as most were sent back to the United States, where they're used on the new digital cameras. But, ultimately, we did get a hold of one.

You also chose to use a Steadicam, which previously Jia had refused to use.

This choice was dictated by the fact that the characters are constantly moving and need to be followed. I'm also not a big fan of the Steadicam, but I do believe it's useful if it goes unnoticed. The movement should appear as a simple tracking shot, even if in fact the Steadicam enables a freedom of movement that would be impossible in a regular tracking shot.

You have been on set with Jia since his first feature film. Have you noticed an evolution in the way he works?

The World was a turning point. For the films before it, Jia was more controlling—lots of rehearsals, scene directions, etc. He had to carefully coordinate the performances of the non-professional actors, their ways of speaking and moving. He was very demanding. Since *Still Life*, another method of working has evolved. Although the majority of actors are still non-professionals, he's become more attuned to the possibilities of the actor, possibilities suggested by the location and the environment. As a result, he's more open to unexpected experiences and trying different options. This feels more relaxed but, in fact, is simply a matter of different expectations. Now the control Jia exerts is more conceptual. He no longer contents himself with just the quality of an individual scene. Rather each scene needs to be integrated into the totality of the film. To date our longest shoot was for *Still Life*.

A Touch of Sin is Jia's first film with primarily professional actors. I presume this prompted further changes to the working conditions?

Yes they're professionals, and even relatively famous. Jia was even more relaxed—it was no longer a question of directing them, but of establishing a real rapport with them. Everything now was coordinated in a much more complex overall design. Consequently he developed a greater conceptual control, no longer needing to get bogged down in all the minute details. On this shoot the crew's work was more specific, and also more piecemeal—Jia needed to exercise a different form of control. He needed to make sure that when delegating a task to someone that person would respect the film's overall design. For Jia it was a new way of working.

As a cinematographer, what do you look for from the performers? Do you think that shooting quickly improves their performance?

No, the speed of the work doesn't matter much. Whether it's for a documentary or for a fiction film, the main thing is the actors' confidence in you, the filmmaker and the cinematographer. This confidence is deeply human, and is essential, whether you are dealing with professionals or non-professionals. We have to gain their trust. After all, in our job we are aiming a camera at them—it scares people! As I'm afraid now![6] Fiction or documentary, it's all the same. What matters is humanity, sensitivity, and perhaps even more, the anticipation of people's movements. This is basic training for making documentaries. One of my professors used to say: "If you haven't proved yourself in making a documentary, you don't have the right to make a fiction film." I wholeheartedly agree!

---

6. During this interview Yu Lik-wai was filmed by Walter Salles and his cameraman, Inti Briones.

Interview with Zhang Yang, Sound Engineer

ZHANG YANG IS the sound engineer on all Jia's films since his earliest work in shorts. He's also worked on twenty or so other films, including several comedies with American actors in China and several major *auteur* films in contemporary Chinese cinema: Diao Yinan's *Night Train* and *Wild Goose Lake*, Vivian Qu's *Trap Street* and *Angels Wear White*.

How long have you known Jia Zhangke?

We were classmates at the Beijing Film Academy. We weren't in the same department as I was studying sound, but we would meet at screenings. I remember that we both greatly appreciated Jean-Luc Godard's *First Name: Carmen*, which was introduced by Alain Sarde, the film's producer. Students from the different departments were there; those from the directing and producing departments asked a lot of questions. The sound department wasn't big on asking questions. The film's producer, a little annoyed, turned to us: "We recorded several hundred tracks; why doesn't anyone ask about the soundtrack?" We were very happy to have a producer drawing our attention to the importance of the sound in a film! We loved Godard's films.

At that time, in the mid-1990s, what kind of material did you have at your disposal?

We were studying at the Film Academy before the digital era. For our school exercises, and even for *Xiaowu*, we worked with a simple four-track tape recorder. It was time-consuming but interesting! For example, if you see a car, we would design the sound like a draftsman, writing on the filmstock: "Here there is a car"! Or, "Here there is a certain vibe," so, in the mixing, I had to push or lower the sound. The work felt both artisanal and painterly. As for our ideas, we had to visualize them in our heads. For our school exercises, four tracks was more than we needed. Of course, subsequently, we were able to increase the number of tracks, but this was time consuming. Initially, having to conceive the film in our minds and anticipate the mixing gave us the same feeling as gambling. You had to imagine everything, and then, in the mixing you would discover the discrepancy between what had been planned and what was really possible.

Did you feel deprived of the necessary means?

At the time of *Xiaowu*, when we were film students, we would dream of synchronous sound. For example, we read articles about how on *Apocalypse Now* each sound was separately stored, and took into account the distance, the location in the frame. That made us think. At the time, we didn't think much about post-production, as we were more focused on capturing the sounds that matched what we were seeing. *Xiaowu* was approached in this frame of mind.

How did the shoot go?

I wasn't there. There was another sound engineer on set, and I only came on board during post-production because his schedule prevented him from finishing the job. Jia asked me if I could help him as we had studied together. We had difficulties due to the loss of a large number of sound recordings. Some of them had to be re-done, and for that we had to view the images. The karaoke singer had to be brought back so she could re-record the song, and we also had to re-record the sound for the scene with the musical lighter. At the time, I didn't think about what was coming from documentary and what from fiction—I focused on what Jia asked for and viewed his images to get an idea of the right sound.

In one scene, Wang Hongwei sends his identity card in the mail, slipping it into a mailbox. The sound for this long take was lost. I memorized the image, so as to maintain the correct rhythm. In the shot Wang passed by children skipping, and walked for a long time, changing direction several times. He crossed several different spaces before slipping his I.D. into the mailbox. I had to remember all of this! In the streets of Fenyang I retraced Wang Hongwei's path with a Nagra tape recorder. Everything was dependent on what I remembered from the images. Once the recording was finished, and the synchronization was done… Wow! It matched! You really would have thought we had direct sound! That's how things were at the time.

You took care of all the post-production.

I was also in charge of the mixing, which I had never done before. The rushes were very dirty and it was my first time! We mixed 120 minutes of the film in one evening and had to work twenty hours or so around-the-clock. Jia would tell me the dialogue as we mixed, translating from the dialect. The scratched-up filmstock with rough sound and atmosphere from the Shanxi province really excited me a lot. I had never seen a film like it. At the time, I was in a rock band and liked things a little rough. The Rolling Stones rather than the Beatles! An incredible energy emanated from this assembly of coarse sounds and unrefined images. When I saw the finished film, I had a completely different response as the image no longer had all its scratches— it was completely clean! So I figured that the soundtrack's job was to restore some of this roughness to the film.

The working conditions and aesthetic are very different in Platform.

They were no longer using a hand-held camera and were working a lot more in wide shots. The image was larger. I remember the first day and the first shot: I didn't think that it would take such a longtime. I couldn't hold the boom any longer and the microphone fell into the frame! I had to find a solution, so placed HF microphones[7] on the actors.

We shot in very different places—along the Yellow River and in very poor neighborhoods, encountering all sorts of unforeseen things. The sound recording itself didn't pose a problem, but sometimes off-camera sounds were heard. For example, in one scene, the characters are standing on a promontory and the female actor shouts out from the mountain. While she shouts, trucks carrying coal were passing way down below. The trucks made a metallic sound while the actor cried out; I felt this metallic sound gave the impression of a ghost in the process of crying. Jia and I were pleased with this unexpected effect and decided to reintegrate it into the editing in the appropriate place. We made use of a lot of sound impressions of this kind without them necessarily being live sound.

At this time, you switched over to digital sound?

Yes. Although it was a very rudimentary device, it allowed me to work quicker during the conceptual phase—I no longer needed to work like an artisan or painter. My digital recorder had sixteen tracks, which still wasn't enough. So I had to continue mentally imagining things without necessarily mixing them all at once. We were required to go through the pre-mix. Jia also wanted to integrate noises that belonged to his memories, to make audible his personal perception of these places. For example, the public announcements in the train stations—in this small, provincial city, hearing the loudspeakers broadcast every day the names of these destinations allowed one to dream, to imagine oneself going there. So I had to record many public announcements.

Music also plays an important role.

---

7. Small microphone transmitters placed directly on the actors, which record the speech of each one. Generally, this system is duplicated by the boom, which records the entirety of the space covered by the camera.

With *Platform*, Jia wanted to cover a decade in Chinese history. Initially we listened to and collected music from different periods and, during the shoot, he would sometimes remember popular music from the time. This music wasn't necessarily a part of my musical universe, but it wasn't entirely unknown to me either. And I had my own memories too, even if they were tied more to my older brother's daily life than mine. I would remember all this—the music, the clothes, the objects of the period—little by little, and for the rest I had to depend on my imagination.

Were there a lot of additional sounds added in the studio?

There were, but I still prefer a rougher sound, like the one that came directly from the loudspeakers. I like to record the sound universe of the set in its entirety, including during the dance scenes. I find it more beautiful, and it's also more accurate—depending on the period, the technique for recording was different. Using sounds that were not organic to the environment would have created a more sterile soundscape, lacking authenticity.

In contrast, the soundscape of The World *is much more constructed, even artificial.*

In visiting the two theme parks—the one in Beijing and the one in Shenzhen—during the location scouting, Jia told me that this time he wanted to make a more dreamlike film. He talked about Fellini, even though the film didn't have much to do with him. In *The World*, there were many extended long takes, so I emphasized the background noises, installing additional microphones to capture the ambiance and the actors' voices. This felt like an appropriate approach given the long takes and the film's overall style. The film also features several dance scenes. I had some regrets concerning *Xiaowu* and *Platform*, so on *The World* I compensated by making adjustments in how I captured the sound by favoring the sonic depth of certain shots. I did the mixing in a good quality studio, which allowed me to really feel the film. In the end, it didn't have the jumps characteristic of *Xiaowu*, or the harshness of *Platform*; instead, it flowed like a single breath, with a dreamlike quality. If *Xiaowu* was the Rolling Stones, *The World*, once it was mixed, was more like Pink Floyd. It had an unreal impression, without suggesting Fellini. It was very interesting, this unique breath.

A complete shift for Still Life…

Initially my preparations for *Still Life* were for a documentary. I decided to abandon DAT cassettes and to record on Compact Flash memory cards, because in a documentary setting, I need to record a lot of sounds and didn't want to risk running out of cassettes. I added mics as I didn't want to be confined. I was haunted by the idea of a *soundscape* and the best way to organize it.

The result is striking, notably in the wide shots with the river and the mountains.

I had not anticipated how beautiful the sound would be at the Three Gorges. There was a frontal sound and then the background too. When the boat's horn rang in the back of the sinuous gorges, the sound wave bounced back on this side, then on the other side, and then behind. If we had been in a studio with reverb or echo effects, it would have been difficult to get a sound as true as that, which we recorded live. So I continued to record on-the-spot, to capture this reverberation and echo with no artifice—this is the kind of sound I want to record. In the edit I must make sure the sound is good for the entirety of the shot. When it is, I can breathe a sigh of relief: Phew! The long take gives me the time to practice sound recording.

A Touch of Sin *required an entirely different approach?*

From the reading of the screenplay and the meetings with Jia and Yu Lik-wai, I could see that we were going in another direction. The sound was going to need to be more theatrical, to express more psychological elements. Very different to the sound in a documentary with long takes. Still, from our first film together up until to *A Touch of Sin*, I always felt that there was no need to get rid of elements of reality. Jia's films are never made entirely of theatricality or artifice.

In A Touch of Sin, *a particular problem arose with the action scenes and the reference to the* wuxia *that Jia wanted.*

At the Beijing Film Academy, we had a small moviola where we would watch, in slow motion, Chinese and Japanese martial arts films from the 1960s and the 1970s. We realized that the fights were achieved largely in the editing, with the sound serving to facilitate the action and offset the fragmentary aspect of the images. The sound is also perceived as a witness of reality; faced with martial arts films or horror films, if what the eye sees is only an illusion, what the ear hears is very real. The work on sound unifies the images, and increases their credibility.

There have been enormous developments in sound technology since you started out. What has that been like for you?

The real problem is each person's place in the process of creation. Recently, I went to Australia; I met colleagues and we discussed the organization of our profession. There are two tendencies: one where the sound engineer takes care of everything from the beginning to the end, and the other where tasks are divided between several people. During my training and throughout my professional trajectory, I've always taken charge of the entire process. This way of operating is closer to my conception of the profession.

Interview with Lin Xudong, Editor

THE PROFESSOR AND editor Lin Xudong belongs to the generation before Jia Zhangke, and played an essential role in the discovery and promotion of Chinese filmmakers in the 1990s. Greatly respected in the film world, he often played a part in obtaining authorizations from the authorities or support from the industry. In some respects he's a mentor to Jia. During our meeting with Lin, Jia was present, before they gave a joint conference in the form of a public conversation at the Central Academy of Fine Arts (CAFA) in Beijing on November 18, 2013.

Could you introduce yourself?

Lin Xudong: I am now an artist, an independent artist. I studied engraving at the Central Academy of Fine Arts in Beijing, but I am primarily interested in a reflection on contemporary art—and on cinema. After my studies, I turned to documentary.

Jia Zhangke: He has three jobs now: as a painter, he's already had several exhibitions; as a critic, he's frequently published, including a book on the history of documentary cinema last year; and finally, as a film editor.

You are also a professor?

Lin: I was a professor. I taught for a long time at the Communication University of China. But not anymore.

How did you meet Jia?

Lin: The first meeting with Jia happened thanks to *Xiaowu*, in the context of a discussion with the cultural attachée of the French Embassy in Beijing. I learned a lot about cinema by regularly attending events there. At the time, there were two screenings of important films every week, on Mondays and Fridays. In addition, we could borrow two videotapes per week from the library. The screenings took place at the Lycée Français in Beijing. Before the massive circulation of bootleg DVDs, it was an invaluable way of getting information on world cinema. This place played an important role for young Chinese filmmakers.

How did you hear about Xiaowu?

Lin: One day, when borrowing videotapes from the Cultural Service Department of the French Embassy, I discussed contemporary Chinese cinema with the audiovisual attachée.[8] She introduced me to some young Chinese filmmakers by lending me some videos. I was particularly impressed by Jia's film. I called her back enthusiastically and she organized a meeting with him. That's how we met for the first time.

What did you say to Jia?

Lin: When I saw him for the first time, I thought he didn't look anything like a director coming from the Beijing Film Academy [*laughter*]. I suggested to the person-in-charge of the French cultural service to organize a screening and to invite directors, teachers, people interested in new experiences. We did this at the Lycée Français in Beijing but in a very limited way. At that time

---

8. Reference to Isabelle Glachant. See also note 29 on page 116.

France and China were supposed to sign an important aeronautical contract—the ambassador indicated that he didn't want our initiative to compromise the negotiation. We were able to screen the film for just fifty people. Notably, Liu Xiaodong, the painter and subject of *Dong*, was in the audience.

Afterwards, did you remain in touch with Jia?

Lin: We saw each other practically every day.

Do you work with other filmmakers or just with Jia?

Jia: He has many, many friends! He's worked extensively with the young generation of Chinese filmmakers, in particular with Zhang Yuan and Wang Xiaoshuai early in their careers.

Lin: But Jia is the only one with whom I work on a regular basis. He's the one with whom I have been closest, the one with whom I have maintained a constant relationship.[9]

Your meeting coincides with the production of Platform.

Lin: I discussed this project a lot with Jia while he was working on the screenplay, by testing many narrative hypotheses.

Jia: Lin also helped me to negotiate with the Shanghai Film Studio,[10] because I was banned from filming at the time.

Lin: First of all, you were not yet banned, because the authorities didn't know about the project. As the screenplay advanced, I was negotiating with

---

9. Lin Xudong would also play a decisive role in the conception and editing of Wang Bing's first film, *West of the Tracks* (2002).
10. The Shanghai Film Studio is one of the three biggest film studios in China; it's the film division of the Shanghai Film Group. [Tr.]

the Studio and I introduced Jia to friends from the film world. We thought we would be able to shoot under normal conditions, but then someone denounced us and the film was banned.

Professor Lin, you also worked on the editing of Platform?

Lin: Yes, as the head film editor. This phase was very long, because there were a lot of rushes. As he had shot on 35 mm, at the end of the shoot Jia went to Hong Kong to transfer everything to Betacam. Then he returned to Beijing for the editing. The equipment back then wasn't as simple to use as today's digital equipment. With a video cassette, you can't decide instantaneously to insert a shot here or there as the entire sequence has to be transferred to another format. Work was still more complicated as, because of the production crew's lack of experience, certain bridging shots hadn't been filmed. We had to figure out a way to construct a coherent narrative and spent a crazy amount of time on this. After the initial edit, the film lasted seven or eight hours; we cut it little by little.

Did you work together again after Platform?

Lin: Starting with *Still Life*, I have worked on the edit of all Jia's films. He had decided to make that film on the spot, as he was inspired by the location. He barely had time to write the screenplay, as the city was in the process of being destroyed. If he hesitated too long, he ran the risk of there no longer being anything to film! So he jumped in. Once the shoot was finished he found out he wasn't really done! Every time he was in the editing room, he would decide to add new shots. Shooting was resumed seven times. He would film and if, in the editing room, he wasn't satisfied, he would start again. It seemed to go on forever. When the film was selected for the Venice Film Festival the post-production wasn't finished. Jia went directly from the post-production studio to the airport—we were all already in Venice but the film still hadn't arrived!

Compared to the other directors with whom you have worked, do you think that Jia has a distinctive approach to editing?

Lin: It's a truism to say that a director finishes their film in the editing room, but with Jia this really is the case. As he rarely follows his screenplays during the shoot, he usually moves away from his original ideas, and, since he's capable of working wonders with improvisation, a lot of work is needed at the editing stage to integrate these additions.

What was your role on A Touch of Sin?

Jia: (answering for Lin) He helped in making a lot of major decisions. The film owes to him, for example, its opening sequence. I had planned to begin with the character of Zhou San (Wang Baoqiang), the motorbike killer. It was Professor Lin who thought that Dahai (Jiang Wu) should be the first to appear. It's a better beginning. You may think that these are just details, but editing is all about such decisions.

Lin: When editing, I rely very often on my training in classical music, for which I have a real passion. I never studied as an editor so music is my point of reference. At the beginning of *A Touch of Sin* it's as if the first note of music is the close up of Jiang Wu playing with an apple. He's like a modest but robust baritone. Then, the camera steps back and this baritone softens a little. In this moment, a quick rhythm is interposed and it's the shot of the motorbike. Then, at the time of the incident, a shrill sound is heard before coming back to the character of Jiang Wu. Afterwards, there's an explosion with a more powerful sound, and the film begins. It's like the overture of an opera.

The initial idea for the film's opening wasn't satisfactory. The first story of the film is Jiang Wu's, and the fact that we first see Wang Baoqiang in the image draws the viewers' attention to him. Then we leave him, while, in the final version, it's clearly said: here is the character we are first going to follow. As for Wang Baoqiang's appearance, it announces the film's theme: violence. Then, we return to the character of the present story. It seems more interesting to me like that.

Does Jia's style pose any particular problems in editing?

Lin: The biggest challenge, especially in *A Touch of Sin*, resides in finding the balance between two opposing aspects: the naturalistic qualities inherent in the film versus its powerful theatricality. In the editing many decisions had to be made. From a narrative perspective, it was often more logical to eliminate shots where the action wasn't progressing, but that would have been harmful to Jia's personal style.

For example, in Wang Baoqiang's story, we witness a dispute between a group of youths gathered in a tearoom. One of the film's distributors felt that this scene weakened the narrative and wanted us to eliminate it. I fought to keep it, even if, from a purely dramatic point of view, it disrupts the flow of the narrative, eliminating it would have harmed the film's atmosphere.

Overall, how do you perceive Jia's filmmaking approach?

Lin: His aesthetic is enriched by all aspects of daily life in China today. And he strives to make ordinary people the protagonists of his films—he's in close contact with the reality of China. In hindsight, I believe that his importance will be clear. Among contemporary Chinese filmmakers, he's the one who continually observes reality with an extreme acuity. Sometimes, while actually experiencing it, we aren't yet aware of the importance of a phenomenon, but Jia has already integrated it into his films. In addition, he manages to structure his perceptions in a purely filmic way. Other filmmakers are sometimes sensitive to one thing then another, but these impressions tend to cancel each other out because they aren't coherently integrated into an overall design. In contrast, Jia succeeds in establishing them within a real filmic structure. He has a global vision. He is, in my opinion, the only Chinese filmmaker to do this. This is what seduced me and it's why I continue to collaborate with him—in working with him, I have reconsidered my perception of reality on many different levels.

by Jia

The Films of My Life
By Jia Zhangke

ON NOVEMBER 18, 2013 *during an exchange with students at the library of the Beijing Film Academy, Jia Zhangke revisited the films and filmmakers that have mattered most to him, and the influence they've had on his own work.*

In 1993 I enrolled at the Beijing Film Academy. At that time in China, it was difficult to see film classics—especially foreign cinema—because the works of the great masters weren't shown. But here, at the Academy, I did have access to these films. There were two ways to see them. The first way was in our Film History course, which was divided into the "History of Chinese Cinema" and the "History of World Cinema." When a filmmaker or a particular period was discussed, we would be shown the corresponding films. The second way was by borrowing VHS tapes from the university videotheque.

There were all kinds of films. The foreign films, for the most part, were translated by our professors, some of whom had studied in Russia. For example, I saw *Ballad of a Soldier* and *The Cranes are Flying*,[1] accompanied by a parallel audio track with a professor's translation. Some of our professors had studied in France, like Hu Bing and Zhang Xianping. We saw Jean-Luc Godard and François Truffaut's films "dubbed" by them. Other films came to us on video from Taiwan and, because we also had professors who had studied in Japan, those of Kenji Mizoguchi and other Japanese masters like Akira Kurosawa, Yasujirō Ozu, and Nagisa Ōshima.

I really benefited from the fact that, at the end of the 1980s, the first students who had graduated abroad returned home and were hired to teach at the Beijing Film Academy. Previously, the Academy had focused mainly on Soviet films, and its teachings followed the Russian model. But in the 1990s this changed as professors talked to us about European cinema, Japanese cinema, and later Korean cinema. In addition, every Tuesday we could watch

---

1. *Ballad of a Soldier* is a 1959 Soviet film directed by Grigori Chukrai; *The Cranes are Flying* is a 1957 Soviet film by Mikhael Kalatozov that won the Cannes Palme d'or in 1958. [Tr.]

two foreign films loaned by the China Film Archive. As several of our professors had studied abroad they remained in contact with the embassies. We saw many films thanks to the French Embassy, which lent feature films like Godard's *Pierrot le fou* and *First Name: Carmen*. I was seeing more and more films, and certain filmmakers began to attract my attention.

I was very impressed with Michelangelo Antonioni. The first film by him that I saw was *Red Desert*, which was shown in class to study color in film. But what really haunted me was the space of the factory, and the intense feeling of loneliness and alienation. Fascinated by Antonioni, I got a hold of all his films at the videotheque. Still today I have a particular fondness for *La Notte* and *Chung Kuo, Cina*. I love *La Notte*'s walking meditation: in leaving the book fair, the heroine roams the streets until she reaches the suburbs. By following her, we see all kinds of spaces. The scene where she sees young people lighting fireworks particularly stands out in my memory. When the fireworks went off, I imagined surreal visions, even planes and aircrafts. Suddenly, I had a revelation about space: how a space itself could be the film's protagonist, conveying emotions and important details. This revelation was entirely thanks to Antonioni.

I liked his films so much that I borrowed books about him from the library. We had a "Hong Kong and Taiwan reading room" at the Film Academy. It was called this because it collected books on cinema published in Hong Kong and Taiwan. I found there Taiwanese books on Antonioni and also interviews with him. In one interview I read that, when making a film, Antonioni would confer with the space for five minutes before filming. I liked this idea a lot as it showed I had understood his use of space. To me it was magical that a filmmaker could communicate with space.

Another important filmmaker for me is Robert Bresson. I like most of his films: *Mouchette*, *L'Argent*, *Diary of a Country Priest*. But the one that influenced me the most was *A Man Escaped*. It introduced me to temporality in cinema. The protagonist's daily gestures in prison—his use of objects— aid the audience in discovering duration as the prisoner himself experiences it. This film made me question the idea of narrative efficacy. Our screenwriting class had underlined the idea—adopted from the American model—that a narrative must be efficient, that every scene, each shot, must advance the plot. We were constantly told that the viewer must be able to follow the narrative from the first minute to the last. Perhaps efficiency is really a capitalist principle, but if you look at the great works of cinema—and this is true of literature too—you will find numerous examples to the contrary. Take Tarkovsky's *Andrei Rublev*: it's clear this kind of efficiency is of no interest to him, that the film is invested with his sensibility.

At the Academy I rediscovered films like Vittorio De Sica's *Bicycle Thieves*. I had seen it as a teenager when it was screened in my hometown, but remembered very little of it. We also watched De Sica's *Umberto D.* and *Miracle in Milan*. I love De Sica's vision of film; there is much instruction that can be drawn from it. For example, *Bicycle Thieves* taught me a lot about how to structure images, that there is a natural order to this structure: the passage from day to night, the wind, the rain, thunder and lightning. In the streets of Rome it suddenly begins to rain and the street vendors flee; the father and son take refuge under an awning and a religious group comes near. To me this is the poetry of daily life; the rain and its sound encourage a poetic moment within the quotidian.

In my last year at school we saw Kieślowski's films. We began with the *Dekalog*, which was the contemporary theory professor's favorite film. I especially liked *Blind Chance*, as it was produced when Poland was still completely closed.[2]

From Abbas Kiarostami I received a great lesson: formal simplicity. It was Professor Xie Fei who brought back two of his films from abroad. One was *Where is the Friend's House?*, and the other was *The Traveler*, a black and white film about a boy who wants to see a soccer game. I found his films very special. What most impressed me was their simple form, and how with this simplicity he reveals an intricate and rich philosophical thought.

Among the Asian directors, I was interested in two Japanese filmmakers. One was Yasujirō Ozu. Although his *Tokyo Story* is perfect, I prefer *Late Spring*, as its human feelings are more familiar to me. Ozu's films show the changes in traditional human relationships caused by industrialization, modernization, and transformation. These transformations in interpersonal

---

2. Kieślowski originally finished *Blind Chance* in 1981. Poland was under Martial law between December 13, 1981–July 22, 1983. The authorities finally released the film, in a censored form, in 1987. [Tr.]

relations, linked to economic and industrial upheavals, are very close to the experience of the Chinese in the 1990s. One example is *The Only Son* where you can see power plants with large smokestacks in the background. The protagonist's mother leaves the countryside to visit her son in Kyoto by train. In the city there is the beginning of train tracks and cars, but you see a horse is attached to a lamppost—a horse bearing witness to the agricultural era—and a child plays under the horse's belly. Yasujirō Ozu's films are always about family, but what inspired me the most is his focus on the change that modernization and industrialization brought to families, the impact these things had on human relationships.

I also like the films of Nagisa Ōshima, especially *Boy*. I like his way of presenting the family and his use of details. I remember a scene of rain, in which the little boy collects water in a hat. Thanks to a copy lent by the Film Archive, I also saw Akira Kurosawa's *Dersu Uzala*, which is about a hunter's life in the forest. I didn't really know what I thought of the film, but something moved me: the hunter leaves salt and matches for those who will later pass by. He's leaving people the means for survival. This most radiant aspect of humanity appears even in such a primitive environment. As I now work with Takeshi Kitano's studio, I often go to Tokyo to attend the Tokyo Filmex International Festival, organized by Shôzô Ichiyama, who co-produces my films. It's through him that I met Mrs. Teruyo Nogami, Akira Kurosawa's assistant. She's a lovely old woman. Every time she sees one of my films, she draws a caricature. I remember the drawing that she made of Wang Hongwei in *Xiaowu*. She also drew Wang Hongwei and Zhao Tao in *Still Life*. She worked with Kurosawa all her life, followed all the stages of his artistic development, and sometimes she tells me stories. She first began working with Kurosawa on *Rashômon* in 1949. In the film world, she represents the style of the older generation. I would really like to interview her—make a documentary about her—so that she can share her love stories and unforgettable memories.

During my studies I also learned more about Chinese cinema. In a Film Academy publication I read an interview with Hou Hsiao-hsien that was accompanied by an article on his work. In the 1980s, Hou Hsiao-hsien taught here, and he donated copies of all his films up until *A City of Sadness*. It was thanks to this that I discovered his films. I remember one morning, when passing by the performing arts building on the way to my class, I saw a bunch of students gathered at a small theater. When I asked them why they weren't going to class, they told me there was going to be a screening of Hou Hsiao-hsien's *The Boys from Fengkuei*. I really wanted to see it so I ran off to the classroom to speak to the professor of classical film theory, Zhong Dafeng. I said to him: "Professor Zhong, there's a film by Hou Hsiao-hsien showing, would you allow me to see it?" Professor Zhong said to the class of twelve students: "You all should go see it. I can hold class another day, a Saturday or Sunday, but it's not every day you have the opportunity to see a film by Hou. Go!"

The Boys from Fengkuei taught me the importance of personal experience in filmmaking, and it stayed in my mind a longtime after I saw it. It's the story of a group of young people in a fishing village in Taizan who leave their village to settle in the big city of Kaohsiung, the provincial capital. This is similar to the experience of many of my friends, including my own. I left a small city in Shanxi to study first in Taiyuan, and then Beijing. It took me a long time to understand how a Taiwanese film could describe my and my friends' life. The innocence and pent-up energy—everything in the film is familiar to me. There is a scene where the youths dance at water's edge, with a stormy sea in the background. The waves remind us of their desires and their passions, that they're difficult to calm. It reminds me of when my friends and I used to cry out to the sky after singing "One Night in Beijing." Our cries were like the boys' dance on the beach in *The Boys from Fengkuei*. Young people's feelings are the same everywhere. I realized how important personal experience was: Hou Hsiao-hsien had filmed his own experience, but its value was universal.

In order to understand what *The Boys from Fengkuei* inspired in me, you have to remember what Chinese cinema was like at the time. Starting from 1949, in accordance with the definition of revolutionary arts, Chinese cinema no longer showed individuals; it had lost its "me." Personal experience no longer had any value. What counted instead was the depiction of heroes, a legendary history had to be told in service to the revolution. Little by little, daily life and the "me" of individuals had disappeared from cinema. And here was a Taiwanese film that gave me access to the experience of someone very different from me, but in whom I recognized myself. It inspired my conception of cinema.

At the Academy I also rediscovered with renewed insight the films of King Hu,[3] films that had stayed with me. During my six years of college and high school I saw a lot of Kung Fu films in the video rooms of Fenyang, and it was his that most impressed me. After I finished my studies at the Beijing Film Academy, I saw *A Touch of Zen*, *Raining in the Mountain*, and *Legend of the Mountain*. Besides the fact they were martial arts films, I was impressed by the filmmaker's imagination in depicting Chinese society from the past; the films allowed me to anchor my understanding of time and space in this distant, half-legendary time. Watching them provided me with a key to the filmmaker. At the beginning of all King Hu's films you see a Chinese landscape: nature, the coastline, mountains, forest. But in reality he filmed everything in Korea or Taiwan! Hu was born on the continent, then left to live in Hong Kong, and filmed in Taiwan and Korea. He worked at the height of the Cultural Revolution when he was not allowed to shoot on the mainland. You feel a profound nostalgia in his films. The mountains and the streams of Korea evoke the mountains and streams of the Chinese countryside.

King Hu's cinema helped me understand the fundamental relationship between man and nature. The traditional Chinese painters appreciated landscapes, something I didn't immediately understand. In the old days people would value knowledge acquired by experience, and travel was an integral part of an education. Traveling from one place to another was a way of establishing a direct contact with the world and appreciating mountain and river landscapes was a way of multiplying experience. These long trips aroused new thoughts, the formation of an aesthetic and personal philosophy. Thanks to the Kung Fu films, I understood this relationship between mountains and water. There is also sadness because, for political reasons, King Hu couldn't film in this land that he never forgot and instead he had to film in South Korea.

---

3. The Chinese filmmaker and actor King Hu (1932-1997), like his older compatriot Mei Fu, was exiled from the mainland. Born in Beijing in 1932, Hu emigrated to Hong Kong after the founding of the People's Republic of China. He is best remembered for his *wuxia* films from the 1960s and 1970s. He worked in Hong Kong, Taiwan, and South Korea, and was offered sponsorship by South Korea if he made two films in a year, which gave rise to two of his best-loved films: *Raining in the Mountain* and *Legend of the Mountain*, both from 1979. He spent the final decade of his life in Los Angeles and died in Taipei in 1997. [Tr.]

When Edward Yang made *Yi Yi* in 2000, I had just finished my second feature, *Platform*. That year, after Zhao Tao and I attended the Toronto Film Festival, we went to Paris where we saw it. I immediately felt Yang had found a great approach for depicting Chinese society, depicting relationships in a just and meaningful way. This was shown in the way the protagonist (played by Wu Nien-jen) behaves with his wife, former mistress, children, and friends. The relationships he has are complex and undergo great changes. Yang was able to reveal the *essence* of the Chinese people. I was deeply moved by his ability to show both the life of a specific individual, and the world to which he belongs.

I also liked Yang's *A Brighter Summer Day*. I especially remember a scene in which two characters are walking in a suburb pushing their bicycles when they see soldiers practicing pistol shooting. This scene is very familiar to me as, when I was little, I would often go to the suburbs with my friends to watch soldiers or militiamen practice their shooting skills. At that time, every work unit had a militia battalion, which would train once a year. In seeing this scene, I noticed the similarity: in Taiwan, under the governance of the nationalist party, as on the continent under the governance of the Communist party, people lived through a period of militarization and tension where a war could break out any day. The shadow of militarized war was a part of daily life. The New Taiwanese Cinema—Hou Hsiao-hsien and Edward Yang's films specifically—helped us to overcome the partisan vision that divided the world up into "friends" and "enemies." Through these films we began to understand everyday life in Taiwan, while before we had been hostile to it. Previously, although we would often speak about Taiwan, it was always in a political or military context. How did people live there? What did they eat? What did they drink? How did they flirt? What were their sorrows and their joys? We knew none of this, nothing of their real existence, but would speak all the time about them regardless.

Just as Hou and Yang's films helped us to understand what was happening in Taiwan, so too the arrival in Taiwan of the first films of the Fifth Generation filmmakers—such as those by Zhang Yimou and Chen Kaige—helped the Taiwanese to better understand us.

For me, Chen Kaige's *Yellow Earth* remains the most important of these. It's the film that encouraged me to become a filmmaker, despite the fact I saw it late. During the 1980s and up until the 1990s, the filmmakers of the Fifth Generation were very creative in their use of filmic language, and in the way they reflected on Chinese history and traditions. Their revolt had an enormous cultural impact, loosening ideological constraints, although from around 1992 or 1993 film censorship did become stricter. The topics addressed by the Fifth Generation reflected the pressures of censorship. Also, from this time, the film industry became stylistically conformist, primarily seeking commercial success. The market and censorship guided this transition, forcing filmmakers to choose more consensus-based subjects and to privilege an approach favored by the general public, far from the ambitions of independent cinema. Chen Kaige with *Farewell My Concubine* and Zhang Yimou with *Shanghai Triad* tried, and succeeded, in making a more commercial cinema. They had chosen a new direction.

My Helpless City, My Homeland
By Jia Zhangke

I WAS TWENTY-THREE years old when I enrolled in the Beijing Film Academy. Most of my classmates were teenagers who had just graduated from high school, and I was five years older. Unlike them, I had no time to lose. For me, it was the end of being carefree. Back home in Fenyang most men of my age were already married and probably had a child. My friends were already proudly sporting the mustache traditionally worn by the head of the family, as they traveled in our provincial city on bicycle with wife and children.

I had already lost interest in playing sports with my classmates. I abandoned boxing, which I had been practicing early in the morning, and also stopped playing soccer in the afternoons. Those around me thought that I had become calm and wise, but actually I was just exhausted by the state of the world, and anxious about the future.

At the end of the day, I would watch my classmates leave the Film Academy in search of adventure. For them, life still had all its freshness but I already felt old. In the evening, my favorite place to be was the study room where we could smoke. I would bring green graph paper and a pen, sit down, light a cigarette, and start to write. There wouldn't be many people there, and everyone seemed sad. At first glance, it was clear that these were the hopelessly single outsiders. We were a handful of intellectuals experiencing hardship.

My cheap pen would make its way over the green graph paper, and, little by little, I would lose myself in my imagination until I forgot who I was. To forget oneself is to want nothing—this gave me a vague feeling of what happiness could be. While my young classmates were having fun, I instead propelled myself into the past: every time I faced a blank piece of paper, my mind would escape to the region where I grew up, this faraway place called Fenyang—my helpless city, my homeland.

I had lived in Fenyang until the age of twenty-one and had tried writing poems and painting there. To escape the ghosts of my past I settled down to write their stories by the pale light of the green lamp on my desk. I began to write *Platform*, which describes the adventures of a theatrical troupe in my hometown in the 1980s. At the time, there were always stories and romantic adventures about this kind of company. I grew up in the 1980s, was ten in 1980, and, from then until now, the changes in Chinese society have been cataclysmic, as violent as sulfuric acid on the ground. I've often wondered why I was so sentimental and nostalgic for this period.

I would cry whenever I was writing. I could hear only the scribbling of my pen, followed by the sound of my tears falling on the paper. This sound is familiar to me. It's the sound of the first summer storm in Fenyang, the sound of water falling on parched earth—white and hard, it would become black little by little from the drops. It was the sound of a downpour hitting the branches of the apple trees in our garden. The rain would nourish the apple trees, making them grow and ripening their fruit. My tears fell on the blank pages of my notebook and nurtured my screenplay, aiding its development until it was done. Works of art need watering just as much as plants.

The finished screenplay consisted of five hundred thousand words and approximately one hundred and fifty scenes. As this amounts to at least three months of shooting, it was clear the film couldn't be made anytime soon.

A landscape always seems more beautiful if perceived from afar, and unhappy people prefer to step back and watch the world from a distance. One evening, while leaning out of my dorm window and gazing into the distance, I noticed that the Beijing Studio was illuminated. In order to ease my anxiety, I donned my military coat and went to watch the shoot. A fire was bursting forth everywhere in the glacial cold of the night—Corey Yuen was shooting *The Legend of Fong Sai-yuk*. Suddenly, a baby's cry was heard. Going closer, I saw Jet Li, who was performing martial arts with dangerous weapons while carrying a newborn before the blazing fire.

At that time the successful formula for a film was "action and love." In thinking about the screenplay I had just written, I questioned who would finance it. So I gave up on the idea of directing it, hoping that one day it would be published in the form of a novel. Time passed in a lightning flash and, as graduation approached, students went off in groups to shoot their films in every corner of the country. I was left alone to endlessly pace back and forth in the hallway of the sixth floor, listening to the sound of my own footsteps in an atmosphere reminiscent of the Coen Brothers' *Barton Fink*.

Around that time it was the Chinese New Year, so everyone, even a penniless fellow like myself, headed home. The highway between Beijing and

Taiyuan hadn't been finished so it took fourteen hours to get to Fenyang by train. Upon my arrival, I was greeted by many large signs plastered to the facades of stores saying things like, "To be destroyed." Finally I reached home, to the delight of my parents. I sat alone, contemplative in the sunshine, while they were busy preparing food. That afternoon of smoke, steam, and fire coming from the kitchen is vivid in my memory. We sat down at the table in front of the family dishes that my parents had prepared, and I told them stories from the outside world. My father said: "You've come at a good time. The old neighborhood is going to be demolished."

I abruptly left the table and ran at full speed toward the city. I looked at the houses that were several hundred years old, the shops I had frequented since childhood. My heart stood still at the idea that all of this would soon disappear. Of course I knew I couldn't prevent these radical changes from taking place. Everyone has their own mission in their time: the abortive Hundred Days' Reform[1] in the last years of the Qing dynasty, the Revolution instigated by the Sun Yatsen generation,[2] the students' May Fourth movement at the beginning of the Republic.[3] For me, confronted with my old neighborhood as it was about to be razed, it became my fate to film the cataclysmic turmoil happening in China. This was the challenge I set myself when I was twenty-seven years old.

At home in Fenyang, I began to write, solitary like a long-distance runner. From the appearance of the first character until the end of the story, you have to write, word after word, alone in the creative act. No-one can help you. As in a marathon, others can certainly encourage you, but it's always you who runs, one step after another—it's the same when you're writing a screenplay. My desk was covered with crumpled up papers as I kept writing and discarding things. Finally, I wrote the line: "A friend of Jin Xiaoyong, a neighbor of the Pin family, son of Liang Zhangyou: Xiaowu." This kind of

---

1. The Hundred Days' Reform took place between June 11 and September 22, 1898. [Tr.]

2. The Chinese Revolution of 1911 led to the end of imperial rule and the Qing dynasty and the establishment of the Republic of China. [Tr.]

3. The May Fourth Movement, which developed from the student protests in Beijing on May 4, 1919, was an anti-imperialist, cultural and political movement. [Tr.]

a title was worthy of the *People's Daily*.[4] During the Cultural Revolution, if you wanted to denounce a "reactionary enemy," you had to expose his private life[5] so it's hardly surprising human relationships were profoundly shaken. This title was interesting but a little long. In the end I withdrew all the specifics, retaining just the given name: Xiaowu.

Once the screenplay was finished, I went to the post office by bike. There, in the long-distance telephone room, the attendant succeeded in reaching a friend of mine in Hong Kong who had a little money. I told him I wanted to shoot *Xiaowu* and asked him if he wanted to finance it. This abrupt request made him uncomfortable—he said he would think about it, and needed to read the screenplay first. To my great surprise there was a fax machine at the post office so I made a momentous decision: I would spend a fortune—five hundred yuans[6]—to fax the screenplay to Hong Kong. The next day, I called my friend in Hong Kong; he said he liked *Xiaowu* and agreed to produce it!

The date of April 10th, the first day of *Xiaowu*'s shoot, is forever fixed in my memory, as if it was the birthdate of my child. It was still cold and the crew was burning incense. In the street, surrounded by this holy smoke, I knelt down and begged for help from all the gods and spirits: the Empress Wu of the Tang Dynasty, the Great Ancestor of the Ming Dynasty, and the Lumière brothers. These prayers allowed me to accomplish one thing: this time, my writings would be transformed into film.

With *Xiaowu* I earned my stripes as a young filmmaker, something I immediately capitalized on by then shooting *Platform*. Somewhat conceitedly I considered *Xiaowu* and *Platform* as the story of my hometown. I then began to think of a third film in order to form a "homeland trilogy," following Gorky's acclaimed three-part model: *My Childhood, In the World,* and *My Universities,* and the Chinese example: Ba Jin's *The Torrent: Family, Spring, and Autumn*.

---

4. The *People's Daily* is an official newspaper of the Central Committee of the Communist Party. Published worldwide, it has a circulation of 3 million. [Tr.]

5. For more on this topic of the profound upset in personal relations during the Cultural Revolution, please see Tania Branigan's article, "China's Cultural Revolution: Son's Guilt over the Mother He Sent to Her Death," *The Guardian*, March 27, 2013. [Tr.]

6. This sum equaled approximately a third of the rural household net income in Shanxi in 1997, which was 1,557 yuans. [Tr.]

The early days of the new century brought major changes to the film industry. First, there was the flood of bootleg DVDs that made film culture accessible to all. Then the arrival of the DV camera triggered a new wave of independent cinema. The International Film Festival of Jeonju in South Korea selected three international directors including me, and financed thirty-minute shorts from us to be shot on DV on the topic of "Space." I looked for inspiration by wandering in the region of the Datong coal mine, beyond the Great Wall, soaking up the atmosphere from the buildings of the planned economy period. Constructed in the 1950s, these mines, factories, and dormitories were the distinguished achievements of a now bygone era. Today, they're desert ruins in a no man's land, divorced from the world. By opening the large door of the workers' club you would find an enormous room with thousands of seats, a room that you can imagine was once very animated during popular gatherings. But today it's just a cavernous space covered with dust. In Datong you often see young people walking around all alone. They're so different from the youths of my childhood! In my day we were always in a group, invading the streets and feasts. Today they hurry along in the streets wearing sports clothes, with headphones fixed to their ears. In the cybercafes you only hear the sound of typing on keyboards. Young people connect to the world through their computers and, even though they're cramped together, no one speaks to each other. Although their lives may be carefree, they're nonetheless prisoners of technology. In this isolated city I decided on my next project: to film this youth.

The world works in mysterious ways. While traveling on a long-distance bus from Beijing, I heard a news item involving a robbery by a young man in northeast China. He wanted to write his last words to his mother, but didn't know how to confess his theft. So he transcribed the words of a popular song called "Ren xiao yao."[7] I didn't know this song, but was very moved by his gesture. Getting off the bus, I ran to the audiovisual market to buy the song. After having heard it, I understood that it was surely the following

---

7. *Ren xiao yao*, the film's original title (international title *Unknown Pleasures*) is a song by the Taiwanese actor and pop star, Richie Jen. The title can be translated as: "I am free and carefree." *Unknown Pleasures* is the title of an album by the English band Joy Division. It was Yu Lik-wai, the film's cinematographer, who suggested its use for the film's international title. Yu Lik-wai also directed a film himself, *Love Will Tear Us Apart*, named after a Joy Division song.

phrase that had touched the young man: "…the hero was born modest and insignificant." It was as if he was speaking about me, a young fellow born in a desolate place who makes films. Yes, the force of youth lies in its disappointment with how the world is.

This "Homeland Trilogy"—consisting of *Xiaowu*, *Platform*, and *Unknown Pleasures*—is the result of my discontent with the current world. With these films I focused on the days, nights, people, and countless unforgettable events in Fenyang, a small, marginal city hidden in the Lüliang Mountains. I made three films about it. My cinema is my country, a world made up of modest characters and even insignificant things.

I would like to make a confession. I've often wondered why I like art. Although I have other undisclosed motives, I have continued to write because there are still so many things that need to be changed, and against which I am fighting. Here is my favorite self-portrait: an exceptionally stubborn intellectual who happens to be a little daft.

How Many Trees Are Needed to Cover Tiananmen Square?
By Jia Zhangke

THE CULTURAL REVOLUTION finished the year before I entered elementary school. Barely had one movement ended, before another one began. Adults at the time were preoccupied with "punishing revolutionary disturbances" in their work units. As they were in meetings day and night, they were rarely at home. So we children were left alone without authority. Aimless and carefree, we overran the streets in groups, multiplying like wild weeds. At the time, it seemed as if only youths occupied the streets: unmonitored children of six to seven years and the young, twenty-year-old unemployed people from peasant and lumber camps. We loitered and wasted time. Other than the cinema we had nowhere to go, so we just had fun in the streets. Young adults, grouped together on corners, would play the harmonica or would read. Although we kids didn't interrupt them, we watched them from a distance so as to vicariously take part in their activities.

Photo: Jia Zhangke at the age of 6.

One day several of us were chatting at an intersection, and the roar of a motorcycle was heard far off. Everyone became quiet and looked off in the direction of the sound. A motorcycle approached: a postal worker delivering a telegram. Our gaze followed the motorcycle as it moved away. After the postal worker disappeared into another street, one of the transfixed older boys said thoughtfully: "That's the dream of my life, to have a motorcycle!" In those days it was a luxury just to have a bicycle; only public authorities at the post office and the prefecture had motorcycles. When the young man made this admission, no one took him seriously as, in those days, wanting a motorcycle wasn't a dream, but pure fantasy.

Then, two years later, for reasons I don't know, there was an influx of motorcycles in the streets. People bought Jialin brand mopeds, which were fabricated in Chongqinq. Even though these mopeds were much smaller than the prefecture's "250 model," they were still the first motor vehicle widely available for personal use. Walking to school I would encounter young people straddling their mopeds, erect as statues in the drivers' seat. Suddenly what had been a utopia was now a reality, a sign of even more magical things to come. Another surprise: some months after having seen in school the film "New Aspects of the Great Fatherland," about the manufacture of washing machines by a Shanghai factory, we had one at home! Life began changing at a breakneck speed. Over the last decade or so, the disruption has been so rapid due to the constant influx of new technology and products that we've had no time to adapt—television, tape recorders, digital watches, washing machines, computers, the Internet have all been parachuted into our lives.

But these new consumer possibilities have not been accompanied by similar surprises in other areas. In middle school I read Lu Yao's novel *Life*.[1] The main character, Gao Jialin, abandons his life as a farmer to go work in a provincial city, but is ultimately sent back to the country by government powers without having earned anything and after sacrificing his love. In reading this novel, I understood why my classmates, who were from the country, worked so hard. Their biggest dream was to pass the entrance exam for the teacher's training college as, once accepted, they would be allowed to permanently live in the city. The novel led me to believe that the unrea-

---

1. First published in 1982 and winner of the Mao Dun Literature Prize. [Tr.]

sonable and inhumane system of "residency permits" would soon disappear, as abruptly as motorcycles had appeared. But I was wrong. The system of "residency permits" still exists. And, recently, the city of Beijing initiated a new policy to monitor buying a car. I have learned it's no longer possible for me to buy a car because I have a "residence" in the Shanxi province. Our life changes as if by magic: it seems some wishes can be granted immediately and miraculously, while many others remain firmly out of reach.

In the 1980s the Chinese people experienced radical, consecutive changes as a result of the economic reforms. These reforms led us to believe life's possibilities were infinite, and were prompted by the organic needs of the system itself. Today, our loss of faith in that system prevents it from evolving, and instead, we base our expectations for change on complete reform. That's the Chinese way, it's how our culture works. Obviously, this has a profound effect on our lives. If we are to change our lives, perhaps we need first to change our culture. Of course we yearn for freedom, democracy, equality, and justice. But it must be done in a Chinese manner, compatible with our history. Of course this rule shouldn't affect what's at stake: freedom is freedom, just like equality is equality *tout court*.

I remember once the architect Ma Yansong was very eager to show me the model for his renovation of Tiananmen Square. In his model this historic site was completely covered with trees, malls, karaoke bars, film theaters, etc. How many trees are needed to completely cover Tiananmen Square? Never mind. The essential idea is to transform this public space once reserved for political rallies into a beautiful site for everyday use and enjoyment.[2]

---

2. Tiananmen Square is a deeply symbolic site. Mao Zedong declared the founding of the People's Republic of China in the square on October 11, 1949. The largest city square in the world, it's occupied by Soviet-style monuments, museums, as well as the mausoleum of Mao Zedong. Tiananmen means the Gate of Heavenly Peace. [Tr.]

afterword

Ulaanbaatar
By Walter Salles

A friend of mine says that if you admire a filmmaker, you like all of their films. This is a precept I would like to follow but rarely manage to. But Jia Zhangke is, for me, the exception that proves the rule. All of his films have transported me to unknown places, resonating for a long time, with repeated viewings only deepening their value. If, as Amos Gitai says, a film begins when the lights in the theater come up, then for me Jia's films never end.

How to talk about a filmmaker who is essential for me? Perhaps by describing the way his films constantly replay in my memory.

In one of *Platform*'s first scenes, a group of young people are talking in a house in Fenyang:

– Where is Ulaanbaatar?
– In the north.
– More exactly?
– In Mongolia. It's the capital.
– And further north, what is there?
– What do you care? The northern sea.
– And still further north?
– You'll find yourself back here, in Fenyang.

This scene leaves an impression of displacement, and also of fascination. It's the first film by Jia that I saw, and it was a revelation. In brilliant long takes the film covers the experiences, over ten years from 1979 to 1989, of a troupe of young actors from northern China. Like all great films, *Platform* is many things at once: a film about a generation longing for a future, about wandering and exile, about the search for our place in the world, the "wider world" that the characters evoke. The film is also a view of a country which, in a decade, had passed brutally from Maoist orthodoxy and a planned economy to a socialist market economy. Furthermore it's a delicate and honed reflection on time, unrequited yearnings, and lost ideals.

Jia treats his characters with a mixture of modesty and affection, but not sentimentality, something which is increasingly rare in cinema. We feel his proximity to the material: each situation is inhabited, seems to possess a dramatic depth, and sets us on unexpected paths. Moments of silence are full and expressive. We find ourselves confronted with the obvious: the emergence of a great filmmaker.

For a film of such complexity, we never feel the presence of the crew. The structure of the script, or of the shot—the position of the camera—never shows. Actors and non-actors perform in the same range. It's as if history is unfolding before our eyes, and could only be told like this. Even when Jia composes sequences as memorable as the one where his two main characters, Mingliang (Wang Hongwei) and Ruijuan (Zhao Tao), timidly talk in front of the walls surrounding the city of Fenyang, nothing seems choreographed. A feeling of lightness, an impression of capturing an unusual state, takes hold of the viewer.

This is thanks to the co-existence of seeming opposites: Jia's cinema is both enormously ingenious and discreet. It's this that enables unparalleled sequences of poetry, like the moment when Ruijuan, working alone in a dusty office, hears a song by Teresa Teng on the radio. She gets up, hazards a few movements—one or two dance steps—and allows herself to be carried away by the melody. The effect is striking but never demonstrative.

As the seasons pass and the group of friends mature, the world seems to shift around them. While the film's action often unfolds in silence, at other times it's brutal. The interior world of the characters deteriorates as the feudal city where they live turns into a huge construction site—modernization accomplished by force. Jia presents this process of deconstruction and loss of identity—as much individual as collective—without ever passing judgment. No one's trajectory is exemplary. His characters simply bear witness to their time, to something that's on the point of disappearing. The camera enables the recording of how this time of turbulent transformation was experienced.

Another element gives rhythm to this unique film: the train, which symbolizes the characters' desire for escape and movement. Early in the film it appears symbolically, when the young actors imitate its whistle. In a circular structure, it then reappears in the last scene of the film, when Mingliang and Ruijuan finally live together under the same roof. But the whistling is no longer their friends' voice: it's the noise of a kettle as the water comes to a boil. The sound is daily and familiar—there is no longer movement or displacement, only waiting and silence.

In a narrative and poetic sense, Jia shows an unusual understanding of filmic space and cinema's possibilities. *Platform* is permeated by a greenish light, the color that characterizes Jia's memories of these years. It is the only one of his films shot on 35 mm, a format that lends itself well to a recreation of the scattered memories of the 1970s and 1980s.

Xiaowu, or *The Stranger*

Xiaowu, Jia's first film, started out at the Berlin Forum where it won the prize for best film. That year my film *Central Station* was also screening at the Berlinale. Discovering the work of other filmmakers at a festival when you are presenting your own work is no easy task, and I didn't see *Xiaowu* until shortly after *Platform*. With both films I felt a shock of discovery, doubly so with *Xiaowu*.

While *Platform* is made up of long takes where time seems to slowly elapse, *Xiaowu* reflects the urgency of its period and is told largely with a handheld camera. At the end of the 1990s, when the story takes place, the city of Fenyang is undergoing a metamorphosis. The word "demolition" appears everywhere in the streets. The new order subjects the characters to the law of the market and privatization. In this world, where competition increases and efficiency is an undisputed value, Xiaowu, the young pickpocket returning to Fenyang, feels like a stranger. He wanders from one place to another without recognizing the streets where he grew up. One of his childhood friends, another pickpocket, has changed profession: he's become a prosperous seller of contraband cigarettes. This friend is preparing his wedding party. His wealth provides him with a secure social standing, something Xiaowu refuses to accept—although a complete cynic and a thief, he's the film's ethical standard bearer. *Xiaowu* is organized around this unexpected contradiction and the brilliant performance of the young actor Wang Hongwei, who would become Jia's alter ego. It runs contrary to the constant action we've become accustomed to experiencing in cinema.

The crux of the plot revolves around simply following the protagonist as he wanders through his hometown. Like Antonioni, Jia understands that suspended time is loaded with meaning and emotion. Bresson's *Pickpocket* isn't far off either, and the film's title in French (*Xiaowu, artisan pickpocket*) reminds us of that. But nothing in Jia is derivative. This is a cinema that expresses a personal and unique vision.

As with *Platform*, the question of love is central to the narrative with Xiaowu's relationship with Meimei, the young woman who works in a karaoke bar, leading one part of the story. Jia's focus on loneliness and the difficulty of finding a foothold in a reality where the past and present are vanishing, reveal him as a sensitive chronicler of his time. But this is no mere chronicle.

The film's strong documentary basis—recording a culture in an accelerated process of upheaval—leads to moments of reflection and bewilderment, where the camera, stationary, looks at Xiaowu from a distance without interference. This manipulation of time, sometimes so fast and brutal, and at other times slow and suspended, enables *Xiaowu* to escape documentary naturalism.

The end of the film reinforces this feeling. Handcuffed, Xiaowu is led to the police station by an officer. After having walked a moment in the street, the policeman ties him to a lamppost. Exhibited to the public, Xiaowu squats down. People stop to watch the scene, staring at him and also at the camera, demolishing cinema's fourth wall. Everything interacts, and suddenly the cinema seems more alive and vigorous than ever before.

Xiaowu is the first collaboration between Jia and his cinematographer, Yu Lik-wai, and was shot on super 16 mm. The coarse grain texture testifies to the violence of a period whose references are fast disappearing, like the centuries-old architecture. A film of great force, *Xiaowu* offers a deconstruction of the past as well as of those who refuse to submit to the new order.

The Floating Ones[1]

The World is Jia's fourth film, and the first to be officially distributed in China. From the opening scene, we know that we are in a Jia film: the camera follows a young dancer Tao (played by Zhao Tao) through backstage corridors, as she looks for a band-aid. The sequence shot reveals the pre-performance chaos, and the young people who work there. But this is no ordinary theater. The dancers are performing in a theme park near Beijing, one where it's possible to visit the Eiffel Tower, the Vatican, the Twin Towers, or the Egyptian pyramids.

What interests Jia here isn't the visitors to the park but the "floating ones," the young people who have arrived from other parts of China to find work in this strange universe. The turmoil of youth, displacement, internal immigration, and loneliness are recurrent themes in Jia's cinema, but here they're expressed differently. While *Platform*'s characters dreamt of the "wider world," in *The World* the unknown no longer exists. The World theme park, with its shrunken models of real buildings, is representative of the spatial and temporal implosion caused by globalization—space and time are here collapsed.

This standardization isn't without consequence. Its effect is painful and touches everyone in the film. In a universe marked by desensitization, Jia manages to endow his characters with a rare humanity. The lack of communication, so important for Antonioni, makes way for the possibility of a dialogue, like the friendship that develops between Tao and Anna, the Russian dancer who has left her two children back home. *Ulaanbaatar* is a leitmotif in Jia's œuvre: here it's a Russian song about a city, unknown to both Tao and Anna, that briefly unites them.

The young people of *The World*, despite the illusion of traveling, are uprooted, disoriented migrants who are stuck in place. Their terrifying predicament is straight out of Orwell. At the same time they're also lured by technology's equally deceptive bait of omnipresence. The brief respite af-

---

1. Salles' reference here evokes the *ukiyo-e*, meaning the floating, fleeting or transient world that describes the urban lifestyle, particularly its hedonistic aspects, of Edo-period Japan (1600–1867) famously immortalized in Japanese woodblock prints. [Tr.]

forded by the Internet and cell phones only proves the opposite. So the characters are imprisoned by both the park *and* technology. Much like the park, the digital world reduces, creating banalizing images and nourishing simulacra. But since we're in a Jia film, where the imagination is given free-reign, animated SMS messages suddenly occupy the entire screen. In this world where everything seems controlled, an unlikely collision between fiction and animation takes place. An impure film, ultimately *The World* is the antithesis of the theme park that it depicts, with its lure of infinite possibilities.

The high-definition video imagery of *The World* reinforces the sanitized nature of the superficial modernization. This digital image abolishes the mishaps and unpredictable grain of celluloid. Everything seems flat and overly exposed, like a magazine's laminated cover. This increasingly dominant representation of the world contrasts with Jia's uncynical vision. It's perhaps this contrast that gives the film its resonance long after it has ended.

In traditional Chinese painting part of the picture would always be enveloped in mist; people were supposed to imagine what existed beyond the visible. The representation of physical space was meant to be incomplete, and reality fragmented. In this film, the universe of simulacrum enters into a collision with this vision of the world, and Jia generously provides us the possibility of finishing the picture and the story through the cinema.

Yangtze, Year Zero

The setting feels unreal. An ancient city in southern China, Fengjie, is about to be devoured by the biggest dam ever built, the Three Gorges. It's there, among hundreds of buildings being demolished and thousands of displaced persons, that we find *Still Life*'s two protagonists. They don't know each other but have a common goal, as both are looking for relatives they haven't seen in a longtime. Sanming is looking for his ex-wife and the sixteen-year-old daughter he's never met. Shenhong (Zhao Tao) is looking for her husband whom she's not heard from in three years. Although both try to save part of their lives, the film's real subject here is the fragmentation of the country's memory. *Still Life* is fueled by the desire to maintain individual memories in the face of the destruction of collective memory. Rossellini isn't far off—although nothing here is derivative of other filmmakers.

A plot resume might lead one to think that such an urgent theme would be shot with handheld camerawork closely following the characters. The unique qualities that Jia achieves with *Still Life* rest in part on the fact that, on the contrary, this delicate odyssey is filmed in long takes with human and physical geographies intertwined. These sequence shots, in which silence is more important than what is said, alternate with documentary shots depicting the demolition of the city, marking the passage of time. The stories of Sanming and Shenhong never intersect, but do constantly reverberate against each other. Things happen without either psychology or explanation, but always have a meaning. The cumulative effect is intoxicating.

In such a gigantic setting, it's the small objects of daily life that have the greatest force of expression. Belonging—what makes us belong to a place—is revealed in the drawing of a river or a mountain on a worn banknote. Even the way one drinks tea is meaningful, revealing as it does one's origins. A cigarette is shared between two people in a small hotel with moldy walls. A caramel. A torn glove on the ground. The contrast between what is mundane—apparently of no importance—with the vast dimension of the construction of the dam is integral to the film, but also of cinema as Jia understands it. These are small clues that encourage reflection on the impermanence of things.

In the midst of such brutal changes, the protagonists can react only with discrete emotion. For example, the moment when Shenhong succeeds in finding her husband is emotionally charged, but no room is left for an overt expression of their feelings in their last moments together. The dignity and vulnerability that Zhao Tao manages to convey in this scene is remarkable. As for Sanming, his physique expresses his way of digesting life's blows and makes him an unusually complex character.

There are moments in *Still Life* when the buildings literally take flight. The first time I saw the film, I was astonished by its combination of special effects with an aesthetic so akin to documentary. Seeing the film again allowed me to understand how these images respond to a logic that's already, by definition, surreal. Such shots also epitomize Jia's unique cinema and the way in which it expresses so clearly an ongoing revolt against the established order.

In a screenplay that he never shot, *Techniquement douce (Technically Soft)*[2] Antonioni wrote: "There is a theory that says man lives in a state of unstable equilibrium, which over the years increasingly stabilizes, until he finds an absolute equilibrium. That is death." In the last sequence of *Still Life*, a man walks on a wire stretched between two buildings. The unstable equilibrium calls to mind what Antonioni said, but what interests Jia is the survival of his characters, their resistance. If there is a way out, Jia shows that it's in humanity.

Imagined Territory

Fragments of Jia's other films recur on a loop in my mind. *24 City* is one of them. Its first image references the birth of cinema, when the Lumière brothers filmed workers leaving the Lumière factory in Lyon in 1895. The beginning of Jia's film shows workers leaving the factory of Chengdu, in the Sichuan province. But this factory's days are numbered. The warehouses where warplanes were once constructed are going to be transformed into luxury residences. Under the new economic order, the factory will be demolished as it's no longer profitable. Consequently, the workers must abandon the world that defines them. With the relationship to their work attenuated, they too will become "floating." *24 City* is a documentary on the loss of identity, and the transient nature of urban geography in contemporary China.

Here, as in other films, what interests Jia is filming the effect of this transformation on human beings, as one world yields its place to another. The testimony of the factory workers melds into the monologues of the four female actors invited to play workers, or the daughters of workers. Fiction and documentary are combined. Some of Yeats' verse fills the screen. During its Cannes screening in 2008, *24 City* baffled many, but perhaps the

---

2. Michelangelo Antonioni, *Techniquement douce*, translated from the Italian into French by Anna Burese and Aldo Tassone (Paris: Albatros, 1978). This work does not appear to have been translated into English. [Tr.]

audience's confusion is actually a signal of its vitality, echoing Antonioni's experiences there.³ From an emotional as well as visual perspective, Jia understands that the cinema needs to reinvent itself in order to survive.

In Public, the medium-length documentary made shortly before *Unknown Pleasures*, is one of those silent masterpieces that reveal unexpected elements at every screening. Shot in train stations, bus stations, and other means of transportation in northern China, *In Public* addresses the displacement of workers. It's one of Jia's films that has most affected me. A great formal freedom leads us from one situation to another, and it's impossible not to become hypnotized by these faces, or imagine what could be happening behind each of these people.

A Touch of Sin made me think of my home country Brazil, and also of Antonioni. In our increasingly globalized world, explosions of violence have become increasingly unpredictable, but also banal, and this is true everywhere. *A Touch of Sin* is about China, but its reality exists close to home for all of us. In the film Jia organizes a quartet of distinct but complementary stories. In several locations in China, we see men and women refuse to continue submitting themselves to a ruling revealed as unjust. Their violence is a form of expression, a way to give voice to those who aren't usually heard.

Again Antonioni comes to mind: "I think that the weapons used by the oppressed against their oppressors are very civilized instruments. And too bad for morality." What distinguishes Jia's perspective is his refusal to judge his characters, even when they're involved in extreme situations. The cinema for Jia isn't a court. Similarly his characters refuse to pose as martyrs. They're ordinary people who sometimes take a stand.

During one of our conversations, Jia wondered what the characters of *Platform*, who dreamt of what lay beyond the walls of Fenyang, would think if they saw *The World*. In addition, he would have liked to know how the character of Xiaowu in the eponymous film would have perceived the documented reality in *A Touch of Sin*. What makes Jia's cinema unique is

---

3. Antonioni's *L'Avventura* was booed in its Cannes premiere but won the Jury Prize and went on to become an international hit. [Tr.]

precisely that he's remained in touch with these extremely rapid and often brutal transformations, and that he's succeeded in conveying them so clearly. Despite being polysemic, his work is extremely coherent. Each film refers to another, like the musical notes of songs that accompany his projects.

The first time that we met in Fenyang, Jia told us that as a child, he was fascinated by the sound of the icy wind coming from Ulaanbaatar. As a student, he asked for a visa to travel there, but never made the trip. Ulaanbaatar is like an imagined territory, never reached. I sincerely hope that Jia never makes it to Mongolia so that his uneasy imagination will continue to transport us to an equally fascinating territory: that of humankind's possibilities.

Songs from Jia's Soundtracks

1. Teresa Teng's "The Moon Represents My Heart"
   https://www.youtube.com/watch?v=-B5gAczFJps

2. Cui Jian's "Nothing to My Name"
   https://www.youtube.com/watch?v=kYwsPt854Xo

3. Dschinghis Kahn's "Dschinghis Kahn"
   https://www.youtube.com/watch?v=pzmI3vAIhbE

4. George Lam's "Dschinghis Khan"
   https://www.youtube.com/watch?v=gPJQUGarDN4

5. Leslie Cheung's "Monica"
   https://www.youtube.com/watch?v=zdx9eFjN7W4

6. Cui Jian's "Let Me Go Wild in the Snow"
   https://www.youtube.com/watch?v=q6LxK4UIkac

7. Cui Jian's "A Piece of Red Cloth"
   https://www.youtube.com/watch?v=OspWXXBEo4A

8. Xin Yue Tuan's "One Night in Beijing"
   https://www.youtube.com/watch?v=6-E-qmtDPKk

9. Richie Jen's "Ren xiao yao" (I am Free and Carefree)
   https://www.youtube.com/watch?v=FbEjRgAoj3I

10. Yang Kun's "The Girl Under the Street Lamp"
    https://www.youtube.com/watch?v=dlrB6X2LWm0

11. Sally Yeh's "Run without Care"
    https://www.youtube.com/watch?v=v3eS-Htswlw

MAPPING JIA'S CINEMA

This map associates the titles of Jia's films with the principal locations where the films take place, and/or were shot. While not exhaustive, this map testifies to Jia's broad and diverse coverage of Chinese territory in his cinema, coupled with a certain presence in the rest of the world, a very rare phenomenon among Chinese filmmakers.

Bashang Grassland (4)

Dunhuang (17)

Kazak Autonomous County of Aksay (17)

Paris (10)

REF	TITLE
(1)	One Day, in Beijing
(2)	Xiaoshan Going Home
(3)	Xiaowu
(4)	Platform
(5)	In Public
(6)	Unknown Pleasures
(7)	The World
(8)	Still Life
(9)	Dong
(10)	Useless
(11)	24 City
(12)	I Wish I Knew
(13)	A Touch of Sin
(14)	Mountains May Depart
(15)	Cry Me a River
(16)	Swimming Out Till the Sea Turns Blue
(17)	Ash Is Purest White

Suggested Further Reading and Viewing

The literature on Jia Zhangke is already extensive. The following directs the reader's attention primarily to monographs, interviews, and general articles in English. Also included are three general works on recent Chinese cinema and Walter Salles' documentary.

Andrew, Dudley. "The Absent Subject of *The World*." *Journal of Chinese Cinemas* 12, no. 1 (2018): 59-73.

Berry, Chris. *Postsocialist Cinema in Post-Mao China: The Cultural Revolution after the Cultural Revolution*. New York: Routledge, 2004.

Berry, Michael. *Xiaowu, Platform, Unknown Pleasures: Jia Zhangke's Hometown Trilogy*, BFI Film Classics. London: BFI, 2009.

Chow, Rey. "China as Documentary: Some Basic Questions (inspired by Michelangelo Antonioni and Jia Zhangke)." In *Poetics of Chinese Cinema*, edited by Gary Bettinson and James Udden, 185–202. East Asian Popular Culture. New York: Palgrave Macmillan, 2016.

Fan, Ho Lok Victor. "Revisiting Jia Zhangke: Individuality, Subjectivity, and Autonomy in Contemporary Chinese Independent Cinema." In *The Global Auteur: The Politics of Authorship in 21st Century Cinema*, edited by Seung-hoon Jeong and Jeremi Szaniawski, 323–42. New York: Bloomsbury, 2016.

Jia, Zhangke. *Jia Zhangke Speaks Out: The Chinese Director's Texts on Film. Texts by and Interviews with Jia Zhangke*. Translated by Claire Huot, Tony Rayns, Alice Shih, and Sebastian Veg. Piscataway, NJ: Transaction Publishers, 2015.

Jia, Zhangke, and Aili Zhang. "Documentary, Fiction, and the Tonalities of Memory: An Interview with Jia Zhangke." *Pacific Coast Philology* (2013) 48, no. 1: 109–124.

Lim, Song Hwee, and Julian Ward, editors. *The Chinese Cinema Book*. London: BFI, 2020.

Mello, Cecília. *The Cinema of Jia Zhangke: Realism and Memory in Chinese Film*. London: I.B. Tauris 2019; e-book Bloomsbury, 2019.

Salles, Walter. *Jia Zhangke: A Guy from Fenyang*, 2014. Kino Lorber; Kanopy, 2019.

Schultz, Corey Kai Nelson. *Moving Figures: Class and Feeling in the Films of Jia Zhangke*. Edinburgh: Edinburgh University Press, 2018.

Stuckey, G. Andrew. "Documentarization and Amplified Realism in Jia Zhangke's Films." In *Metacinema in Contemporary Chinese Film*, 78-99. Hong Kong: Hong Kong University Press, 2018.

Wang, Xiaoping. *China in the Age of Global Capitalism: Jia Zhangke's Filmic World*. London: Routledge 2019.

Yang, Li. *The Formation of Chinese Art Cinema 1990–2003*. 1st ed. 2018. Cham, Switzerland: Springer International Publishing; Imprint: Palgrave Macmillan, 2018.

Zhang, Hongbing. "Ruins and Grassroots: Jia Zhangke's Cinematic Discontents in the Age of Globalization." In *Chinese Ecocinema: In the Age of Environmental Challenge*, edited by Lu Sheldon H. and Mi Jiayan, 129-54. Hong Kong University Press, 2009.

Zhang, Zheng. *The Urban Generation: Chinese Cinema and Society at the Turn of the Twenty-First Century*. Durham: Duke University Press, 2007. E-Duke.

Filmography

One Day, in Beijing (You yitian, zai Beijing)
China/1994/BETAMAX
Director: Jia Zhangke
Image: Jia Zhangke, Zhu Jiong
Production: Wang Hongwei
Length: 15 mins.

Xiaoshan Going Home (Xiaoshan Hui Jia)
China/1995/BETACAM
Director and Screenwriter: Jia Zhangke
With: Wang Hongwei, Yao Sheng, Zhu Liqin, Dong Shuzhe, Zhou Xiaomin
Image: Hu Xin
Length: 58 mins.

Dudu
China/1996/VHS-C
Director and Screenwriter: Jia Zhangke
With: Lin Xiaoling
Image: Liang Meng
Production: Wang Hongwei
Length: 50 mins.

Xiaowu
China/1997/16 mm
Director and Screenwriter: Jia Zhangke
With: Wang Hongwei, Zuo Baitao, Hao Hongjian, An Qunyan, Liang Yong-hao
Image: Yu Lik-wai

Art Direction: Liang Jingdong
Sound: Lin Xiaoling
Editing: Lin Xiaoling
Production: Jia Zhangke, Wang Han-bin, Li Kit-ming
Length: 108 mins.

Platform (Zhantai)
China, Hong Kong, Japan, France/2000/35 mm
Director and Screenwriter: Jia Zhangke
With: Wang Hongwei, Zhao Tao, Liang Jingdong, Yang Tianyi, Han Sanming
Image: Yu Lik-wai
Art Direction: Qiu Sheng
Music: Yoshihiro Hanno
Sound: Zhang Yang
Editing: Kong Jinglei
Executive Producer: Masayuki Mori
Producers: Shôzô Ichiyama, Li Kit-ming
Co-producers: Joël Farges, Élise Jalladeau
Associate Producers: Chow Keung, Yu Lik-wai
Length: 154 mins. & 193 mins.

"Dog's Condition" ("Gou De Zhuangkuang")
China/2001/DV
Director and Screenwriter: Jia Zhangke
Length: 6 mins.

In Public (*Gonggong Changsuo*)
South Korea/2001/ DV
Director and Screenwriter: Jia Zhangke
Image: Yu Lik-wai, Jia Zhangke
Sound: Zhang Yang

Production: Cha Seoung-Jae, Sidus, Jeonju International Film Festival
Length: 30 mins.

Unknown Pleasures (Ren Xiao Yao)
China, Japan, France, South Korea, 2002/DIGIBETA
Director and Screenwriter: Jia Zhangke
With: Zhao Weiwei, Wu Qiong, Zhao Tao, Zhou Qingfeng,
    Wang Hongwei
Image: Yu Lik-wai
Sound: Zhang Yang
Editing: Chow Keung
Executive Producers: Masayuki Mori, Hengameh Panahi, Paul Yi
Producers: Shôzô Ichiyama, Li Kit-ming
Co-producer: Yuji Sadai
Associate Producer: Chow Keung, Fumiko Osaka, Yu Lik-wai
Length: 113 mins.

The World (Shijie)
China, Japan, France/ 2004/HDCM
Director and Screenwriter: Jia Zhangke
With: Zhao Tao, Cheng Taisheng, Han Sanming
Image: Yu Lik-wai
Music: Lim Giong
Sound: Zhang Yang
Editing: Kong Jinglei
Executive Producers: Masayuki Mori, Hengameh Panahi,
    Chow Keung,
Producers: Shôzô Ichiyama, Takio Yoshida, Ren Zhonglun
Length: 133 mins & 108 mins.

Still Life (Sanxia Haoren)
China/2006/HDV

Director and Screenwriter: Jia Zhangke
With: Zhao Tao, Han Sanming, Xiang Haiyu, Ma Lizhen, Li Zhubin, Wang Hongwei
Image: Yu Lik-wai
Music: Lim Giong
Sound: Zhang Yang
Editing: Kong Jinglei
Executive Producers: Ren Zhonglun, Chow Keung, Dan Bo
Producers: Zhu Jiong, Wang Tianyun, Xu Pengle
Co-producer: Director and screenwriter: Jia Zhangke
Associate Producer: Ma Ning, Liu Xiaodong, Song Jing
Length: 108 mins.

Dong
China/2006/HDV
Director: Jia Zhangke
With: Liu Xiaodong
Image: Jia Zhangke, Yu Lik-wai, Tian Li, Chow Chi-sang
Music: Lim Giong
Sound: Zhang Yang
Editing: Zhang Jia, Kong Jinlei
Producer: Chow Keung
Co-producer: Dan Bo
Length: 66 mins. Documentary

Useless (Wuyong)
China/2007/HDCM
Director: Jia Zhangke
Starring: Ma Ke
Image: Jia Zhangke, Yu Lik-wai
Music: Lim Giong
Sound: Zhang Yang
Editing: Zhang Jia

Executive Producers: Chow Keung, Kang Jianmin, Mao Jihong
Producers: Youyishanren, Yu Lik-wai, Zhao Tao
Length: 80 mins. Documentary

"Our Ten Years" ("Wo Men De Shi Nian")
China/2007/HDV
Director and Screenwriter: Jia Zhangke
With: Zhao Tao, Tian Yuan, Liang Jingdong
Image: Lu Sheng
Music: Lim Giong
Producer: Chow Keung
Length: 9 mins.

24 City (Er Shi Si Cheng Ji)
China, Japan/2008/HDCM
Director: Jia Zhangke
Screenwriters: Jia Zhangke, Zhai Yongming
With: Joan Chen, Lü Liping, Chen Jianbin, Zhao Tao
Image: Yu Lik-wai, Wang Hu
Music: Yoshihiro Hanno, Lim Giong
Sound: Zhang Yang
Editing: Kong Jinglei, Lin Xudong
Executive Producers: Ren Zhonglun, Chow Keung, Tang Yong
Producers: Shôzô Ichiyama, Jia Zhangke, Wang Hongwei
Co-producers: Satoshi Kubo, Ma Ning, Masayuki Mori, Yuji Sadai, Xu Pengle, Takio Yoshida, Zhu Jiong
Length: 112 mins.

Cry Me a River (He Shang De Ai Qing)
China, Spain, France/2008/HDCM
Director: Jia Zhangke
With: Wang Hongwei, Zhao Tao, Hao Lei, Guo Xiaodong

Image: Wang Yu
Sound: Ren Jiajia
Length: 20 mins.

Black Breakfast (Hei Se Zao Can)
Switzerland/2008/HDCM
Director: Jia Zhangke
Screenwriter: Zhao Jing
Starring: Zhao Tao
Image: Yu Lik-wai
Sound: Zhang Yang
Producers: Zhang Dong, Eva Lam
Length: 5 mins.

Remembrance (Shi Nian)
China, 2009/HDCM
Director and Screenwriter: Jia Zhangke
With: Zhao Tao, Yu Entai
Image: Yu Lik-wai
Music: Lim Giong
Executive Producers: Jia Zhangke, Shao Zhong
Producers: Eva Lam, Ou Ning, Zhang Dong
Length: 12 mins.

I Wish I Knew (Hai Shang Chuan Qi)
China, 2010/DIGITAL RED ONE
Director and Screenwriter: Jia Zhangke
With: Chen Danqing, Yang Xiaofu, Zhang Yuansun, Du Meiru, Wang Peimin, Wang Toon, Chang Lingyun, Lee Chiatung, Chang Hsini, Hou Hsiao-hsien, Zhu Qiansheng, Huang Baomei, Wei Ran, Wei Wei, Barbara Fei, Rebecca Pan, Yang Huaiding, Han Han, Zhao Tao, Lim Giong

Image: Yu Lik-wai
Music: Lim Giong
Sound: Zhang Yang
Editing: Zhang Jia
Executive Producers: Ren Zhonglun, Chow Keung, An Gang, Li Peng
Producers: Wang Tianyuan, Yu Lik-wai, Meg Jin, Lin Ye, Xiong Yong
Length: 138 mins.

Yulu
China/2011/DIGITAL RED ONE and 5D MARK II
Directors: Jia Zhangke, Chen Tao, Chen Zhiheng, Song Fang, Chen Tao, Chen Cuimei, Wang Zizhao, Wei Tie
Title of Jia Zhangke's segment: "Pan Shiyi"
Image: Yu Lik-wai
Music: Lim Giong
Sound: Zhang Yang
Editing: Tan Chui Mui, Bu Yang, Bu Peng-zheng, Shun Zi, Shen Ao, Wang Jing, Xie Qi, Zhou Jingjing
Producer: Jia Zhangke
Length: 88 mins; length of Jia's segment: 3 mins.

Alone Together ("3.11 A Sense of Home Films")
Japan, China/2012/5D MARK II
Director and Screenwriter: Jia Zhangke
With: Zhao Tao, Liang Jindong
Image: Yu Lik-wai
Sound: Li Danfeng
Executive Producer: Naomi Kawase
Length: 3 mins.

A Touch of Sin (Tian Zhu Ding)
China, Japan/2013/DIGITAL ALEXA

Director and Screenwriter: Jia Zhangke
With: Jiang Wu, Wang Baoqianq, Zhao Tao, Luo Lanshan
Image: Yu Lik-wai
Art Direction: Liu Weixin
Music: Lim Giong
Sound: Zhang Yang
Editing: Matthieu Laclau, Lin Xudong
Executive Producers: Jia Zhangke, Masayuki Mori, Ren Zhonglun
Producer: Shôzô Ichiyama
Associate Producers: Kazumi Kawashiro, Yuji Sadai, Liu Shiyu, Jia Bin
Co-Producers: Eva Lam, Qian Jianping, Zhang Dong, Gao Xiaojiang
Length: 128 mins.

Mountains May Depart (Shan he gu ren)
China, Japan, France/ 2015/ ALEXA
Director and Screenwriter: Jia Zhangke
With: Zhao Tao, Zhang Yi, Liang Jindong, Dong Zijian, Sylvia Chang, Han Sanming
Image: Yu Lik-wai
Art Direction: Qiang Liu
Music: Yoshihiro Hanno
Sound: Zhang Yang
Editing: Matthieu Laclau
Producers: Shôzô Ichiyama
Executive Producers: Nathanaël Karmitz, Jia Zhangke, Ren Zhonglun, Liu Shiyu
Length: 126 mins.

The Hedonists
Director and Screenwriter: Jia Zhangke
With: Han Sanming, Liang Jingdong, Yuan Wenqian, Jia Zhangke
Image: Yu Lik-wai

Production: Youku and Hong Kong International Film Festival
Length: 26 mins.

Ash Is Purest White (jiānghú érnǚ)
Director and Screenwriter: Jia Zhangke
With: Zhao Tao, Liao Fan, Xu Zheng, Feng Xiaogang, Diao Yinan
Music: Giong Lim
Image: Éric Gautier
Sound: Zhang Yang,
Editing: Mathieu Laclau, Lin Xudong
Art Direction: Weixin Liu
Special Effects: Rodolphe Chabrier
Producers: Josie Chou, Ping Dong, Shôzô Ichiyama, Jia Zhangke, Olivier Père, Nathanaël Karmitz, et al.
Length: 136 mins.

Yi Ge Tong
2019. iPhone XS.
Director and Screenwriter: Jia Zhangke
With: Li Xuan, Jiang Zhen
Image: Yu Lik-wai
Editing: Su San Pao
Produced by: Xie Chen
Coproduced by: Michael Wong
Length: 6 mins.

Swimming Out Till the Sea Turns Blue
  (Yi zhi you dao hai shui bian lan)
China/2020
Director: Jia Zhangke
Screenwriter: Jia Zhangke, Wan Jiahu
With: Duan Hufan, Jia Pingwa, Yu Hua, Liang Hong

appendix 249

Image: Yu Lik-wai
Sound: Zhang Yang
Editing: Kong Jinlei
Producer: Zhao Tao
Beijing Production: Huaxia Film Distribution, Beijing, Shanghai Group Corporation, Shanghai, Shanxi Film and Television Group, Shanxi, Huaxin Kylin Culture Media, Beijing, Wisharty Media, Beijing, Huayi Brothers Pictures, Beijing, Shidian Culture Communication, Tianjin, We Entertainment, Xiamen.
Length: 112 mins.

Visit
China/Greece/ 2020
Director and Screenwriter: Jia Zhangke
With: Lian Yirui, Casper Liang, Jia Zhangke
Image: Tian Li
Sound: Zhang Yang
Editing: Zhang Juan
Jia's segment of the omnibus film commissioned by Thessaloniki Film Festival Spaces #2 | *7 films inspired by the book "Species of Spaces" by G. Perec and the days of quarantine*
Length: 4 mins

index

Film Titles

24 City 29, 31, 59–61, 74fn18, 138, 138fn35, 140–143, 230, 236, 245
36th Chamber of Shaolin, The 101, 101fn21
400 Blows, The 133
Adieu Philippine 44, 44fn4
All Tomorrow's Parties 27, 177
Andrei Rublev 205
Apocalypse Now 188
Ash is Purest White 13, 71–74, 249
Avventura, L' 106, 231fn3
Ballad of a Soldier 203, 203fn1
Barton Fink 212
Beijing Bastards 25, 95
Berlin: Symphony of a Great City 46
Better Tomorrow, A 52
Bicycle Thieves 98, 205
Black Peter 44, 44fn4
Blind Chance 205, 205fn2
Boy 206
Boys from Fengkuei, The 44, 207
Brighter Summer Day, A 209
Bumming in Beijing: The Last Dreamers 25
Central Station 225
Chung Kuo, Cina 66, 66fn15, 184, 204
City of Sadness, A 206
Cranes are Flying, The 203, 203fn1
Crows and Sparrows 99, 99fn14
Cry Me a River 61–63, 63fn12
Dead Souls 64, 64fn13
Dekalog 205
Dersu Uzala 206
Ditch, The 64, 64fn13
Dolce vita, La 133

Dong 29, 31, 32, 53–56, 75, 77, 116fn31, 135, 140, 140fn37, 147, 148, 181, 196, 236, 244
Douro, Faina fluvial 46, 46fn6
Escrava Isaura 93, 93fn5
Dudu 107, 241
Farewell My Concubine 210
Fengming, a Chinese Memoir 64, 64fn13
Fidaï 158
First Name: Carmen 187, 204
Forgetting to Know You 158
Girl from Hunan, A 113fn26
Goddess, The 142
Good-for-Nothing 44, 44fn4
Guerillas Sweep the Plain 98, 98fn8
Hello Mr. Tree 158–159
I Vitelloni 44, 159
I Wish I Knew 19, 29, 30, 63–66, 67, 77, 115, 175, 183, 184, 236, 246
In Public 28, 29, 31, 43, 45–46, 54, 73, 75, 126, 127, 129, 144, 148, 231, 242
Isaura the Slave Girl 93, 93fn5
Last Bridge, The 98, 99fn12
Last Emperor, The 161
Late Spring 205
Legend of Fong Sai-yuk, The 212
Legend of the Mountain 208, 208fn3
Legend of the White Serpent 85
Love Will Tear Us Apart 27, 124fn32, 177, 178, 179, 215fn7
Mama 25
Man Escaped, A 204
Man with a Movie Camera 46
Manhatta 46
Maple Tree, The 99, 99fn15
Memories Look at Me 158
Metropolis 51

Miracle in Milan 205
Mountains May Depart 13, 69–71, 74, 162, 164, 166, 236, 248
Neon Goddesses 38fn1, 178
Night Train 187
Notte, La. 204
Old Well 100, 100fn19
One Day, in Beijing 37–38. 107, 241
Only Son, The 206
Piano, The 106
Pickpocket. 38, 226
Pierrot le fou 204
Platform 18, 19, 27, 29, 31, 32, 40–46, 51, 57, 71, 75, 83, 84,
    86, 87–88, 90, 91, 92–100, 115, 116, 118, 120–125, 129, 138, 139,
    142,144, 148, 163, 166, 167, 169, 170, 175, 178, 179, 179fn5, 180,
    181, 189, 191, 196, 197, 209, 211, 214, 216, 223, 225, 226, 231, 238
Pulp Fiction 45
Raining in the Mountain. 208, 208fn3
Rashômon 206
Red Desert. 204
Red Detachment of Women, The 98, 98fn9
Red Sorghum. 24, 101fn19, 119
Rome 11 o'clock. 98, 98fn11
Saturday Night and Sunday Morning. 44, 44fn4
Shanghai Triad. 210
Shaolin Temple, The 100
Sorrow and the Pity, The 65
Spring in a Small Town 30, 30fn4, 62, 66, 66fn16, 142, 142fn38
Springtime in a Small Town 30fn4
Square, The. 25, 37
Still Life 15, 16, 17, 18, 28, 29, 31, 50–53, 54, 55, 60, 67,
    73, 91, 1234, 135, 135, 137, 138, 138fn35, 139, 144, 148, 151, 173,
    182, 183, 185, 192, 197, 206, 228, 229, 230, 236, 243
Street Angel 142, 142fn38
Summer Palace. 62
Swimming Out Till the Sea Turns Blue 13, 74–78, 249

Tears of the Yangtze 99, 99fn14
"Tender is the Night" 146, 146fn42
Tokyo Story 205
Touch of Sin, A 12, 17, 28, 30, 32, 58, 67–69, 71, 83, 85, 102, 119, 139, 141, 144, 145, 147, 148, 149, 150, 151, 152, 155, 160, 165, 167, 175, 184, 185, 192, 193, 198, 199, 231, 236
Touch of Zen, A. 150, 150fn44, 208
Trap Street 187
Traveler, The 205
Umberto D. 205
Unknown Pleasures. 19, 27, 29, 32, 43–49, 91, 102, 124fn32, 129, 138, 144, 175, 182, 215fn7, 216, 231, 236, 243
Unscrupulous Ones, The. 44, 44fn4
Useless 32, 55, 56–58, 77, 102, 144, 147, 244
Vagabond, The 99, 99fn13
Walter Defends Sarajevo 98, 98fn12
Where is the Friend's House? 205
Women from the Lake of Scented Souls 113fn26
World, The 15, 16, 19, 20, 21, 28, 29, 46–49, 53fn8, 60, 84, 91, 130, 131, 132, 133, 134, 136, 139, 144, 171, 172, 173, 173fn2, 175, 182, 185, 191, 192. 227, 228, 231, 236, 238, 243
Xiaoshan Going Home 23, 37–38, 157, 178, 241
Xiaowu 9, 19, 26, 30fn3, 31, 38–43, 48, 67, 72, 95, 108, 110, 112, 113, 114, 115, 116, 117, 119, 121, 123, 124fn32, 142, 144, 146, 148, 163, 178, 179, 182, 188, 191, 192,195, 206, 213–214, 216, 225, 226, 2312, 238, 241
Yellow Earth 24, 25, 29, 101, 101fn19, 114, 210
Yi Yi 209

People

Antonioni, Michelangelo . . 31, 204, 226, 227, 230, 230fn2, 231, 238
Ba, Jin 214
Bazin, André 21, 24, 143

index

Bei, Dao 96
Bertolucci, Bernardo 160
Brecht, Bertolt 30
Bresson, Robert 26, 31, 204
Briones, Inti 12, 186fn6
Bruno, Maria Carlota 20
Cakoff, Leon 11, 13
Campion, Jane 106
Chan, Peter 167
Chang, Cheh 100, 155
Chang, Sylvia 167, 248
Chen, Jianbin 59, 245
Chen, Joan (aka Chen Chong) 60, 138, 138fn35, 245
Chen, Kaige 24, 25, 101fn19, 101fn20, 119, 209, 210
Cheung, Leslie 94
Chevassu, Philippe 116
Chow, Keung 27, 38, 242, 243, 244, 245, 247
Chow, Yun-fat 9, 52
Coen Brothers 212
Corey, Yuen 212
Cui, Jian 94, 95, 116, 235
Dahai 152, 153, 198
de Almedia, Renata 11, 12, 13
Deng, Xiaoping 25, 25fn1, 41, 94
Diao, Yinan 27, 249
Dong, Zijian 167
Farges, Joël 179fn5, 241
Fei, Mu 30, 62, 66, 66fn16, 142, 142fn38
Fellini, Federico 44fn4, 191, 192
Ferrari, Florencia 20
Ferrasson, Annette 116
Gitai, Amos 11, 223
Glachant, Isabelle 13, 116, 194fn1
Godard, Jean-Luc 31, 186. 187, 203
Gorky, Maxim 214

Gu, Cheng 96
Gu, Zheng. 105, 108
Guo, Xiaodong 61, 62, 245
Han, Jie 158, 159
Han, Sanming. 32, 51, 52, 53, 54, 121, 122, 123, 137, 138, 139, 242, 243, 244, 248
Hao, Lei. 61, 245
He, Yi 26
Hou, Hsiao-hsien 9, 39, 44, 66, 115, 206, 207, 209, 246
Hsu, Feng 150
Hu, Bing 203
Hu, King 30, 100, 150, 150fn44, 184, 208, 208fn3, 209
Hui, Ann 100, 100fn18, 167
Ichiyama, Shôzô. . 13, 28, 115, 123, 124, 156, 156fn51, 157, 206, 242, 243, 245, 248, 249
Jackson, Michael 94
Jen, Richie. 215fn7, 235
Jiang, Wen. 26, 28
Jiang, Wu 198, 248
Kapoor, Raj 42, 99fn13
Karmitz, Nathanaël 167, 248, 249
Kiarostami, Abbas 19, 114, 205
Kieślowski, Krzysztof. 114, 205fn2
King, Hu 30, 100, 150fn44, 184, 208, 208fn3, 209
Kitano, Takeshi. 71, 115, 156fn51
Kurosawa, Akira .104, 203, 206
Lam, George 43
Lau, Kar-leung 101, 101fn21
Leone, Sergio 67
Li, Danfeng. 13, 247
Li, Jet 100
Li, Kit-ming. 157, 157fn52, 179, 242, 243
Liang, Jingdong. .242, 245, 247
Lin, Xudong. . . .13, 64, 83, 116, 116fn30, 121, 194–99, 245, 248, 249
Liu, Jiang 26

Liu, Xiaodong 53, 55, 56, 116fn31, 135, 136, 147, 197, 244
Lou, Ye 26, 28, 66
Lu, Yao 218, 218fn1
Lü, Liping. 59, 245
Luo, Lanshan 150, 248
Ma, Yansong 219
Mao, Zedong 53, 219fn2
Méliès, Georges. 143
Mizoguchi, Kenji 203
Nietzsche, Friedrich. 69, 93
Nogami, Teruyo. 206
Ōshima, Nagisa 203, 206
Ounouri, Damien 158
Ozu, Yasujirō 203, 205, 206
Peixoto, Mário 11
Pialat, Maurice 39
Qu, Vivian. 187
Quan, Ling 158
Rembrandt 55
Ren, Zhonglun 134, 243, 244, 245, 247, 248
Rodin, Auguste 105
Rossellini, Roberto 31, 54, 143fn39, 229
Saijo, Hideki 94, 94fn6
Salles, Walter 11, 20, 21, 83, 186fn6, 223–232
Sarde, Alain. 187
Shu, Ting 96
Song, Fang 27, 158, 247
Tang, Emily. 27
Tarantino, Quentin 67
Tarkovsky, Andrei. 107, 205
Teng, Teresa. 94, 224, 235
Tian, Zhuangzhuang 24, 28, 30fn4, 118, 119, 167
To, Johnnie 150
Truffaut, François. 203
Tsai, Ming-liang .9, 114, 114fn27

Tsui, Hark 100, 167
Wang, Baoqiang 150, 198
Wang, Bing 48fn7, 64, 196fn9
Wang, Chao 26
Wang, Hongwei 13, 32, 37, 40, 42, 52, 61, 88, 96, 100, 105, 107, 108, 110, 111, 121, 122, 124fn32, 138175, 176, 189, 206, 224, 225, 241, 242, 243, 244, 245
Wang, Xiaoshuai 15, 26, 53fn8, 118, 196
Wong, Kar-wai 66
Woo, John 52, 100, 150
Wu, Tianming 24, 100, 101fn19
Wu, Wenguang 25
Wu, Yonggang 142, 142fn38
Wu, Zeitan 214
Xie, Fei 113fn26, 205
Yang, Edward 30, 115, 167
Yeats, W.B. 61, 61fn11, 230
Yu, Lik-wai 9, 13, 27, 38, 46, 65, 115, 121, 124fn32, 144, 152, 153, 153fn47, 157, 162, 177–186, 186fn6, 192, 215fn7, 226, 241, 242, 243, 244, 245, 246, 247, 248, 249, 250
Yuan, Muzhi 142
Zhang, Di 94
Zhang, Ming 26
Zhang, Xianping 203
Zhang, Yang. 93fn4, 113fn24, 121, 187–193, 242, 243, 244, 245, 246, 247, 248, 249, 250
Zhang, Yimou 24, 25, 76, 100fn19, 116, 116fn31, 119, 209, 210
Zhang, Yuan 15, 25, 118, 196
Zhao, Tao 12, 16, 19, 29, 32, 42, 45, 49, 51, 52, 59, 61, 62, 64, 67, 68, 69, 71, 73, 74, 85, 88, 96, 111, 121, 131, 131fn34, 132, 136, 136, 138, 144, 150, 154, 163, 166, 169–176, 184, 206, 209, 224, 227, 228, 229, 242, 243, 244, 245, 246, 247, 248, 249, 250
Zhong, Dafeng 207

Songs

"Cry Me a River" 63
"Dschinghis Kahn" 43, 94, 96, 235
"Für Elise". 39
"Girl under a Street Lamp, The" 94
"Go West". 69, 69,fn17, 165, 235
"I Am Free and Carefree". 215fn7, 235
"I Wish I Knew" 65
"Internationale, The" 61
"Let Me Go Wild in the Snow". 95
"Monica" 94, 235
"Moon Represents My Heart, The". 94
"Nothing to My Name". 94, 235
"One Night in Beijing" 103, 207, 235
"Piece of Red Cloth, A". 95, 235
"Platform". 66
"Run without Care". 165, 166
"The Vagabond". 99
"Union Makes Us Strong" 94
"We are the Builders of Communism" 94
"We are the New Generation of the 1980s". 94
"Workers, We Have the Strength" 94

Other

798 Art Zone in Beijing. 125, 125fn33
animation 47, 100, 228
Bangkok. 55, 131, 140, 140fn37
Beatles, The 189
Beijing Film Academy . . . .
    18, 20, 24, 27, 30fn3, 37, 95, 104, 110, 117, 122, 139, 149, 187, 193, 195, 203, 205, 208, 211
Beijing Film Institute. 106

Beijing Film Studio 118
Berlin, Berlinale, and Berlin Forum 25, 76fn19, 113, 113fn25, 114, 114fn26, 115, 116, 119, 123, 225
Bund of the Concessions 65, 65fn14, 66, 66fn16
Cannes International Film Festival 21, 25, 27, 64fn13, 73, 76, 150, 162, 176, 203fn1, 230, 231fn3
Central Academy of Drama. 167, 167fn2
Central Academy of Fine Arts (CAFA) 83, 194
centrally planned economy 26, 41, 140, 142, 145, 145fn41, 215, 223
Centre de l'audiovisuel in Brussels (CBA) 178
Chengdu. 59, 68, 230
China Film Administration. 158, 158fn53
China Film Archive. 67fn16, 204
Chongqinq 145, 218
Clermont-Ferrand. 65
Communication University of China 195
Connaissance du cinéma 116
Cosac Naify 12, 13
Cultural Revolution. 24, 29, 67fn16, 76, 89–92, 89fn3, 98, 98fn8, 98fn9, 99, 99fn15, 101fn20, 208, 214, 214fn5, 217, 238
Cultural Thaw. 91
Datong 17, 29, 44, 45, 46, 73, 127, 129, 144, 215
Dazibao 89,89fn3
documentary 11, 12, 13, 16, 25, 26, 29, 37, 38fn1, 41, 45, 48, 48fn7, 56, 60, 66fn15, 68, 72, 74, 77, 107, 129, 135, 136, 138fn35, 141, 143, 148, 178, 178fn4, 179, 180, 182, 183, 184, 186, 189, 192, 194, 206, 226, 229230, 231, 238, 244, 245
Dream of the Red Chamber. 61, 61fn10
Factory 420 . . . . .59, 61
Falun Gong 44, 44fn5
Fengjie. 136, 174, 228
Fenyang 12, 19, 21, 26, 39, 41, 42, 42fn3, 43, 44, 57, 75, 83, 84, 85, 87, 89, 93, 95, 97, 98, 100, 101, 102, 107, 108, 109, 110, 112,

120, 121, 122, 126, 129, 139, 146, 147, 152, 160, 163, 189, 208, 211, 212, 213, 216, 223, 224, 225, 231, 232, 239
Festival des Trois Continents 27
fiction 12, 13, 17, 25, 29, 32, 37, 48, 60, 64, 68, 71, 74, 128, 129, 136, 137, 143, 148, 178, 182, 184, 186, 189, 228, 230
Fifth Generation 24, 29, 101fn19, 101fn20, 113, 113fn26, 114, 116fn31, 119, 209, 210
First Generation. 24
Fourth Generation 24, 30, 101fn19
Golden Lion. 28
Great Leap Forward. 64
Great Wall 215
Guangdong 68, 128, 145, 145fn40
Guan Gong aka Guan Yu. 164, 164fn1
Guangzhou 56, 58, 86, 146fn40, 147, 171fn1
Guizhou. 106
gun fu 106
Henan. 77, 106
Hong Kong 9, 23, 25, 27, 30, 42, 43, 59, 65, 66, 66fn16, 93, 94, 100, 100fn18, 115, 131, 145,145fn40, 157, 172, 177,178, 179, 184, 197, 204, 208, 208fn3, 214, 240, 242, 249
Hong Kong Arts Development Council 178
Hong Kong Independent Short Film and Video Awards. . 38, 178fn4
Hubei 73,145
Hundred Days' Reform .213, 213fn1
Hutong Films. 157, 179
INSAS 177, 177fn3
Italian Neorealism. 24, 26, 54, 98fn11
Jeonju International Film Festival 45, 215, 243
Jialin mopeds 218
Kaohsiung. 207
Karaoke 53fn8, 98, 109, 110, 189, 219, 226
Korean War 59
Kuimen Gate 50, 53
Kuimen mountains 31

Kuomintang 66
"Legend of the White Serpent, The" 85
Lishui 147
Louis Vuitton 56
Lüliang 84, 216
market economy 18, 140, 142, 172fn1, 223
martial arts 30, 55, 71, 100, 100fn17, 101fn21, 106, 145, 150, 193, 208, 212
May Fourth Movement .213, 213fn3
Mekong River 140, 140fn37
Ming Dynasty 31, 154, 154fn50, 214
Mongolia 46, 84, 126, 223, 232
National Film Bureau 20, 117, 118, 119, 125, 134
Office Kitano . .28, 71, 115, 116, 124, 156, 156fn51, 157, 167, 179fn5
Organisation internationale de la Francophonie 178
Peace Hotel 65, 65fn14
People's Daily 214, 214fn4
Pet Shop Boys 69, 69fn17, 165
Pingyao 42, 83, 121, 122
Pingyao International Film Festival 15, 27, 31, 75, 103fn22
Pink Floyd 192
postmodernism 105, 146
Red Guard 99
Reform Era 24, 25, 41, 76, 94, 180, 219
Rolling Stones 189, 192
Scar Literature 99
School of Fine Arts in Taiyuan (Shanxi University) . . .103, 105, 120
Second Generation 30
Shaanxi province 77, 101fn20
Shanghai Film Group 134, 167, 196fn11
Shanghai Film Studio 134, 196, 196fn11
Shanghai World Expo 19, 184
Shanxi province 16, 17, 18, 19, 20, 26, 39, 41, 48, 51, 57, 58, 68, 73, 75, 76, 77, 83, 84, 91, 95, 99, 101fn19, 101fn20, 102, 106, 113, 116, 117, 119, 120, 129,

    130,131, 139, 145,147, 154, 165, 169, 171, 176, 189, 207, 214fn6, 219, 250

Shenzhen 42, 46, 62, 131fn34, 133, 150, 171, 171fn1, 172, 191

Shenzhen All Star Rock 41

shuoshu. 149, 150

Sixth Generation 15, 25, 26, 29

Steadicam 153, 184, 185

"Strike Hard" Campaign 87, 87fn1

structuralism 105, 146

Sun Yatsen generation. 213, 213fn2

Suzhou 61, 62, 63, 63fn12, 87

Taiwan. . 9, 65, 93, 94, 100, 115fn28, 184, 203, 204, 208, 208fn3, 209

Taiyuan . . 91, 95, 97, 101, 103, 105, 120, 126, 169, 171, 172, 207, 213

Taizan 207

Third Generation 24

Three Gorges Dam 16, 29, 51, 53, 55, 73, 135, 136, 137, 139, 140fn37, 145, 147, 192, 228

Tiananmen Square 18, 25, 37, 43, 44fn4, 62, 95, 97, 97fn7, 107, 116fn31, 120, 217, 219, 219fn2

Tianjin. 89, 250

Tokyo Filmex International Festival 206

Toronto Film Festival. 124, 209

Triad. 65, 71, 210

Turin 68

Ulaanbaatar 46, 84, 85, 120, 223–232

Venice Film Festival. 27, 123, 124, 167, 197

Village People 69, 69fn17, 94fn6

Water Margin 150, 150fn43

Weibo 28, 103

Wham! 94

White-Haired Girl, The. 98, 98fn10

Window on the World Park, Shenzhen. 131, 171, 172

Wolf of Zhongshan, The. 86

World of Lakes and Rivers 145, 145fn41

World Park, Beijing. 131, 139, 171, 172

wuxia 72, 100, 145, 145fn41, 150, 150fn43, 150fn44, 154
Xiaoyi 88
Xstream Pictures 27, 157, 158, 167, 179
Yamagata Documentary Festival 178, 178fn4
Yangtze River 51, 52, 54, 99, 140, 140fn37, 144, 145, 228
Yellow River. .69, 120, 126, 190
Youth Experimental Film Group 27, 37, 105
Yu Garden. 65
Yulin. 120
Yunnan 117
Zhejiang. 77, 94

about the author

Jean-Michel FRODON is a journalist and film critic, who was a writer for *Le Point* (1983-1990), and *Le Monde* (1990-2003), before becoming the editorial director of *Cahiers du Cinéma* (2003-2009). He now regularly writes for *Slate.fr* along with many journals and magazines, both in print and online, in France, but also the USA, South Korea, Spain and the Balkans. He is a professor at Sciences Po Paris (Political Sciences Institute) and an Honorary Professor at the University of St. Andrews, Scotland. As a cinema historian, he is the author or editor of many books, including *La Projection nationale, Hou Hsiao-hsien, Conversation avec Woody Allen, Horizon cinéma, Le Cinéma chinois, Cinema and the Shoah* (SUNY Press), *Robert Bresson, Gilles Deleuze et les images, La Critique de cinéma, Amos Gitai Genèses, Le Cinéma d'Edward Yang, Le Cinéma français de la Nouvelle Vague à nos jours, Assayas par Assayas, L'Art du cinéma, Que fait le cinéma?, Cinemas of Paris, New York mis en scènes, Jafar Panahi Images/Nuage, Chris Marker, 13xOzu, Abbas Kiarostami l'œuvre ouverte*. He also acts as a programmer and curator for many festivals and exhibitions.

Photo: Jean-Michel Frodon and Jia Zhangke. © Walter Salles